Goethe

Essays on Art and Literature

GOETHE

Selected Poems
Faust I & II
Essays on Art and Literature
From My Life: Poetry and Truth (Parts One to Three)
From My Life: Poetry and Truth (Part Four) • Campaign in France 1792 • Siege of Mainz
Italian Journey
Early Verse Dramas and Prose Plays
Verse Plays and Epic
Wilhelm Meister's Apprenticeship
Conversations of German Refugees & Wilhelm Meister's Journeyman Year or The Renunciants
The Sorrows of Young Werther • Elective Affinities • Novella
Scientific Studies

Collected Works in 12 Volumes

Goethe's Collected Works, Volume 3

Johann Wolfgang von

GOETHE

Essays on Art and Literature

Edited by John Gearey
Translated by Ellen von Nardroff
and Ernest H. von Nardroff

Princeton University Press
Princeton and Oxford

Published by Princeton University Press
41 William Street, Princeton, New Jersey 08540
99 Banbury Road, Oxford OX2 6JX

press.princeton.edu

GPSR Authorized Representative: Easy Access System Europe - Mustamäe tee 50, 10621 Tallinn, Estonia, gpsr.requests@easproject.com

First published 1986
First Princeton paperback printing, 1994
New paperback and e-book editions, 2026

Paperback ISBN 978-0-691-29218-2
ISBN (epub) 978-0-691-29697-5
ISBN (PDF) 978-0-691-29219-9

This is volume three in the Collected Works of Johann Wolfgang von Goethe

Cover images: Courtesy of INTERFOTO / Alamy and Rawpixel

The Library of Congress has cataloged an earlier edition of this book as follows:
Goethe, Johann Wolfgang von, 1749–1832.
[Works. English. 1994]
Goethe's collected works
p. cm.
Originally published: Cambridge, Mass. : Suhrkamp, 1983–1989. Includes indexes.
Contents: v. 1. Selected poems—v. 2. Faust I & II—v.
3. Essays on art and literature.
ISBN 3-518-03058-2 (v. 3 hardback)
ISBN 0-691-03657-8 (v. 3 paperback)
I. Title.
PT2026.A1C94 1994
831'.6—dc20 93-27617

CONTENTS

PREFACE

The essays in this volume are broadly representative of the views on art and literature that Goethe developed over a long career of concern with both. He had wanted to become a painter, an ambition he abandoned only in his fortieth year.

The broadness of the selection reflects both scholarly consensus and opportunity. It is generally agreed that Goethe presents himself best in his development, in motion, as it were. The essays are thus taken from his early, middle and late periods. Included are those that play an important part in the understanding of Goethe and are often cited to illuminate his poetic works as well as those that are important in their own right or of general historical significance.

The opportunity for broadness was afforded by the position of this volume in the much larger undertaking which is the Suhrkamp New York multi-volume edition of Goethe's works in English translation. It was possible within this context not only to include many more of the essays on art and literature than have ever before been collected in English but to offer them complete and unabridged. Some appear for the first time in English in this form. A number appear for the first time in any form in English. All have been newly translated.

J.G.

Goethe
Essays on Art and Literature

PART ONE
Essays on Art

I
ARCHITECTURE

On German Architecture[1] (1772)

On a pilgrimage to your grave, noble Erwin, I searched for the tombstone with the inscription, *Anno Domini 1318. XVI Kal. Febr. Obiit Magister Ervinus, Gubernator Fabricae Ecclesiae Argentinensis.*[2] But I could not find it, nor were any of your countrymen able to help me. And I was saddened to the depth of my soul, for I had come to pour out my veneration for you at that hallowed place. My heart, younger then, warmer, more foolish and better than now, solemnly vowed that once in due possession of my inheritance, I would build you a memorial of marble or of sandstone, whichever I could afford.

Yet you need no memorial! You erected your own, a magnificent one. And though the throngs crawling about it like ants know nothing of your name, you are like the Great Architect who piled up mountains into the clouds.

Few have been blessed with a mind capable of conceiving a Babel-like vision—whole, great, inherently beautiful to the last detail, like God's trees—and even fewer with the good fortune to encounter a thousand willing hands, to excavate the rocky foundations, to conjure up towering structures and, with their dying breath, tell their sons: I will remain with you in the works of my spirit. Complete what is begun, until it reaches into the clouds.

You need no memorial! Certainly not mine! When the rabble utter sacred names, it is superstition or blasphemy. The feeble esthete will feel forever giddy in the presence of your colossus, robust sensibilities will understand you without an interpreter.

Now then, worthy Erwin, before I venture back to sea in my fragile bark, more likely to encounter death than prosperity, behold this grove where I engraved the names of beloved friends, there I will cut yours into a beech tree slender and soaring like your tower, and in its branches I will hang by its four corners this handkerchief full of gifts. It resembles the sheet that was let down from the clouds to the holy apostle, full of clean and unclean beasts.[3] So mine will be filled with flowers, blossoms, leaves, but also dry grass and moss and toadstools sprung up over night—everything I gathered while walking through an uninteresting region, collecting specimens simply to pass the time. I now commit them to decay as an offering in your honor.

"What immature taste," says the Italian and walks on. "Childish nonsense," parrots the Fenchman and triumphantly flicks open his snuffbox à la Grècque.[4] What right have you to show contempt?

Did not the genius of the ancients rise from the grave and fetter your own, Italian? You crept among the mighty remains like a beggar, hoping to learn of proportion, you patched together villas from sacred rubble, and you consider yourself the custodian of the secrets of art because you are able to give an account of the measurements of gigantic buildings, down to the last inch! Had you felt more and measured less, had you been inspired and not simply overawed by these massive structures, you would not have merely imitated them because they were created by the ancients and are beautiful. You would have created your own plans with their own inherent truth, and natural living beauty would have emanated from them.

Instead you applied a thin veneer of truth and beauty to your buildings. You were struck by the magnificent effect of columns, so you wanted to put them to use and embedded them in walls. You wanted colonnades too, so you encircled St. Peter's Square with marble walks which lead nowhere. And mother nature, who despises the inappropriate and hates the superfluous, drove your rabble to prostitute all that splendor by transforming it into a public sewer. Now everyone averts his eyes and holds his nose when approaching this wonder of the world.

And so things go: the artist's fancy serves the rich man's caprice, the travel writer gapes, our esthetes, called philosophers, always fashion principles and histories of art from the stuff of fairytales, while their evil genius murders true human beings at the threshold of revelation.

Principles are even more damaging to the genius than examples. Individual artists may have worked on individual parts before him, but he is the first from whose soul the parts emerge grown together into an everlasting whole. Yet school and principle fetter all powers of perception and activity. Of what use to us is the knowledge, you philosophizing expert of the new French school,[5] that the first man, inventive in his need for shelter, rammed four stakes into the ground, joined them with four poles and made a roof of branches and moss? From this you derive the appropriateness of our own buildings, as if you wanted to rule your new Babylon with a simplistically patriarchial attitude!

And it is wrong to boot. This hut of yours was not the first in the world. Two poles crossed at the top in front, two in the back and a fifth as a ridgepole, as we can see every day from huts in fields and vineyards, that is clearly a far earlier invention, from which you could not even derive a principle for your pigsties.

Thus none of your conclusions are able to ascend to the realm of truth, but merely float in the atmosphere of your own system. You want to teach us what we should use, because what we do use cannot be justified according to your principles.

The column is very dear to your heart, and in another part of the world you would be a prophet. You say: "The column is the first, essential component of a building, and the most beautiful. What exquisite elegance of form! What pure and varied grandeur when they stand in a row! But beware of using them inappropriately; their nature is to stand free. Woe to those wretches who welded their slender shape onto bulky walls!"

And yet it seems to me, dear Abbé, that you should have been concerned when you encountered the unseemliness of walled-in columns so often, and saw that moderns even walled up the intercolumniations of antique temples. If your ears were not deaf to the truth, these stones would have preached the truth to you.

The column is by no means a natural component of our dwellings, on the contrary, it contradicts the character of all our buildings. Our houses did not develop from four columns in four corners, but from four walls on four sides. The walls are in place of columns and exclude columns, and where columns are tacked on, they are a superfluous encumbrance. This is also true of our palaces and churches, with a few exceptions, on which I need not elaborate.

Your buildings present mere surfaces which, the further they extend and the bolder they soar to the sky, inevitably oppress the soul with ever more unbearable monotony. Fortunately, Genius came to our aid and inspired Erwin von Steinbach, saying: Diversify the immense wall, raise it toward heaven so that it soars like a towering, widespreading tree of God. With its thousands of branches and millions of twigs and as many leaves as sand by the sea, it shall proclaim to the land the glory of the Lord, its master.

When I first came to visit the cathedral, my head was filled with general notions of good taste. Based on what I had heard others say, I praised the harmony of mass, the purity of form, and I was a sworn enemy of the confused arbitrariness of Gothic adornment. Under the heading 'Gothic,' as in an entry in the dictionary,[6] I listed all the synonymous misconceptions that I had ever encountered, such as indefinite, disorganized, unnatural, patched-together, tacked-on, overladen. No wiser than a nation which calls the world it does not know barbaric, I called everything which did not fit into my system Gothic: from the elaborate figures and colorful ornaments on the houses of our would-be nobility to the somber remains of early German architecture. A few bizarre curlicues prompted me to join in the general chorus: "Smothered by ornamentation!" So I shuddered, anticipating a misshapen, grotesque monster.

But what unexpected emotions seized me when I finally stood before the edifice! My soul was suffused with a feeling of immense grandeur which, because it consisted of thousands of harmonizing details, I was able to savor and enjoy, but by no means understand and explain. They say it is thus with the joys of heaven, and how often I returned to savor such joys on earth, to embrace the gigantic spirit expressed in the work of our brothers of yore! How often I returned to view its dignity and magnificence from all sides, from every distance, at different times of day! It is hard for the mind of man when his brother's work is so sublime that he can only bow his head and worship. How often the gentle light of dusk, as it fused the countless parts into unified masses, soothed my eyes weary from intense searching. Now all stood before my soul, simple and great, and I, full of bliss, felt develop in me the power at the same time to enjoy and understand. Then I sensed the genius of the great builder. "Why are you so amazed?" he whispered, "All these masses were necessary. Don't you see them in all the older churches of my city? I have merely elevated the arbitrary vastness to harmonious proportions. Above the main portal dominating the two smaller ones on either side, see the broad circular window! Once there was only a small hole to let in light, and now it harmonizes with the nave of the church. See the belltower high above—it demanded smaller windows. That was all necessary, and I lent it beauty. But oh, when I float through these dark and sublime side apertures which appear to be empty and useless! In these bold, slender forms I have concealed the mysterious forces which were to raise two towers high into the air. Alas! but one stands there forlorn, without the five crowning pinnacles I had planned, so that the surrounding provinces would do homage to it and its royal brother!" And so he departed from me, and my heart was filled with sympathy and melancholy, until the birds of the morning who live in the thousands of openings greeted the sun with jubilant songs and awakened me from my slumber. How fresh was its radiance in the misty shimmer of morning light, how happily I stretched out my arms toward it and looked at the vast, harmonious masses animated by countless components! As in the works of eternal nature, down to the smallest fiber, all is form, all serves the whole. How lightly the immense, firmly-grounded edifice soars into the air, how like filigree everything is, yet made for eternity! I owe it to your instruction, noble genius, that I no longer reel when confronting your profundities, that my soul is touched by the blissful calm of a spirit who can look down on such a creation and say, as did God, "It is good!"

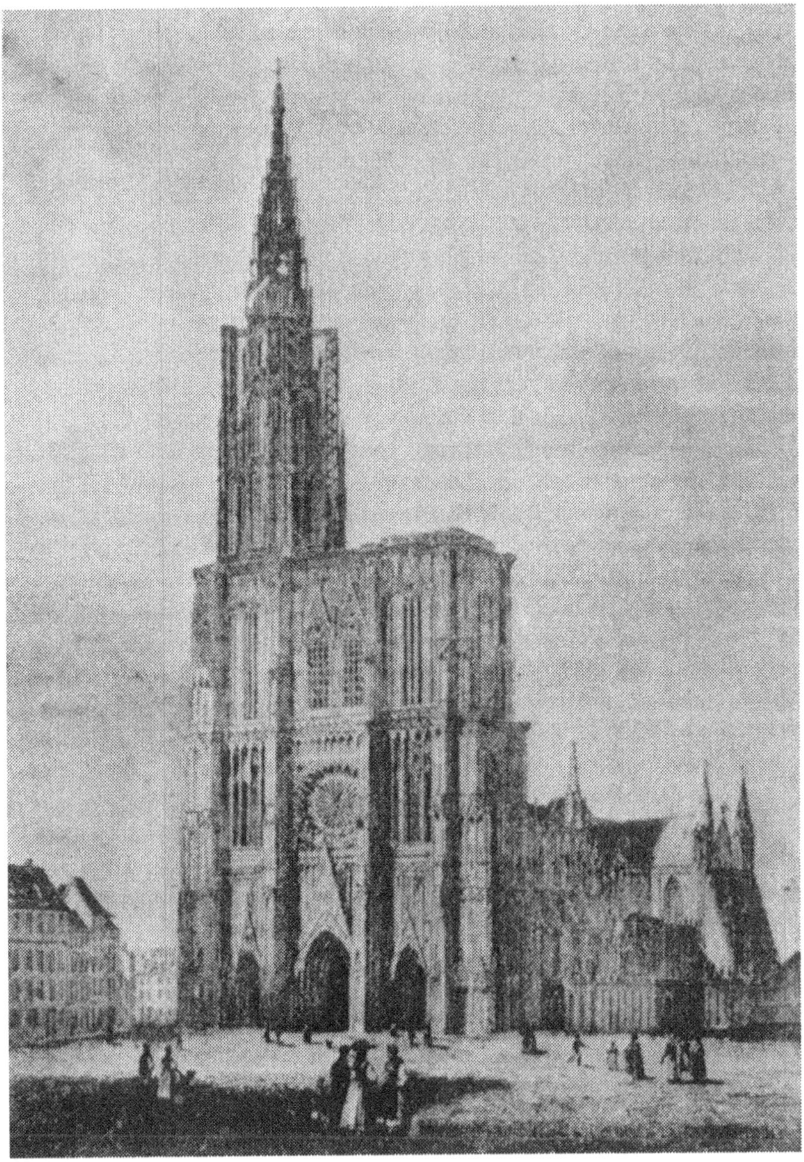

Strasbourg Cathedral. (Courtesy of the Picture Collection, the Branch Libraries, New York Public Library.)

And should I not grow angry, divine Erwin, when a German scholar, on the word of envious neighbors, fails to see his advantage and belittles your work with the misunderstood term Gothic, when he ought to thank God for being able to proclaim: This is German architecture! Our architecture! The Italians cannot boast one of their own, much less the French. And if, Professor, you are not willing to admit this advantage, then show us that the Goths really built in this style, which will prove quite difficult. And in the end, if you cannot establish that there was a Homer before Homer,[7] we will gladly grant you your theory of minor trial-and-error efforts, and approach with reverence the work of the master who first created a living whole out of scattered elements. And you, my dear brother in the quest of truth and beauty, close your ears to all pretentious prattle about art—come, enjoy, behold! Beware of profaning the name of your noblest artist and hasten here to see his magnificent work. If you feel repelled, or feel nothing at all, then farewell, harness your horses and be on your way to Paris.

But I will gladly join you, worthy youth, who stands there moved, unable to reconcile the contradictions clashing within your soul, now feeling the irresistible power of the great whole, now calling me a dreamer for seeing beauty where you see only strength and roughness. Do not let a misunderstanding separate us. Do not let the effete doctrine of our modern esthetizisers so enfeeble you that you can no longer bear what is meaningful but rough, lest in the end your sickly sensibility can tolerate only what is polished but meaningless. They would have you believe that the fine arts sprang from our supposed inclination to beautify, to refine, the things around us. That is not true! For it is the common man and the artisan who use these words in the only sense they could be true—not the philosopher.

Art is creative long before it is beautiful. And yet, such art is true and great, perhaps truer and greater than when it becomes beautiful. For in man there is a creative force which becomes active as soon as his existence is secure. When he is free from worry and fear, this demigod, restless in tranquility, begins to cast about for matter to inspire with his spirit. And thus savages decorate their coconut-fiber mats, their feathers, their bodies, with bizarre patterns, ghastly forms and gaudy colors. And even if this creative activity produces the most arbitrary shapes and designs, they will harmonize despite the apparent lack of proportion. For a single feeling created them as a characteristic whole.

This characteristic art is in fact the only true art. If it springs from a sincere, unified, original, autonomous feeling, unconcerned, indeed unaware of anything extraneous, then it will be a living whole, whether born of coarse savagery or cultured sensitivity. You see endless variations of this in different nations and individuals. The more the soul develops a feeling for proportion, which alone is beautiful and eternal, whose fundamental harmony we can prove but whose mysteries we can only feel, in which alone the life of the god-like genius dances to blissful melodies, and the more deeply this beauty penetrates the mind so that both seem to have originated as one and the mind can be satisified with nothing but beauty and produces nothing but beauty—then the more fortunate is the artist, the more glorious is he, and the deeper we bow before him and worship God's anointed one.

No one will dislodge Erwin from his pedestal. His work stands before you. Approach it and experience the profoundest feeling of truth and beauty of proportion, sprung from a strong, rough-hewn German soul in the setting of the gloomy petty-clericism of the Middle Ages.

And our own age? It has renounced its genius, sent forth its sons to collect foreign produce at their peril. The flighty Frenchman, who borrows even more heavily, has at least ingenuity enough to lend his meager pickings a semblance of oneness. He is building a magic temple to his Sainte Madeleine[8] with Greek columns and German vaults. One of our own artists was asked to create a portal for an old German church, and I saw the model he proposed: stately antique columns.

I will not dwell on how much I detest our dainty doll-painters.[9] Through theatrical poses, fake complexions and colorful costumes they have caught the eye of women. Manly Albrecht Dürer, the neophyte sneers at you—but to me, even the crudest of your woodcut figures is more welcome!

And you yourselves, the privileged, to whom it was given to enjoy the highest beauty and who now come among us to proclaim your revelations, even you do harm to the genius. He does not want to be borne up and carried off on wings not his own, though they be the wings of morning.[10] He must provide his own strength, developed in childhood dreams and honed during youth, until, strong and lithe like a mountain lion, he can hasten forth to seek prey.[11] Nature above all must be his teacher, since you pedagogues will never devise a setting diverse enough to challenge and delight him as his abilities develop.

Hail to thee child who art born with an eye for proportion, ready to practice your talent on all nature's forms. When you gradually awaken to the joyful life around you and share the jubilant pleasure man feels after toil and fear and hope—the vintager's lusty song as the riches of autumn swell his vats, the reaper's lively dance after he has hung his idle sickle high on the beam—when the powerful forces of desire and suffering guide your brush in manlier strokes, when you have striven and suffered enough and have enjoyed enough, and when you are sated with earthly beauty and worthy to rest in the arms of the goddess, worthy to feel in her embrace the sensation which gave birth to the deified Hercules—then receive him, heavenly beauty, you mediator between gods and humans! And then, more than Prometheus, may he bring down the bliss of the gods upon our earth.[12]

On Gothic Architecture[1] (1823)

There must be something fascinating about the architectural style which Italians and Spaniards for a long time, but we Germans only recently, have called "German" (*tedesca, germanica*). It was used for buildings of all sizes for centuries, adopted by most of Europe and utilized by thousands of artists and tens of thousands of craftsmen; it helped greatly in furthering Christianity and had a powerful effect on spirit and mind. This style, then, must possess something great, something profoundly felt, fully thought-out and developed, and must both conceal and reveal[2] interrelationships whose effects are irresistible.

We were struck, therefore, by the testimony of a Frenchman whose own style was at odds with the one so extolled above and whose time held it in low esteem. Nonetheless, he said the following:

"Any gratification we derive from a beautiful work of art depends on whether regularity and symmetry are observed, because satisfaction is produced solely by proportions. If proportion is wanting, no amount of external ornamentation will compensate for the lack of inner beauty and charm. We may even say that ugliness becomes more obnoxious and unbearable if one tries to enhance the effect of ornamentation through intricate workmanship or costly material.

"I am inclined to go further and maintain that beauty, which stems from symmetry and proportion, does not at all need precious material and fine workmanship to win admiration; on the contrary, beauty shines forth, calling attention to itself in the midst of the tangled confusion of material and technique. Thus we look with pleasure at those sections of Gothic structures whose beauty seems to derive from the symmetry and proportion of the whole in relationship to its parts, and of the parts among themselves. Beauty is evident despite, and even in defiance of, the ugly embellishments which abound on those edifices. But what most convinces us is that upon careful examination of these sections, we generally find the same proportions as in the buildings which were constructed according to the rules of good architecture and are so pleasant to behold." (François Blondel, *Cours d'Architecture*, Cinquième partie. Livre V. Chap. XVI. XVII.)[3]

In this context, those years past come to mind when the Strasbourg Cathedral impressed us so greatly that we could not refrain from giving written expression to our delight.[4] The same conclusion which the French architect had reached after customary measurement and examination, we came to intuitively. After all, there is no law requiring that one account for impressions which take one by surprise.

It is not difficult to cite reasons why these buildings stood there for centuries as relics from the past, without making a particular impression on the public at large. But how powerful was their impact in recent times with the revival of interest in this style! The young and old of both sexes were overwhelmed by the sight of such structures and were inspired not only to seek pleasure and edification from repeated visiting, measuring and sketching, but also to have this style actually incorporated in the subsequent construction of buildings dedicated to the needs of real life. Here they found satisfaction in evoking the feeling of being back in the time of their ancestors.

Now that the interest in these achievements of the past has been aroused, we owe thanks to those who have made it possible for us to feel and understand the merits of this style in the real sense, that is, from a historical perspective. I feel in a position to offer a few remarks on this subject because of my close study of such important edifices.

After my departure from Strasbourg I saw no other major work of this type that I found imposing, and the impression faded. I hardly remembered the state of mind which had made it possible for me to react with such intense enthusiasm to the sight of the cathedral. My stay in Italy could not revive those feelings, especially since the modern alterations on the cathedral of Milan had changed its original character, and for many years I felt remote, if not alienated from this form of architecture.[5]

Then, in 1810, through the good offices of a distinguished friend, I entered into a close relationship with the Boisserée brothers.[6] They shared with me some of the outstanding results of their efforts. There were carefully executed drawings of the Cologne Cathedral, a ground plan and several elevations, which acquainted me with an edifice that, after thorough examination, I would say deserves recognition as the foremost example of this style. I resumed my studies of past years, acquired information through an exchange of visits with friends and the conscientious inspection of engravings, drawings and paintings of buildings from this period, so that I finally felt at home in that world once again.

But given the nature of the matter, and especially considering my age and position, the historical aspect of the whole undertaking necessarily became most important to me. In this regard, important collections owned by friends proved most helpful.

As good fortune would have it, Mr. Moller,[7] a highly cultivated and perceptive artist, also developed a lively interest in the enterprise and contributed significantly to it. A recently discovered architect's plan of the Cologne Cathedral lent the affair new interest. The lithograph of the cathedral, and particularly the counterproofs which made it possible through joining and coloring to represent visually the entire twin-towered edifice, produced a significant effect. At the same time—highly gratifying to the historically-minded—the excellent man undertook to present us with a chronological series of illustrations from earlier and more recent times, enabling us to follow easily the development of the style in question from its origin to its zenith and finally its decline. As a result our study of the subject has been greatly facilitated, especially since the first part of his work has now been completed and sections of the second, which is to deal with individual buildings in this style, have been made available to us.

We hope the public receives the endeavors of this perceptive and active man favorably, for now is the time to be concerned with such things and we must take advantage of the opportunity if we and generations to come are to arrive at a complete understanding of the matter.

And so we hope, too, that the Boisserée brothers' important work, the first installment of which we announced on a previous occasion, receives the same attention and interest.

I am most gratified to see the general public enjoy the benefits which I have been privileged to share for thirteen years, the length of time I have witnessed the Boisserées' laborious and persistent efforts. I was frequently privy to newly drawn plans as well as older drawings and engravings relevant to this style. But especially important were the proofs of major plates which were in the process of being produced by outstanding engravers.

As pleased as I was that the enthusiasm of my early years had been rekindled by the project, the greatest impetus was nonetheless provided by a brief visit to Cologne which I was fortunate to make in the company of Minister von Stein.[8]

I must admit that seeing the exterior of the Cologne Cathedral aroused a certain apprehension in me which I could not explain. A significant ruin has a venerable quality, and we sense and actually see in it the conflict between a noble work of man, and time that with silent force spares nothing. Here, on the other hand, we are confronted with an edifice which is unfinished and prodigious, and precisely its incompleteness reminds us of man's insufficiency when he attempts the colossal.

Even the interior of the cathedral, although impressive, frankly strikes us as inharmonious. Only when we enter the completed choir do we encounter a surprising harmony. Then we are happily amazed, then we are joyously startled and experience a sense of complete fulfillment.

But since I had already studied the ground plan at length and discussed it in detail with friends, I was able to closely follow here on location the traces of the original concept, because almost the entire

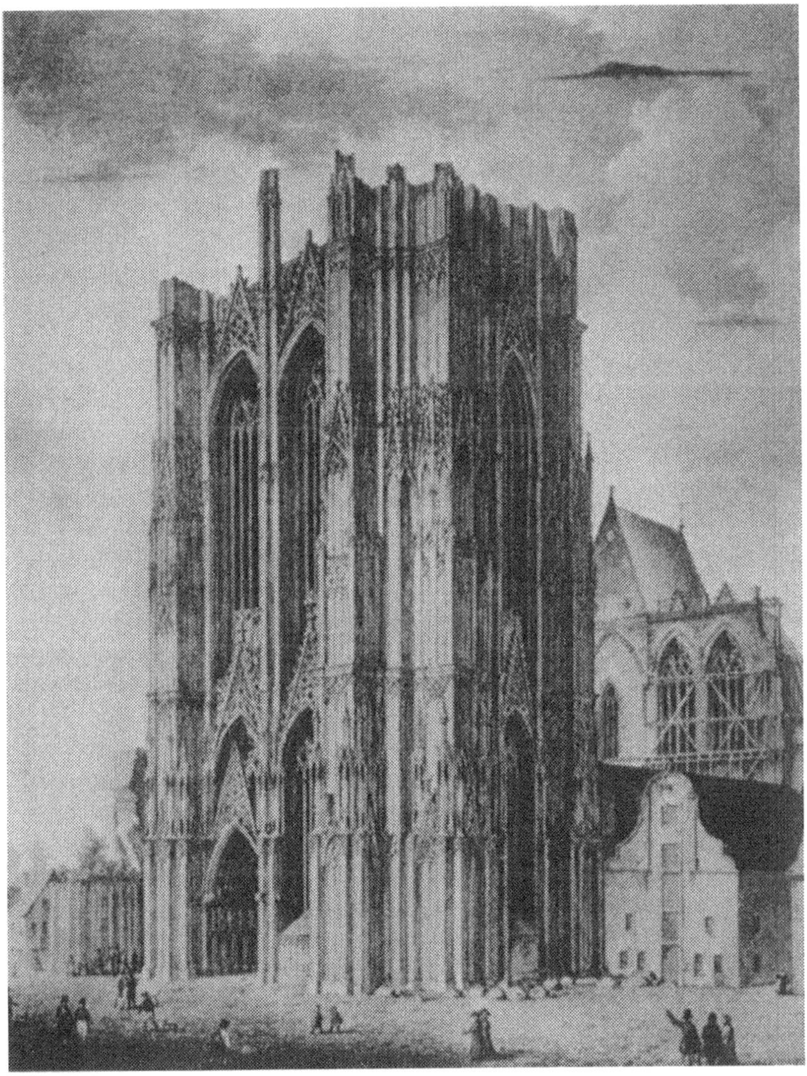

Cologne Cathedral. (Courtesy of the Picture Collection, the Branch Libraries, New York Public Library.)

foundation had been laid. The proofs of the side elevations and the drawing of the front elevation were also of some help in visualizing the entire structure. Yet what was missing still seemed so colossal that it was impossible to soar mentally to such heights.

However, now that the Boisserées' work is approaching completion, and illustrations and commentary will be available, the true art lover will have an opportunity, though he may live far away, to convince himself completely that the Cologne Cathedral represents the pinnacle of this architectural style. Should he some day visit the wondrous site, he will no longer succumb to his own particular feelings, to vague prejudice or even outright aversion. As an informed insider, an initiate, the visitor will be able to reflect on what is before him and substitute in his thoughts what is missing. I, at least, felt fortunate after fifty years of study to have reached this level of clarity through the effort of patriotic, imaginative, diligent and indefatigable young men.

It is quite natural that in resuming my studies of German architecture of the twelfth century my earlier admiration for the Strasbourg Cathedral often came to mind, as did the essay I wrote in 1773, the expression of my initial enthusiasm. On re-reading it I was pleased to discover that I had no cause to be ashamed, for I had been intuitively aware of the inner proportions of the whole, had grasped the natural evolvement of the ornamentations from this whole, and had concluded after lengthy and repeated observation that the single tower, although of sufficient height, was nonetheless unfinished. All this corresponded well with my friends' recent views as well as with my own. If the essay is somewhat rhapsodically rambling, that is perhaps excusable when one tries to express the inexpressible.

We will have occasion to return to this subject often. We conclude our present discussion by expressing our gratitude to those who did the painstaking preliminary work: Mr. Moller for his interpretative remarks on the engravings in question, and Mr. Büsching[9] for his 'Introduction to the History of Early German Architecture.' As another welcome resource I now have on hand the expert treatise written by Mr. Sulpiz Boisserée as introduction and commentary to the engravings.

Meanwhile, we wish a reprint of that aforementioned early essay of mine might soon appear; it would serve as a striking illustration of the difference between the first budding and the ripe fruit.

II
ANCIENT ART

On the *Laocoon* Group[1] (1798)

A genuine work of art, like a work of nature, will never reveal all its mysteries to the human mind. We view it, and it touches our soul. It speaks to our mind, yet we cannot comprehend it totally. Any attempt to express in words its essence and merits is even more futile. The following remarks on the *Laocoon* group, therefore, by no means presume to do justice to the subject or to present a critical discussion of this excellent work; they were simply inspired by it. It is to be hoped that the sculpture will soon again be exhibited in such a way that everyone can enjoy it and express his own views about it.[2]

If we want to speak about an outstanding work of art, we are practically compelled to talk about art in general, for such a work embodies all aspects of art, and anyone, according to his ability, can derive general rules from a specific case. Therefore, let me begin with some general observations.

All great works of art portray some aspect of man. The preferred subject of the plastic arts is the human body, and our present discussion is limited to them. Art has many levels, and on each one excellent artists may be found. However, a great work comprises all qualities that are normally found only separately.

The greatest works of art show us:

Highly Developed Human Forms.[3] We expect above all a knowledge of the human body, of its parts, proportions, its internal and external functions, its form and movement in general.

Individuation. Knowledge of the variations in appearance and functions of these parts. Particular qualities are isolated and highlighted; as a result, individual characters emerge. Through this, a significant relationship can be established among various works of art, and, in the case of a composite work, its individual components can exhibit a significant relationship among themselves. The subject can be:

At Rest or in Motion. The whole work of art or its components can either be represented complete within themselves, at rest, just existing, or they can be presented in motion, acting, expressing strong feelings.

The Ideal. To achieve ideal presentation, the artist must be profound, thorough, and persevering in his endeavors. Yet he must also possess the intellectual breadth to grasp his subject fully and to find the best moment to be portrayed. Such an artist can raise his subject above the limitations of the here and now and make it part of an ideal world, lending it the restraint, moderation, immediacy and dignity that befit this ideal world.

Grace. The subject and the manner in which it is portrayed must, however, obey the physical laws of art: order, clarity, symmetry, positioning, and so forth, which render it beautiful to the eye, that is, aesthetically graceful.

Beauty. The subject must also follow the law of spiritual beauty which results from restraint; an artist trained to portray or create beauty knows how to subject everything, even extremes, to this law.

These are the characteristics we expect of a great work of art. I do not believe I am overstating the case if I assert that the *Laocoon* group fulfills all these requirements, and that we can even derive all of the above laws from this particular work.

It would be superfluous to submit detailed proof of the artists'[4] knowledge of the human body and their ability to portray its characteristic features, as well as to show expression and passion. Their lofty and idealized concept of the subject will become evident in the course of our discussion; the beauty of the work is obvious to anyone who perceives with what restraint the extreme physical and mental suffering is presented here.

However, many readers will find it paradoxical if I maintain that the *Laocoon* group has grace as well. Let me elaborate briefly:

Every work of art must be identifiable as such; this is only possible if it exhibits what we call physical beauty, or grace. The artists of antiquity were not laboring under our present-day misconception that a work of art must appear to be a work of nature; rather, they identified their works of art as such by a conscious arrangement of components, employed symmetry to clarify the relationship among these components, and so made a work of art comprehensible. Through slight variations in symmetry and positioning the most effective contrasts became possible, and their painstaking efforts to juxtapose diverse subjects and particularly to achieve harmonious positioning of bodily extremities in groups were most judicious and successful. As a result, each one of their works pleases the eye, even if we disregard the content or see it only in general outline from a distance. Antique vases provide us with hundreds of examples of such graceful groupings, and it would no doubt be possible to illustrate the scope of such symmetrically artistic and visually pleasing compositions by comparing various examples, ranging from the most tranquil vase grouping to the extremely animated *Lao-*

coon group. Therefore, I say again that this work, in addition to all its other merits, is at one and the same time a model of symmetry and diversity, tranquility and motion, contrasts and gradations. The viewer perceives these varied qualities as a whole that is partly physical, partly spiritual, and—because of the sublime pathos of the subject—they arouse pleasurable feelings and finally calm the storm of suffering and intense emotions with their grace and beauty.

It is a great advantage for a work of art to be self-contained, complete in itself. A subject at rest presents solely itself, and therefore is complete by and in itself. Jupiter with the thunderbolt in his lap, Juno reposing with sovereign womanly dignity, Minerva lost in thought—all are subjects which, so to speak, have no contact with the outside world but are completely self-contained. Subjects like these are the sculptor's favorites. But within the glorious sphere of the mythical art world, where these self-contained beings reign in splendid isolation, there are also smaller spheres where figures are conceived and created in relation to others. For example, the nine Muses and their leader Apollo are conceived and created individually, yet each becomes more interesting if perceived as a member of a diverse group. If the artist seeks to portray exalted feelings, he can proceed in the same way: either he presents a group of figures who have a deeply felt relationship to each other, such as Niobe and her children persecuted by Apollo and Diana, or he shows us the motion together with its cause in a single figure. The examples that come to mind are the graceful boy removing a thorn from his foot, *The Wrestlers,* two groups of fauns and nymphs at Dresden, and the magnificent, animated *Laocoon* group.[5]

Sculpture deserves our high esteem because it can and must achieve ultimate perfection in the representation of its subject, since it divests man of all inessential elements. Laocoon lends only his name to the sculpture, since the artists have stripped him of his priesthood, his Trojan nationality, and of all poetic and mythological attributes. He is not Laocoon as portrayed in fiction, but simply a father who, together with his two sons, is about to fall prey to two deadly serpents. Nor are these animals here divine messengers, but simply snakes capable of overpowering several human beings. Neither in appearance nor in action are they supernatural creatures bent on vengeance or punishment. They approach stealthily, as snakes do, and coil themselves tightly around their victims. Only when one of them feels provoked does it bite. If I were ignorant of the Laocoon legend and had to classify this sculpture, I would call it a tragic idyl. A father was sleeping next to his two sons; they were attacked by two snakes, and, now awake, they are trying to extricate themselves from this reptilian net.

The great significance of this work lies in its presentation of a particular moment. If a sculpture is to convey to the viewer a sense of real movement, it has to portray a fleeting moment. We must be convinced that no part of the whole was in its present position just prior to this instant, and that no part will be in the same position just afterwards. If this is so, the sculpture will forever be a living image for countless millions.

In order to experience this sense of movement in the *Laocoon* group, I would suggest that you face the sculpture from a proper distance, eyes closed. If you open and then immediately close your eyes, you can see the whole marble in motion, and you will even expect the whole group to have changed its position before you glance at it a second time. I would describe the sculpture as a frozen lightning bolt, a wave petrified at the very instant it is about to break upon the shore. The effect is the same if the group is viewed at night by torchlight.

In portraying the particular situation of the three figures, the artists used a most ingenious technique of gradation. Only the extremities of the oldest son are ensnared, while the second is encircled several times and his chest is tightly bound. He tries to free himself by moving his right arm and with his left hand does no more than push the snake's head back slightly to prevent the creature from encircling him completely. The snake is about to slip out from under his hand, but it does *not* bite. The father, on the other hand, is trying by force to free himself and his sons from this entanglement: he squeezes the other snake and provokes it, so that it bites him in the hip.

The best way to explain the father's position both in general and in detail, it seems to me, is to say that the sudden pain from the bite is the primary cause of his movement. The snake is just in the act of biting, and, what is more, biting a sensitive part of the body, above and just behind the hip. (The position of the restored head of the snake does not correctly convey the actual biting; fortunately, the remains of both jaws on the back part of the statue have been preserved, and it is to be hoped that these most important remains will not be destroyed during the current woeful restoration efforts.) The snake wounds the unfortunate man in an extremely sensitive spot where even a slight irritation would produce the movement which is caused here by the bite: the body strains in the opposite direction, the abdomen is drawn in, the shoulder is forced down, the chest thrust out, and the head is inclined toward the afflicted side. Since the fettered feet and wrestling arms indicate the situation or action immediately preceding, we have a combination of struggle and flight, activity and passivity, resistance and surrender—a combination which would perhaps not be possible under any other circumstances. We are amazed at the artists' wisdom when we try to imagine the bite being inflicted somewhere else. All of Laocoon's gestures would then be different, and yet we cannot conceive of them being more appropriate than they are here. Therefore, we can

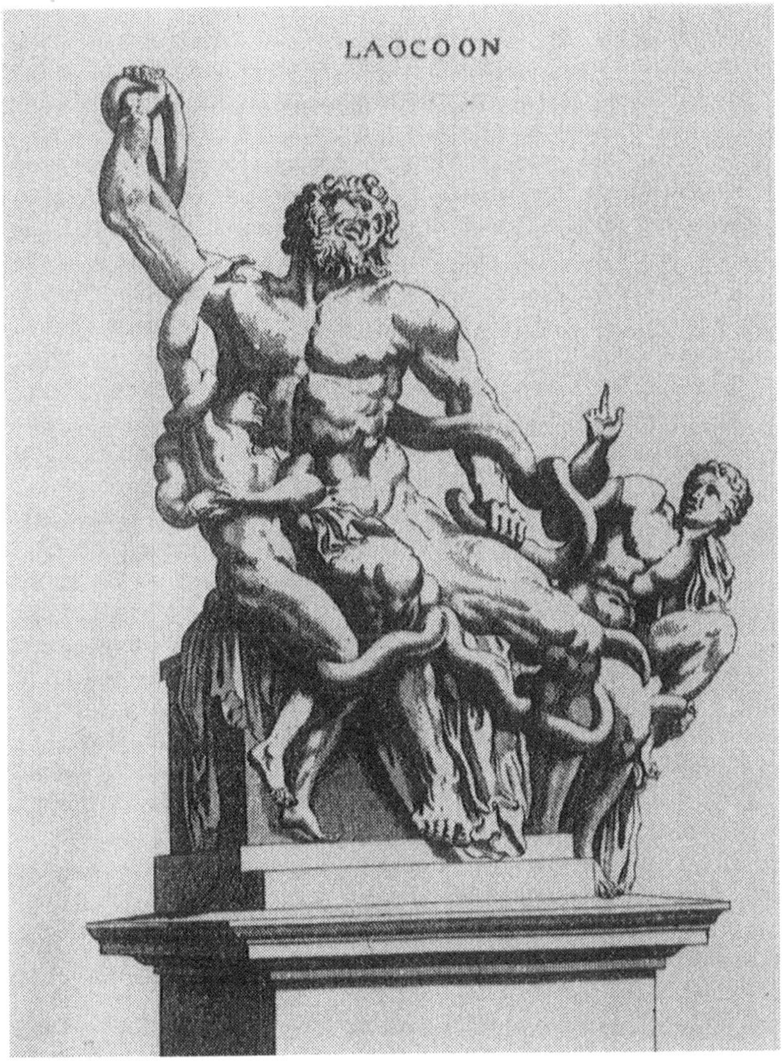

Engraving of the Laocoon statue from Montfaucon's *L'Antiquité expliquée*, Paris 1719–1724. (Courtesy of the Trustees of the Boston Public Library.)

infer the following: the artists have protrayed a physical effect together with its physical cause. I repeat, the location of the bite determines the present movement of the body: the evading motion of its lower part, the contraction of the abdominal muscles, the outward thrust of the chest, the lowering of the shoulder and the head. Even the facial expression is determined by this sudden, painful, unexpected stimulus.

Far be it from me to dispute the unity of mind and body. I do not deny the role of the mind in this splendid physique, nor do I fail to recognize the struggle and suffering of a great spirit. I do see that anxiety, fear, terror and paternal love rush through this man's veins, grip his heart and furrow his forehead, and I gladly admit that mental as well as physical suffering are protrayed to perfection. Yet, we must be careful not to confuse the effect the work of art has on us with the work itself. In particular, we should not imagine seeing the effect of venom in a body which is only at this moment feeling the snake's fangs. We must not imagine a death struggle taking place in the splendid, writhing healthy body which is scarcely wounded. At this point, permit me to interject something that is of importance for the plastic arts. The most sublime expression of pathos which art can achieve is to be found in the transition from one condition to another. A good example would be a child running along, full of vitality and joy of life, who is suddenly struck hard by a a playmate, or otherwise hurt physically or emotionally. The new sensation has the impact of an electric shock on his entire body. This moment of sudden transition has genuine pathos and can only be appreciated fully if one has experienced it. Obviously, it is a spiritual as well as physical effect. If during such a transition there remains a clear indication of what the previous condition was like, we have an ideal subject for sculpture, as in Laocoon, where struggling and suffering are combined in a single moment. Another example would be Eurydice cheerfully strolling over the meadows, carrying the flowers she has picked, and suddenly stepping on a snake which bites her in the heel. This would be a good subject for great pathos if the sculptor could express the dual condition of cheerful strolling and painful stopping. He would have to express this state not only by means of the flowers Eurydice drops but also through the position of her limbs and the swaying of the pleats in her garment.

Now that we have dealt in detail with the central figure of the *Laocoon* group, we can more easily analyze relationships, gradations and contrasts in all parts of the work.

The artists' choice of subject is one of the best imaginable. Human beings are battling against dangerous creatures which do not have to rely on large numbers or tremendous strength, but rather attack separately on separate fronts. Hence, concentrated resistance is ineffective; indeed, the snakes, because of their elongated bodies, are capable of rendering three people almost defenseless without injuring them. As a result of the figures' immobility, a certain sense of tranquility and unity pervades the group despite all movement. There is a gradation in the activity of the snakes, one only coiling itself around the victims, the other provoked and causing injury. The three human beings are also wisely chosen: a strong, well-built man, but past the prime of life and therefore no longer as capable of withstanding pain and suffering. (If we imagine in his place a robust young man, the group loses all its effectiveness.) His companions in suffering are two boys who are disproportionately small compared to him, and thus, like him, suggest two characters susceptible to pain.

The younger son struggles helplessly; he is frightened, but not injured. His father struggles valiantly but ineffectively, and his efforts produce just the opposite result: he provokes the snake and is wounded. The older son is the least entangled and experiences neither the snake's constriction nor any pain. But he is startled by his father's injury and sudden movement and cries out while trying to free one foot from the snake's tail. This son, then, plays the part of spectator, witness of the action and sympathetically involved onlooker, thus rounding out the work.

I would now like to remark further on what I have touched upon above. All three figures are engaged in a twofold action and are therefore participating in extremely varied activities. The younger son wants to extricate himself by raising his right arm and with his left hand pushes back the snake's head. He wants to make his present predicament more bearable and prevent a worse one—the highest degree of activity possible in his captive state. The father struggles to disengage himself from the snakes, and at the same time his body recoils from the bite. The older son is startled by his father's movement and tries to free himself from the loose hold of the snake.

I mentioned before that the choice of the highest moment of expression is a great achievement of this work, and I would like to discuss this point in more detail.

We assumed that natural snakes had entwined a father and his sons while they were asleep, since we wanted to determine the most suitable moment, the climax in a series of events. The first moments of being entwined while asleep are ominous, but insignificant for art. Perhaps the sleeping infant Hercules could be protrayed entwined by snakes, but then the depiction of his relaxed body would indicate what we could expect when he awakes.

If we now proceed and imagine the father awakening and realizing that he and his children have been entwined by snakes, then there is only one single moment of highest interest: when one of them has been rendered helpless by the snakes' entanglement; when the second is still able to defend himself although injured; and when the third still has a glimmer of hope for escape. The first is the younger son's situation, the second the father's, and the third the older son's. There is no other conceivable situation, nor can there be other roles than these for this cast of characters.

If we now visualize the action from the very beginning, we recognize that it has reached its climax at this point and that during the next and all subsequent moments the group must change. We also realize that there is no other moment artistically more significant than this one. The younger son will either be suffocated by the snake, or, helpless as he is, be bitten if he should provoke it. Either case would be unbearable because they are extreme situations which should not be portrayed. As for the father, he will either be bitten in another place, which would considerably change his body's position and cause the first wounds either not to be noticed or, if they were visible, to be felt as loathsome; or the snake could turn and attack the older son, which would divert his attention to himself. The scene would then lose its sympathetic onlooker, and the last vestige of hope in the group would be destroyed—it would no longer be a tragic presentation but a cruel one. The father, who is now self-contained in his greatness and suffering, would have to turn to his son and thus be a secondary figure, a sympathetic onlooker.

A human being reacts with only three kinds of emotion to his own suffering or that of others: fear, terror, and pity, that is to say, anxious anticipation of approaching evil, sudden awareness of present suffering and compassion for present or past suffering. All three reactions are represented as well as evoked by this work, and they are portrayed with appropriate gradations.

Since plastic art always aims at portraying one particular moment, the artist who chooses a tragic subject will always select the one that evokes terror. Literature, on the other hand, prefers subjects that evoke fear and pity. In the *Laocoon* group, the father's suffering evokes terror, indeed in the highest degree—sculpture has here reached its pinnacle in achieving this end. However, partly in order to have the viewer experience the whole gamut of emotions, and partly in order to soften the violent impact of terror, the artists evoke pity for the younger son and fear for the older by allowing a glimpse of hope for him. Through this diversity, the artists have managed to lend their work a certain balance; they have softened as well as strengthened one effect by means of other effects. And they have achieved a spiritual as well as a physical totality.

In brief, we are justified in saying that this work exhausts its subject and fulfills to perfection all the requirements for art. It teaches us the following: even though a master sculptor can imbue tranquil and simple subjects with his sense of beauty, he can reveal this sense most forcefully and majestically if in the creation of diverse characters he always tempers and restrains passionate outbursts of human nature. In a later discussion we will give a more detailed description of the statues known as the *Niobe* group, as well as the *Farnese Bull*.[6] They are among the few remaining ancient sculptures representing subjects that evoke feelings of pathos.

As a rule, modern artists have shown poor judgment in their choice of such subjects. Milo[7] with his hands caught in the cleft of a tree and attacked by a lion is not a subject to evoke pure compassion. Twofold pain, futile exertion, a helpless condition, and inevitable death can only evoke abhorrence, if they affect us at all.

And finally, a few remarks concerning this subject in relationship to poetry.

We are doing a great injustice to Virgil and poetry in general if we compare, even for a moment, the most self-contained of all sculptural masterpieces with the episodic treatment the subject receives in the *Aeneid*. Since Aeneas, the unfortunate exiled hero, is the narrator and must tell us himself that he and his compatriots committed the unpardonable folly of bringing the famous horse into their city, the poet is obliged to provide him with an excuse for this action. That is the poet's sole concern, and the story of Laocoon is only a rhetorical argument in which exaggeration, if it serves a purpose, is certainly acceptable. Monstrous serpents with crested heads emerge from the sea and rush upon the children of the priest who had damaged the horse, wind themselves around them, and bite and beslaver them. When their father rushes to their aid, the snakes wrap themselves around his chest and neck and hold their heads high in triumph, while the unfortunate father, thus encoiled, screams in vain for help. The people are horrified at the sight and flee; no one dares to be a patriot any longer. After listening to this imaginative and loathsome account, we are quite willing to agree that there was no alternative to bringing the horse into the city.

In Virgil, therefore, the Laocoon story serves merely as a means to an end; and in any event, it is highly debatable whether this episode is a subject for poetry at all.

Myron's Cow[1] (1818)

About 400 B.C., a Greek sculptor named Myron made a bronze cast of a cow. Cicero reports having seen the statue in Athens, and in the seventh century Procopius saw it in Rome. Thus, for over a thousand years the work had attracted attention. Although considerable information concerning this statue has come down to us, none of it is of much help in forming a clear idea of the original. Even more surprising is the fact that some thirty-six epigrams on the subject[2] are not more useful in this respect either and are only worthy of note as examples of the kind of confusion which poetically inclined viewers can cause. These epigrams are dull and neither descriptive nor informative, and for this reason tend to be more misleading than helpful when used as a basis for visualizing and defining the lost bronze. The named and unnamed authors seemingly tried to outdo each other in producing rhythmic pleasantries rather than address themselves seriously to the work itself. The best they can say is that they feel compelled to extol the statue's remarkable realism. But such praise by dilettantes is highly suspect.

It was certainly not Myron's goal to achieve a realism that vies with nature. As a direct successor of Phidias and Polyclitus,[3] he had loftier aspirations. He portrayed athletes, and even Hercules, and was no doubt able to lend a style to his works which set them apart from anything found in nature.

It is safe to assume that in antiquity no work gained fame which did not reveal superior creativity. For it is creativity that delights the connoisseur as well as the general public. How then did Myron manage to turn a cow into an important and significant work of art which attracted and fascinated so many through the centuries?

To be sure, all epigrams praise the statue's realism and naturalness, and the poets rival each other in assuring us that it would be easy to mistake the bronze cow for a real one. A lion is tempted to attack it, a bull to mount it, a calf to nurse from it, a herd to follow it. A herdsman tries to drive it on by throwing a stone and whipping it and blowing his horn. A peasant gets harness and plow for the cow to work in the field. A thief wants to steal it, a horsefly alights on it, and even Myron himself cannot distinguish it from the other cows in the herd.

Obviously the poets were trying to surpass each other in empty rhetorical flourishes. What the cow actually looked like and what it did remains obscure. It is even described as lowing—the very thing to make it realistic! Yet a lowing cow, if it were possible to portray it as a piece of sculpture, is such a base and, what is more, undefined motif that the high-minded Greek could not possibly have used it.

That it is a base subject is obvious to everyone. But it is also undefined and insignificant, for the cow may low yearning for the pasture, the herd, the bull, its calf, the stable, the milkmaid, and who knows what else. To be sure, the epigrams do not say that it actually lowed, only that it would low if it had lungs, just as it would move if it were not cast in bronze on a pedestal.

Perhaps we can reach our goal of visualizing the work despite these

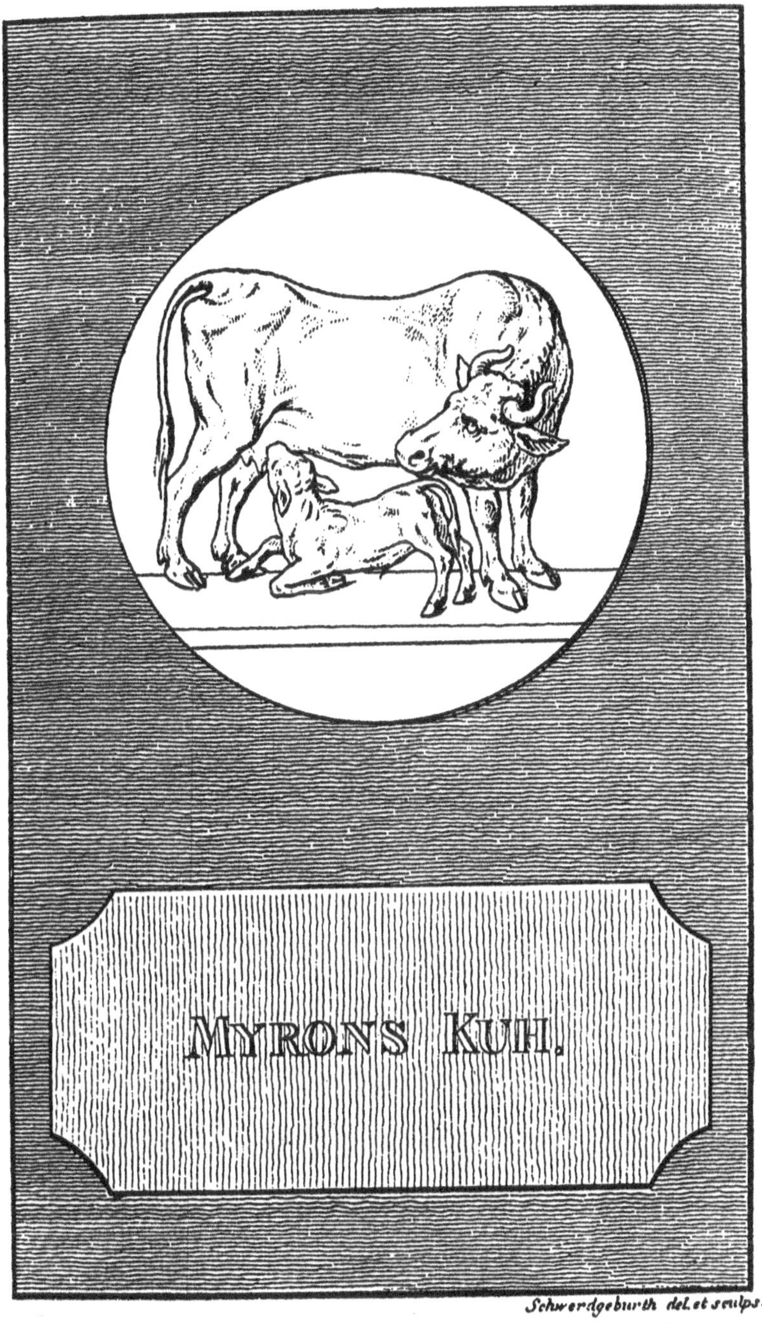

Myron's Cow. The drawing is by K. A. Schwerdgeburth, a contemporary of Goethe's. (Courtesy of the Harvard College Library.)

obstacles if we disregard all the misleading assumptions the epigrams make about the cow, and try to focus on the actual sculpture.

Either as complement or as contrast to the cow, it is impossible to imagine a lion, a bull, a herdsman, the rest of the herd, a peasant, a thief or a horsefly. But there is one living creature the artist could have permitted to associate with the cow, indeed the only suitable one—a calf. It was a nursing cow because only a nursing cow has significance for the herdowner, as a symbol of propagation and nourishment, as a provider of milk and calves.

If we eliminate all the misleading attributes with which the poets tried to embellish the statue (perhaps without ever having seen it), we are still left with some epigrams which explicitly mention that it was a cow with a calf, a nursing cow.

> Myron the wanderer created a cow; a calf, upon seeing her
> Approached to be nursed, believing that she was its mother.

> Poor calf! Why come you to me with such pitiful bleating?
> Art did not furnish my udder with milk.

Were we to doubt the specific description in these two epigrams and maintain that the calf, just like the other fictitious companions, was only a poetic adornment, we could find irrefutable confirmation in the following:

> O herdsman, shun the cow and let your flute be still,
> So that her calf may nurse in peace.

The word flute probably refers to the horn the herdsman sounds to move his herd, but he is not to sound it near this cow, for she must not be disturbed. The calf is not imaginary, but actually perceived by the poet and addressed as a living being, like the cow.

If all doubts are now eliminated and we are on the right track, having separated the true attributes from the fanciful ones, the sculptural adornments from the poetic ones, how much more delighted we are to see our theory confirmed and our efforts crowned by the existence of an illustration handed down from antiquity. It has been frequently reproduced on coins from Dyrrhachium and is identical in its major features on all of them. We enclose a sketch and would wish that a skillful artist would create the relief portrait once again as a statue.[4]

Since the magnificent work is now accessible, even though as an inexact reproduction, I need not point out the excellence of the composition at length. The cow, sturdy on her legs as if on pillars, provides with her splendid body protection for the nursing calf. The hungry young creature is sheltered as if in a niche, a cell, a sanctuary, and occupies with utmost grace the space that is organically defined by the cow's body. The half-kneeling position is reminiscent of a supplicant. The upturned head, both pleading and receiving, the gentle effort, the restrained vigor—everything is faintly suggested in the best of these copies, but it must have been perfect beyond imagination in the original. And now the mother turns her head towards the center, and the whole composition is perfectly rounded and complete. It attracts our attention and holds our interest, so that we do not want to, and indeed cannot, imagine anything else outside or next to it. For, like any true work of art, it excludes and momentarily eliminates anything extraneous.

The compositional talent revealed in this work—the balance to be found in apparent imbalance, the contrast to be found in things which are similar, the harmony to be found in things which are dissimilar, and everything which defies expression in words—that is what the sculptor should strive for. But here we dare say that it was the naiveté of the concept, and not naturalism in execution, which delighted all of antiquity.

Nursing is animal behavior, and in four-footed animals a very graceful act. The passive, uncomprehending amazement of the nursing mother and the vigorous, purposeful activity of the offspring offer a magnificent contrast. A foal, already grown to considerable size, still kneels down to be able to obtain the desired nourishment by energetic sucking. The mare, half irritated, half relieved, turns her head, and this movement results in the most intimate scene. City dwellers rarely have the opportunity to see a cow nursing her calf or a mare her foal. Yet during a walk on a spring day we may observe this act with delight in ewes and lambs, and I urge every art and nature lover to pay more attention to such scenes in pastures and fields.

But to return to our sculpture. I think we can generalize and say that animals, individually or in groups, are effective as artistic subjects if the artist depicts them from the side to which the head is turned, because our attention is focused there. For this reason, such portrayals are suited for statues and paintings, as well as bas-reliefs. That explains why Myron's cow could be so perfectly reproduced even on coins.

From animal statuary, rightly held in high esteem, we turn to the gods. It would have been impossible for a Greek sculptor to represent a goddess in the act of nursing a child. The poet, on the other hand, who describes Juno suckling Hercules is not to be censured, since he produces such a superb effect by having the Milky Way created from the milk the divine mother has spilled. The sculptor, however, must reject such subjects. To have Juno or Pallas Athena in marble, bronze or ivory together with a baby son would have demeaned their divine majesty.[5] In high antiquity, Venus, because of her girdle the eternal virgin, has no son. To be sure, Eros, Amor and Cupid, products of an earlier time, appear in the company of Aphrodite, yet they do not seem closely related to her.

At most, beings of lower rank in the mythological hierarchy, such as mortal heroines, nymphs and fauns, who were assigned the roles of nursemaids and tutors, may be portrayed tending a child. For example, Jupiter himself was nursed by a nymph or, as was sometimes said, by a goat, and other gods and heroes were similarly raised in a remote wilderness. Amalthea and Chiron and many others come to mind as examples.[6]

Sculptors have best demonstrated their fine artistic sense and taste by portraying the animal activity of nursing in semihuman subjects. Zeuxis' centaur family is a splendid example. The centaur woman is reclining on the grass, suckling her youngest hybrid offspring while another is being nursed by a mare, and the father in the background displays his prey, a young lion. A family portrait of water-gods, a lovely engraved gem, has also been preserved, probably an imitation of one of Skopa's famous groups.[7]

A triton couple calmly wades through the waves, with one of their offspring, half fish, half boy, cavorting in the water in front of them. Another, disliking perhaps the taste of salty water after having nursed, clamors for his mother to pick him up, which she does while clasping the youngest to her breast. We can hardly imagine anything more graceful, in concept and in execution.

We pass over many similar examples by which the ancients have taught us what excellent subjects nature provides on all levels, whether her head touches the heavens where the gods reside, or her feet the earth where the animals dwell.

There is still one other subject that we must not omit: the Roman she-wolf.[8] No matter how it is depicted, even in the crudest imitation, it is always a source of great pleasure. Two children of heroes receive their nourishment from the full teats of the wild beast, and the savage creature of the forest gazes maternally at her adopted children. Human beings in most intimate contact with a wild animal, a ferocious monster as their mother and nurse—we can certainly expect a miraculous effect on the world from such a miracle. It may well be that the legend was first conceived by an artist who recognized the sculptural potential of such a scene.

But how weak, in comparison with such a grandiose concept, appears a madonna and child. . . .[9]

The Greeks' goal is to deify man, not humanize gods—it is theomorphism, not anthropomorphism! Furthermore, the animal in man is not to be ennobled, but rather the human element in animals emphasized, so that we can delight in them in a higher, artistic sense. After all, we already do this with real animals which, following an irresistible instinct, we are fond of choosing as our companions and servants.

Returning once more to Myron's cow, we would like to mention our speculation that the sculptor portrayed a young cow who has calved for the first time, and furthermore, that the statue may have been less than life-size.

We repeat what we said above, namely that an artist like Myron would not have attempted to outdo nature for the purpose of crude deception, but rather that he knew how to perceive the essence of nature and express it. Because his work communicates itself in an absolutely natural way, we can forgive the ordinary viewer or the dilettante, the orator or the poet, if they see as pure nature what in reality is the product of the highest, deliberate art, namely the harmonious effect which makes the viewer's mind and senses focus on one point. But it would be unforgivable if we maintained even for one moment that the high-minded artist Myron, the successor of Phidias and the predecessor of Praxiteles, lacked artistic insight and grace of expression in creating his statue.

In conclusion we take the liberty of quoting some modern epigrams which refer to this work. The first is by Ménage,[10] who describes Juno as being jealous of this cow because she sees in it a second Io. This worthy poet of modern times was the first to notice how many idealized animal figures there were in antiquity and, what with all the love affairs and metamorphoses, how well they were suited to facilitate encounters between gods and humans. This is an important artistic concept which we should note in judging works from that period. Ménage's lines are as follows:

> When she observed your small cow, the bronze one, O Myron,
> Juno grew jealous, believing her Inachus'[11] daughter.

And lastly, a few rhythmic lines which may give a summary of our view:

> That you are most splendid and could be the jewel of Admetos'[12] herd;
> That you seem to come from the drove of the sungod himself:—
> All this fills me with wonder and moves me to praise of the artist.
> But that you can also show motherly feelings—that touches my soul.

A Grave Near Cumae[1] (1812)

Once again, my good sir, you have presented lovers of art with a beautiful, no doubt unique gift, and I for my part hasten to express my profound gratitude. In addition to publishing your extremely important findings, you have done everything possible to interpret and explain them with reference to ancient traditions.

Permit me to indicate here briefly how I, enlightened by your article, have endeavored to understand in my own way these reliefs that have so delighted me. Please excuse my brevity, but I am preparing to depart for Karlsbad.

The tomb you discovered is probably that of a celebrated dancer who, to the distress of her friends and admirers, departed much too early from the stage of life. I regard the three pictures as a cycle, a trilogy. The talented performer appears in all three. In the first, she entertains a rich man's guests, awakening in them the joy of life. The second shows her in Tartarus, the region of decay and limbo-like existence, barely able to continue her art. In the third she is seemingly restored to life, having arrived in the eternal bliss of the shades. The first picture and the last allow no other interpretation; the interpretation of the second derives for me from the other two.

Is it really necessary to examine in detail these beautiful artistic products which appeal so directly to the mind, the emotions and to artistic taste? Yet, on the other hand, it is not easy to tear oneself away from something charming, and so I take pleasure in expressing those thoughts and feelings which are revived every time I look at these lovely works of art.

The first relief shows the spirited dancer as the crowning attraction at a banquet, where guests of all ages watch her with amazement. Uninterrupted attention is the highest form of applause bestowable by the elderly, who, though just as receptive as the young, are not as easily prompted to express themselves. Middle age conveys admiration with a modest hand gesture, as does youth. The young man here, in addition, hunches forward with feeling, and the youngest of the group actually starts forward and claps his hands to applaud the performance.

We turn now from the effect produced by the dancer, which because of its gradations first caught our eye, to the dancer herself. She is portrayed in one of those striking positions by means of which dancers manage to delight us so thoroughly in performance. The beautiful fluidity of movement that we admire in such artists is here fixed for the moment, so that we simultaneously see previous, present and subsequent movements, and are already transported into a different world. Here, too, art triumphs by changing common sensuousness into a higher form, so that hardly a trace of its earlier state is noticeable.

There is little doubt that the dancer is portraying a bacchante[2] and going through a set of characteristic positions and actions. On a side table are the accessories she needs to lend the different parts of her presentation variety and expressiveness. The bust hovering in the

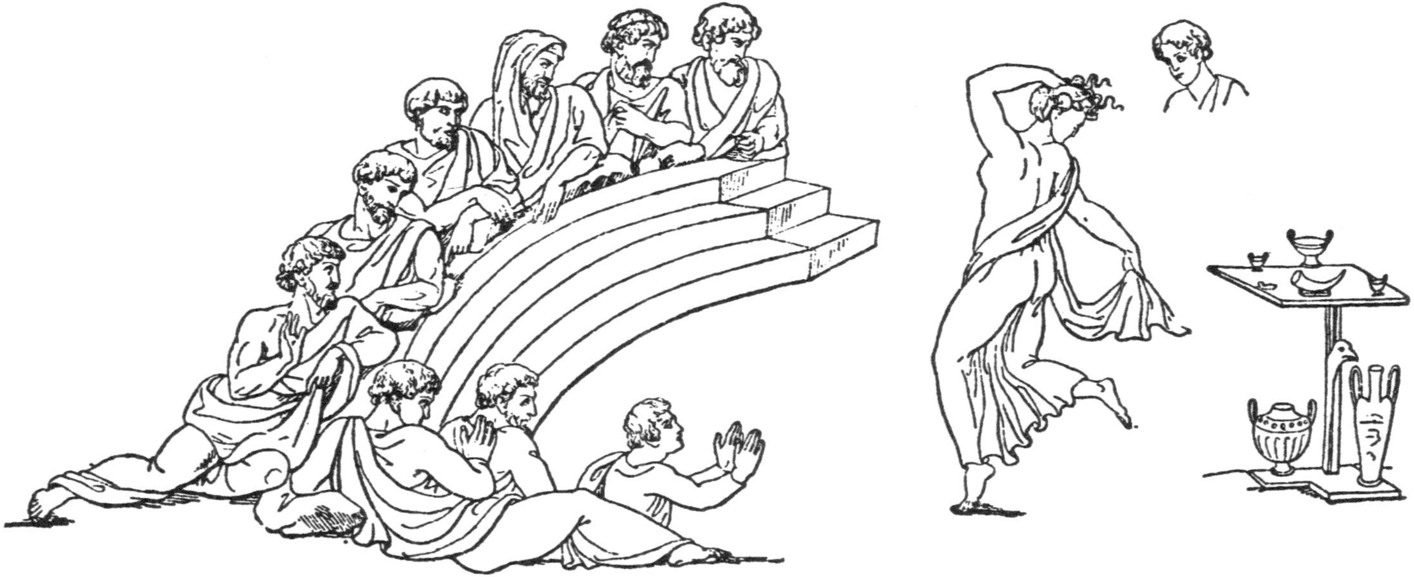

Greek grave near Cumae. (Courtesy of the Harvard College Library.)

background seems to indicate an assistant who hands the props to the main figure and now and then plays the part of an extra. Everything suggests to me a solo performance.

Now to the second print. While in the first the dancer appeared lively and vivacious, full-figured, lithe, graceful, undulating and fluid, here in the dismal realm of the lemures we see quite the opposite. To be sure, she again stands on one leg, but she presses the other against the thigh of the first as if for support. Her left hand is resting on her hip as though it did not have enough strength to hold itself up. We find here the unaesthetic cruciform, the limbs are zigzag, and even the raised right arm, moving into what in life would have been a graceful position, adds to the strange effect. The supporting leg, the hand on hip, the bent knee pressed against the thigh, everything gives the impression of being stationary, movable yet immovable—a true portrait of the lamentable lemures who have just enough muscle and sinew to be able to move and not to appear as complete skeletons which must ultimately collapse.

But even in this repulsive condition the dancer still seems attractive, artistic and invigorating to her audience. The eagerness of the crowd hurrying to see her, the applause of those calmly watching her are exquisitely symbolized by the two half-ghosts. Each figure individually is superbly done, and all three as a group harmonize, convey a single meaning and produce a single effect.—But what is this meaning, what is this effect?

Art, which is god-like in that it ennobles and elevates, will not reject the repulsive and the loathsome. Here is just where it will exert its divine prerogative. But it has only one way of doing so: art can only master ugliness by treating it comically. Zeuxis comes to mind, who is said to have died from laughter at his supremely ugly rendering of Hecuba.[3]

In life, an artist such as this dancer had to be versatile enough to master all dance forms and portray all roles. We know from experience that the funny and roguish impromptu performances of such a talent often entertain us more than the serious and dignified presentations which require much preparation and effort.

Fit out this ghostly monstrosity with the muscles and flesh of a young woman, cover her with glowing skin, dress her in an appropriate garment—all of which any tasteful artist today can do with ease—and we will see one of those comical poses with which Harlequin and Colombine have always amused us. Proceed the same way with the secondary figures, and we realize that they are intended to represent the common crowd usually attracted to such shows.

I hope I will be forgiven for having gone into more detail than perhaps necessary. But not everyone would grant me at first glance my inter-

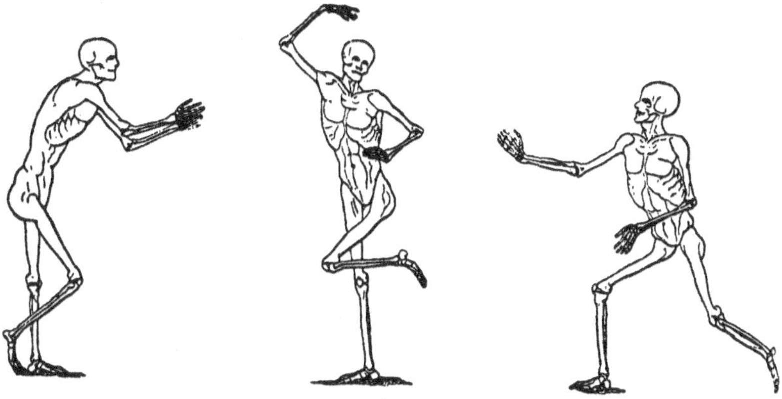

Greek grave near Cumae. (Courtesy of the Harvard College Library.)

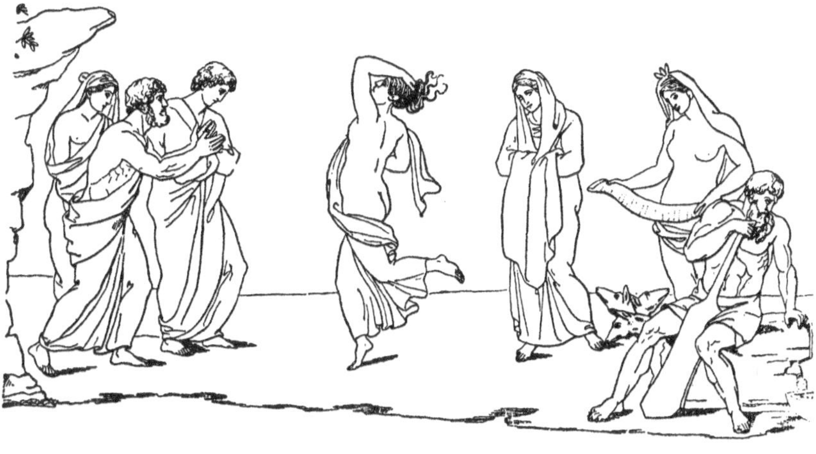

Greek grave near Cumae. (Courtesy of the Trustees of the Boston Public Library.)

pretation of this humorous stroke of genius from antiquity, whose magical power interposes a ghostly farce between a human drama and a spiritual tragedy, interjects a grotesquerie between the beautiful and the sublime. I admit that I cannot easily think of anything more admirable than the aesthetic juxtaposing of these three states containing everything that man can know, feel, imagine and believe about his present and future.

The last picture, like the first, speaks for itself. Charon has ferried the artist into the realm of the shades and is looking back to see if perhaps new passengers are waiting. A divine figure, who is favorably disposed to the dead and thus records their merits in the realm of forgetfulness, examines with satisfaction an open scroll that may well list the roles for which the dancer had been admired in life. For, since monuments were erected for poets and the titles of their tragedies inscribed on tablets next to their statues,[4] should not the performing artist have enjoyed a similar privilege?

And particularly an artist such as this, who continues and perfects her activities here, as Orion[5] continued his hunts. Cerberus[6] remains silent in her presence. Already she has attracted new admirers, perhaps some from her former life who have preceded her to these dark regions. Nor does she lack a servant: here also one is in constant attendance and, continuing her former duties, holds a shawl ready for her mistress. These figures are grouped and positioned beautifully and tellingly. And yet, as in the other prints, they are merely the frame for the actual center of attention, the figure that here as elsewhere emerges as dominant. The dancer makes a forceful impression with a maenadic movement which might well represent the finale of her Bacchic dance, because movement any more frenetic would result in distortion. In the midst of the artistic enthusiasm which inspires the dancer even in Hades, she seems to feel the difference between her present condition and the one she has just left. Her position and expression are tragic, and now she could just as well be representing a woman in despair as one powerfully inspired by a god. While in the first picture she appeared to tease her audience by deliberately averting her face, here her mind is distracted. Her admirers stand applauding in front of her, yet she pays no attention to them. She is aloof to everything around her, withdrawn completely into her inner self. And so she concludes her dance by expressing, mutely to be sure, but in clear pantomime, a tragic, truly pagan value she shares with Achilles of the *Odyssey*, namely that it is better to carry the shawl for a dancer among the living than to be considered the best dancer among the dead.[7]

If I should be accused of having read too much[8] into these pictures, I would say that should my essay be unacceptable as an interpretation of these pictures, it could be considered a poem about a poem, from the comparison of which new enjoyment might be derived.

I do not, of course, wish to deny that beneath the sensuous-esthetic surface of these pictures, something else may be hidden. Although it may not be visible to the eye of the artist and the art lover, once it is discovered by scholars of antiquity, we should accept it gratefully as an aid to deeper understanding.

Despite my detailed interpretation of concept and execution of these reliefs, I believe I have cause to doubt their great antiquity. If they had been produced by ancient Greek inhabitants of Cumae, they would have to be placed in the time before Alexander, when art in general had not yet attained such facility and subtleness. If we consider the elegance of the dancer found at Herculaneum,[9] we are tempted to attribute the Cumae discovery to artists of that period, all the more so since there are works among the Herculanean findings comparable in artistic intent and composition.

The Greek word-fragments found in the tomb do not seem convincing proof to me because the Romans were also quite fluent in that language; it had been commonly spoken in the area since early times and was probably also used on more recent monuments. Indeed, I must confess that the lemurian jest simply does not seem genuinely Greek to me. I am more inclined to say it dates back to those times from which the older and the younger Philostratos[10] got their more or less fictive stories, their poetic and rhetorical descriptions. I will not venture to say more in support of this opinion. Whether I am right or wrong does not of course detract from the excellence of the pictures themselves, and there is no question that with repeated observation and contemplation our gratitude to the discoverer and editor increases.

I hope these remarks are kindly received. I intended to be briefer, but if we try to be too concise on such a subject, we run the risk of becoming like lemures ourselves.

III
EUROPEAN ART

Giuseppe Bossi: On Leonardo da Vinci's *Last Supper* at Milan[1] (1817)

The author of this important treatise, Giuseppe Bossi, was born in Milan in 1777. An intelligent and gifted child, he exhibited considerable artistic interest and talent, which he seems to have developed both on his own and by using Leonardo da Vinci's art as a model. We know that after a six-year stay in Rome he returned to his native city, where he was appointed director of an art academy which was to be reorganized there.

Since he was interested in the theory as well as the practice of art, he became well versed in basic artistic principles and in art history. This made him eminently qualified to take on the difficult project of producing an accurate copy of da Vinci's famous painting, *The Last Supper,* which was to be reproduced in mosaic to preserve it for posterity. In his treatise Bossi gives an account of his working procedures. We intend to provide a brief summary of these.

In general, Bossi's book has enjoyed a favorable reception. We here in Weimar are fortunate to be in a position to evaluate it in greater detail. Let me explain why. Because Leonardo's original was of no use for his project—it was thoroughly ruined and painted over—Bossi had to examine all available copies carefully. He prepared tracings of the heads and probably the hands of three of these copies and tried to immerse himself as deeply as possible in the spirit of his great predecessor to divine his intentions. Guided by his own expert judgement, discrimination and intuition, he finally succeeded in completing a preliminary drawing for the now finished mosaic. Those tracings are all here in Weimar because His Royal Highness, the Grand Duke of Weimar, acquired them on his last journey to Lombardy. How great their value is will become apparent in our subsequent discussion.

Some Remarks on Leonardo's Life

Vinci, a castle and manor in the Arno valley near Florence, belonged in the mid-fourteen hundreds to a man named Piero, who had a natural son by an unidentified woman. The boy, Leonardo, was endowed with all the knightly virtues: physical strength, athletic skills, gentility and fine manners. But most pronounced were his passionate love of art and his artistic ability. Accordingly, he was dispatched to Florence to study with Verrochio, a man of intellect, well-grounded in the theory of art. To his teacher's distress, Leonardo soon surpassed him as a painter.

At that time, art had reached a point where any promising artist could begin a career and enjoy respect and admiration for his achievements. For more than two centuries, art had struggled to break free from the sterile formality of the Byzantine school[2] and had gained new life through the imitation of nature and the expression of pious and moral sentiments. Artists produced excellent works, but were unaware of artistic principles. They followed the prompting of their genius, guided by intuition and their particular level of artistic sophistication. However, none of them was yet able to account for his excellence or his shortcomings, even though he may have sensed or noticed them. Everyone had an eye for truth and naturalness, but an organic harmony was lacking. We find the most exquisite subjects, and still, none of the works was conceived as a perfect unit or was thoroughly developed. Everywhere we see randomness and incongruity. Standards and principles had not yet been established by which the artists could have judged their own works.

Into these times Leonardo was born. Because of his innate talent it was easy for him to imitate nature, but his penetrating mind soon told him that behind the externals, which he could recreate so well, there lay secrets which he should do his utmost to unveil. So he tried to establish the laws of organic structure, the principle of proportion; he worked to determine the rules of perspective and composition, the proper positioning and coloring of his subjects in a given space—in short, he tried to fathom the basic components of art. What fascinated him most was the expressiveness of the human face, which reflects a person's permanent character as well as his momentary passions. That is the point we wish to dwell on in most detail in connection with the *Last Supper*.

Leonardo's Public Works

The political unrest in Florence caused by the incompetent Piero Medici forced Leonardo to move to Lombardy. There, after Duke Francesco Sforza's death, his successor, Lodovico ('The Moor'), intended to pay hommage to his predecessor—as well as to himself—by following Sforza's practice of glorifying his reign through works of art. Immediately, Leonardo was commissioned to create a gigantic equestrian statue, which took a number of years to complete and was widely admired. While it was being paraded during a festival as the most splendid example of the art of sculpture, it was so badly damaged that Leonardo was forced to begin work on a new statue. When this was completed, the French invaded Italy, and soldiers used the statue for target practice and demolished it. Thus nothing remains of those two works which had taken sixteen years to complete. From this example we see that vain ostentation as well as barbarous ignorance proves to be highly detrimental to the arts.

We refer only in passing to the 'Battle of Anghiari,' for which Leonardo made a preparatory drawing in Florence in competition with Michelangelo, and to the picture of St. Anne, where grandmother, mother and grandchild are artfully grouped, sitting lap in lap.[3]

The Last Supper

We turn now to the main subject of our discussion, the *Last Supper*, a mural in the monastery Santa Maria delle Grazie in Milan. Our remarks regarding the whole picture or details of it may be easier to follow if the reader consults Morghen's print,[4] which should prove adequate for this purpose.

The place where the picture is painted will be considered first of all, for the choice of location reveals perfectly the essence of the artist's wisdom. Could there be a more appropriate or better conceived subject for a painting in a refectory than a farewell supper, which was destined to become eternally sacred to the whole world?

On a journey some years ago, we had the opportunity to see the dining hall when it was still intact. The prior's table stood at the far end of the hall, along the short wall of the room opposite the entrance. The monks' tables, all raised one step from the floor, were along the long wall on both sides. When the entering visitor turned, he saw on the fourth wall, above two doors of medium height, a painting of a fourth table: Christ and his disciples, as if they were part of the group of diners. It must have been an impressive sight at mealtime, when the prior's table and Christ's faced each other, and the monks found themselves between them. Leonardo must have anticipated this effect and made the wise decision to use the monks' tables as a model. We also can be sure that the tablecloth with its pleated folds, its striped pattern and knotted corners came from the monastery's linen closet, and that the bowls, plates, cups and other utensils are similar to those used by the monks.

In this setting, trying to approximate the costuming of a distant time was out of the question, and it would have been highly inappropriate to have this holy group recline on cushions. Clearly, the diners had to appear as contemporary as possible—Christ was simply having supper in the company of Dominican monks in Milan.

The painting must have been quite striking in other respects too. The thirteen figures are positioned about ten feet above the floor, are one and one-half times life-size, and occupy a space twenty-eight feet in length. Only the two persons sitting at opposite ends of the table are seen full-length; all the others are half-figures. The artist turned even this necessary positioning to his advantage, for a deep emotion is expressed exclusively by the upper part of the body, and then the feet usually prove distracting. Here Leonardo created eleven half-figures, keeping their laps and knees covered by the table and the tablecloth, and making their feet scarcely discernible in the shadow.

If we imagine ourselves there in the hall, in the decorous, peaceful atmosphere customary in a refectory, we must admire the artist who was able to lend his painting powerful emotions and passionate movement and, while making his work as life-like as possible, was able at the same time to contrast it with its immediate surroundings.

The means the artist used to arouse such passionate reactions in the tranquil, sacred group are the words of the Master: "There is one among you who will betray me."[5] The words have just been spoken, and now there is general consternation among the disciples. The Master, however, bows his head, with eyes downcast. His posture, the movement of his arms and hands, everything repeats with divine resignation, and his silence itself confirms, those fateful words: "Verily, verily! There is one among you who will betray me."

Before proceeding any further, however, we must analyze an important technique which is the primary means Leonardo employs to enliven his picture: hand movements. Only an Italian would have thought of that. For Italians, the entire body speaks; all parts contribute to the expression of feelings, passion, and even thought. They use various hand gestures and motions to express: "What do I care!—Come here!—He's a crook, watch out!—To hell with him!—This is important, listen closely!" Leonardo, an eager student of characteristic expressions, was obviously keenly aware of this national trait, and the *Last Supper* is unique in that it provides inexhaustible evidence of this awareness. The harmonious interplay between physiognomy and gesture is masterfully rendered, as are the positioning and the contrasting movements of arms and hands, which is readily discernible to the viewer.

The figures on either side of the Lord can be divided into two groups of three, but are still conceived of as individuals who are placed in complementary as well as contrasting positions. The first group on Christ's right consists of John, Judas and Peter.

Of the three, Peter, the short-tempered disciple, is sitting furthest from Jesus. Upon hearing His words, he rises quickly and leans forward behind Judas' back. The latter, looking up with a start, leans over the table, clutching a closed purse tightly in his fist, and with his left hand makes a convulsive gesture as if to say, "What does this mean? What is this?" Peter meanwhile has seized John, who is leaning toward him, by the left shoulder and, pointing at Christ, seems to be urging the

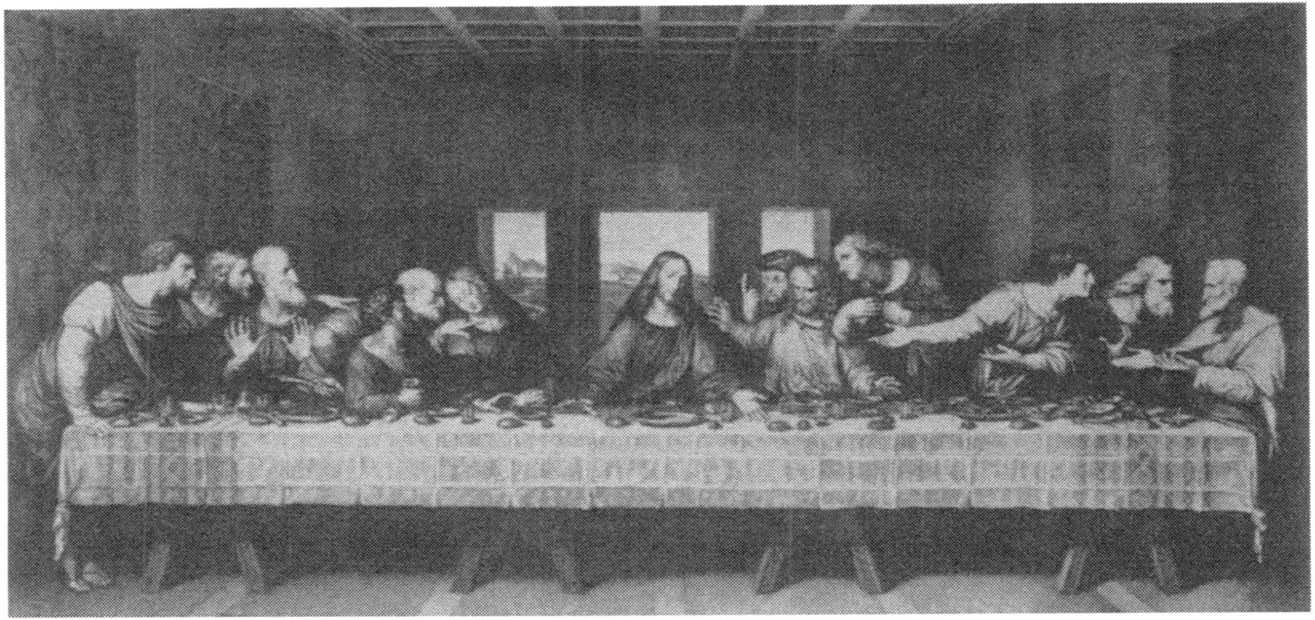

Leonardo da Vinci's *Last Supper*. Engraving by Raphael Morghen.
(Courtesy of the Trustees of the Boston Public Library.)

beloved disciple to ask the Lord who the traitor is. Holding a knife in his right hand, Peter accidentally jabs Judas in the ribs with its handle. This unintentional jab precipitates Judas' startled lurch forward, which in turn causes him to knock over a saltcellar. This group may have been the first conceived by the artist, for it is the best realized.

While desire for immediate revenge is expressed with moderate movement on Christ's right, intense horror and outrage at the betrayal are evident on his left. James the Elder recoils in terror, stretches out his arms, lowers his head and stares into space, as if his eyes were already seeing the abomination that his ears have just heard. Thomas peers from behind his shoulder and raises his right index finger to his forehead while approaching the Saviour. Philip, the last of the three, rounds out the group superbly. He has stood up and, bending toward the Master, lays his hands on his chest as if insisting: "Lord, not I! You know that! You know my heart is pure. Not I!"

The second group on this side presents us with new subject matter to consider. The three disciples are discussing among themselves the terrifying words they have just heard. Matthew turns his face eagerly towards his two companions on his left, while extending his hands quickly in the other direction towards Christ. By this admirable artistic device, Leonardo has linked this group to the first one. Thaddaeus shows utmost surprise, doubt and suspicion. He has placed his left hand on the table, palm up, and raised his right as if he were about to bring the back of it down into his left. This is a gesture we can still observe today among simple people if, after something unexpected, they want to say: "Didn't I tell you! I knew it!" Simon, with great dignity, is sitting at the end of the table so that his entire figure is visible. He, the oldest of the disciples, is dressed in a garment rich in folds. His face and motions indicate that he is pondering what he has just heard and is troubled by it, though not shaken and certainly not agitated.

If we now look at the opposite end of the table, we see Bartholomew leaning forward, standing on his right foot, his left crossed over, both hands resting calmly on the table, supporting his body. He is listening, probably to hear what John will find out from the Lord, since everyone on Christ's right seems to be urging the beloved disciple to ask the question. James the Younger, next to Bartholomew but partly hidden by him, places his left hand on Peter's shoulder, just as Peter puts his on John's. But James does so gently, only asking for clarification, while Peter threatens revenge.

And just as Peter extends his hand behind Judas, James the Younger reaches behind Andrew. The latter, one of the most prominent figures, raises his hands, palms forward—an unambiguous expression of horror. This gesture appears only once in the picture, whereas in other works, less ingenious and less well thought-out, it is unfortunately overused.

Technical Procedures

Although we have by no means exhausted the subject of figures, faces, movement and costume, let us proceed to the next and, unfortunately, somewhat disturbing part of our discussion, namely the mechanical, chemical and technical aids the artist used in producing his magnificent work. The most recent investigations have made all too clear that the picture was painted on the wall in oil. This technique, already accepted and proven successful at that time, must have been welcome to an artist like Leonardo, who with his innate, keen perception of nature endeavored to penetrate nature's essence in order to recreate it in his works.

How ambitious, perhaps even presumptuous this undertaking was becomes evident when we consider that nature works from within and must engage in endless preparations before it is capable of developing organic structures sufficiently evolved to produce, after thousands upon thousands of attempts, a form as complex as that of a human being. The human form indeed manifests outwardly the highest inner perfection, but it seems to deepen rather than solve the mystery behind which nature hides.

To represent the inner world faithfully in the external world was the highest and sole aim of only the greatest masters. They not only sought to recreate the essence of the object exactly, but the copy was to replace nature itself, and even to surpass it in impact. To realize this goal, absolute accuracy of detail was essential, and that could only be achieved in stages. Furthermore, it was indispensable that the artist be able to make corrections while in the process of painting. Oil painting offered all these and many other advantages.

After careful investigation it was determined that Leonardo used a mixture of mastic, pitch and other ingredients, which he applied with a hot iron tool to the plastered wall. In addition, to obtain a perfectly smooth surface, and as further protection against external damage, he applied a thin coating of white lead mixed with fine yellow aluminea. Yet it was precisely this precautionary measure that seems to have caused damage to the work. To be sure, the thin oil coating lasted well initially while the colors of the picture imparted enough of their oil substance to help preserve it, but when the oil gradually dried, the undercoating lost its resilience and began to crack. Then the dampness of the wall was able to penetrate and produce the mold which gradually effaced the picture.

Location

What is more lamentable is the fact that the destruction of the picture, even at the time it was painted, could have been predicted from the condition and location of the building. Duke Lodovico, either by intent or caprice, had forced the monks to rebuild their decaying monastery at this disagreeable place. As a result it was built poorly, as if by slave labor. In the old cloisters, for example, we can see shoddy workmanship on the pillars, big arches alternating with small ones, and worn, uneven tiles which had been salvaged from leveled buildings. If such things were allowed to happen in the exterior, prominently visible areas, it is to be feared that the interior walls, which were to be plastered over, were treated in an even worse manner. It is possible that old, weather-beaten bricks and materials with harmfully high salt content were used, permitting the moisture to penetrate to the inside, with dire consequences. Furthermore, the wall which was to receive such a great masterpiece faced north and was close to the kitchen, storage-rooms and pantry. How sad it is that an artist who was so scrupulous in choosing his colors and in purifying his varnishes was forced by circumstances to disregard or underestimate the importance of the picture's location—the most crucial consideration of all.

In spite of all this, the result would have been less disastrous had the monastery been situated on a hill. But it is actually located in a low-lying area, with the refectory lying lowest of all the buildings. As a result, during a rainy period in 1800, the refectory was under two feet of water, which leads us to conclude that the same thing happened during the great flood of 1500. Even if we assume that the monks did their best to drain the building, the walls must have retained quite an amount of moisture—and this at a time when Leonardo was still working on the painting.

About ten years after the completion of the picture, a terrible epidemic ravaged the city, and we cannot expect hard-pressed monks, alone and in mortal danger, to have taken care of the painting in their refectory.

The unsettling effects of war and the countless other misfortunes that befell Lombardy during the first half of the sixteenth century contributed to a general neglect of art works. Leonardo's painting was especially vulnerable; the above-mentioned flaws in the wall, the oil undercoating, and perhaps the painting technique itself predestined it for destruction. About the middle of the sixteenth century, one traveler reported that the picture was half ruined, while another saw only one faded spot. Others reported the work as good as lost and claimed it was difficult, if not impossible, to make out details; still others called it completely spoiled, and subsequent reports were in a similar vein.

But the picture was still there, even though only a shadow of its former self. As the years passed, people began to fear that it might become completely ruined. The cracks started to break up into innumerable, small, crust-like segments which threatened to come off piece by piece. Fortunately, Cardinal Federigo Borromeo became alarmed by the condition of the painting and in 1612 commissioned a copy to be made. More of this later.

Progressive Deterioration

However, it was not the passage of time or the above-mentioned conditions that caused most damage to the painting. The owners themselves, who should have been the work's guardians and protectors, were the main culprits, and by their actions they disgraced themselves for all time. The door leading to the refectory seemed too low to them; this door and a second one had been set symmetrically in the lower part of the wall, the foundation on which the picture rested. They demanded a majestic entrance for their beloved dining hall.

A door, far bigger than necessary, was broken into the center of the wall, and without respect for the painter or the sacred group in the painting, they destroyed the feet of some of the apostles, and even of Christ himself. And now the actual ruination of the picture began. Since they wanted an arch over the door, they had to break out a part of the wall much larger than the door itself. As a result, not only was more of the painting sacrificed, but in addition the entire surface was so shaken by the hammering and hacking that in many places pieces broke off, which were then re-attached with nails.

Later on, the picture was further demeaned by yet another display of insensitivity. A shield with the sovereign's coat of arms was suspended from the ceiling so that it almost touched Christ's head. The door from below and the shield from above now both encroached on the Lord and dishonored him. From that time on, there was constant talk of restoration, but nothing was done until much later. What real artist would want to assume such a responsibility? Unfortunately, in 1726 a certain Bellotti[6] offered to undertake the restoration. He was an artist endowed with little talent but, like many of his ilk, with a good measure of arrogance. Like a peddler hawking his wares, he boasted of a secret process with which he could bring the fading picture back to life. With a small-scale demonstration he bedazzled the naive monks, and they entrusted him with their treasure. Bellotti immediately concealed the picture behind a wooden partition where, hidden from view, he committed the blasphemy of re-doing it completely. The good monks were very impressed by the result, so—to complete his deception—he presented them with an ordinary varnish, assuring them that it contained a secret ingredient and would prove invaluable in the event of future difficulties.

It is not known if the monks actually made use of this 'precious' varnish when the picture soon began to fade again. But it is certain that the painting was retouched here and there with water colors on more than one occasion, as is still noticeable today.

Meanwhile the picture continued to deteriorate, and again the question of how to preserve it was debated, often acrimoniously, by artists and administrators. De Giorgi,[7] a modest man of average talent, yet an intelligent and passionate connoisseur of true art, steadfastly refused to tamper with Leonardo's work.

Finally, in 1770, as the result of a well-intended but insensitive order carried out by a subservient courtly prior, an artist by the name of Mazza[8] bungled the job thoroughly. The few original places still intact, although already subjected to two restoration attempts, proved offensive to his wide-ranging brush, so he scraped them smooth to make room for his own brazen strokes. Several heads suffered this kind of treatment.

Art lovers in Milan were stirred to protest by the result, and there was a public outcry against sponsor and client. Vocal critics agitated, and the discontent spread. Mazza had started with Christ's right-hand side and worked so fast that by this time he had reached the figures on the left. Only the heads of Matthew, Thaddaeus and Simon remained untouched, although here too he had intended to cover up Bellotti's repair work—no doubt to compete with him for the title of a Herostratus.[9] However, as fate would have it, the servile prior accepted a position elsewhere. His successor, an art lover, dismissed Mazza on the spot, and we are indebted to him for having saved the heads of these apostles which had been restored by Bellotti, so that we can still judge the latter's methods. This circumstance probably gave rise to the legend that three heads of Leonardo's original had been preserved.

Subsequently there were many consultations and discussions, but no action was taken. This was just as well, for nothing of the 300-year-old corpse was left to embalm. In 1796, Napoleon led his army victoriously across the Alps. Young and ambitious, he was attracted by things of renown, and Leonardo's name drew him to our monastery.

He immediately gave instructions not to use it for shelter or damage it in any way, and he signed the order on his knee before mounting his horse. Shortly thereafter, another general disregarded Napoleon's command, had the door broken down and the refectory turned into a stable.

Mazza's embellishments had already faded, and the steam from the horses, worse than the steam from the monks' kitchen, constantly kept the walls damp and caused new mold to form on the picture. The amount of moisture finally became so great that it condensed and trickled down the walls, leaving white streaks. Later on, the hall was used for storing hay and for other, exclusively military, purposes.

Finally, the administration succeeded in having it closed down, even walling up the entrance. The result was that for quite some time anyone wanting to see the *Last Supper* had to enter the room by climbing down a ladder from the pulpit, which was accessible from the outside and which had formerly been used for mealtime Bible recitations.

When the great flood of 1800 came, it turned the refectory into a veritable swamp, increasing the moisture level tremendously. In 1801, Bossi, in his capacity as Secretary to the Academy, ordered a door installed, and the administration promised to be more attentive in the future. Finally, in 1807, the Viceroy of Italy[10] gave instructions to restore the hall to its original splendor. Windows were installed, part of the floor was replaced, scaffolding was erected to examine the painting to see if anything could be done, and the position of the door was changed to the side wall. Since that time there have been no major changes, although a careful observer will notice that, depending on the light, the picture appears sometimes more, sometimes less, faded. Since the original is as good as lost to us, may at least its remains be preserved for future times as a melancholy but worthy memorial.

On Copies in General

Before we proceed to a discussion of the almost thirty[11] copies of the *Last Supper,* we must consider the question of copies in general. Copies of works of art were not commonplace until there was unanimous agreement that art had reached its pinnacle, at which time lesser talents, viewing the works of the greatest masters, despaired of their ability to produce anything comparable, either from models or their own imagination. Art at that point, having deteriorated into a craft, began to copy its own creations. Art lovers soon became aware of the lack of genius in most artists and, since they could not always turn to first-rate painters for original works, preferred to commission lesser talents to paint copies of recognized works rather than settle for inferior originals. In this way they were assured of at least getting something for their money.

Clients as well as artists promoted this new genre, the clients because it was cheap, the artists because it was fast. Thus art deliberately debased itself by making copying a matter of principle.

In the fourteenth and fifteenth centuries, on the other hand, artists held themselves and their art in high esteem and did not lightly stoop to copying someone else's work. This is why there were hardly any copies from that time—a circumstance which art historians may well note. To be sure, some handicrafts did make use of important models for works in niello and other forms of enameling. And if for religious or other purposes a copy was called for, an approximate imitation was considered acceptable, one that expressed the sense of movement, action, form and color of the original only in a general way. For this reason, even in the richest galleries, no copy from before the sixteenth century can be found.

Then came a time when art achieved perfection in all respects thanks to a few extraordinary artists, of whom Leonardo must surely be recognized as the first. Artistic perception and judgment improved, and the demand for copies of outstanding works could be easily satisfied, especially in those art schools which attracted many students and where the works of the master teaching there were sought after. Yet at that time the demand for copies was limited to smaller works, which could be easily exhibited next to the original for comparison and evaluation. In the case of larger paintings, the situation then—and later too—was very different. Since the original could not be compared with the copies, there were few orders for reproductions of that kind. Artists and art lovers were satisfied with imitations on a smaller scale. Here, the copyist was free to use his own judgment, and the result of this license can be seen very clearly in the few cases where large-scale reproductions were demanded. Such copies were almost always based on others executed on a smaller scale, probably far from the site of the original, often just based on sketches, or perhaps done from memory. More and more hack-painters were willing to do the job for a low price. Owning a painting became a status symbol, taste deteriorated, and more and more reproductions crowded the walls of lobbies and stairways. Hungry apprentices painted for a pittance, recreating great works of art on any scale; some painters even made a career of it. In every copy there were deviations from the original due to the client's desires, the artist's whim or perhaps the arrogance of his wanting to improve on the original.

The increased use of ornate tapestry posed another problem. Paintings now had to contain gold to be deemed effective, and people considered the most magnificent picture unattractive and paltry if it was simple and austere. The copyist had to supply buildings and landscapes to enhance the background, had to adorn figures with jewelry, golden rays of light or with crowns, and add strange-looking children, animals, chimera, unusual objects and other foolishness of that sort. Sometimes an artist, confident of his own creativity, received a commission for a copy from a client who was not at all aware of the artist's talent. The painter carried out the assignment, although with reluctance. But he also wanted to demonstrate his originality here and there and made alterations and additions, inspired by insight or vanity. No doubt, changes of that kind were also made to satisfy the requirements of time and place. Some figures were made to serve purposes quite different from those originally intended. Through a few additions, profane subjects were changed into sacred ones; pagan gods and heroes had to submit to being turned into martyrs and evangelists. Frequently, an artist copied a figure from a famous work for practice and edification, and then added something of his own to make it saleable. Finally, the invention and the misuse of engraving may also be said to have contributed to the corruption of art. This new technique gave second-rate painters easy access to reproductions, so that no one bothered to study the originals anymore, and in the end painting deteriorated to such a degree that it was looked upon as not much more than a technical skill. After all, engravings deviated from the originals, and when the prints were copied, the changes were multiplied according to the artist's or client's conviction or whim. Drawings suffered the same fate. Artists sketched out the most remarkable subjects in Rome or Florence, only to return home and reproduce them arbitrarily.

Copies of The Last Supper

These facts give us some notion of what to expect of the copies of the *Last Supper,* even though the earliest ones were contemporary with the original. For the work was a sensation, and other monasteries wanted one similar.

Of the copies cited by Bossi we shall discuss only those three on which the traced copies at Weimar are based. However, all three are in turn based on a fourth, which we shall consider first.

Marco d'Ogionno[12] was a pupil of Leonardo's, but of modest talent. Nonetheless, he was highly regarded in his school, especially for his copies of the heads of the *Last Supper,* although his work here is not always consistent. Around 1510, he made a small-scale copy which he later wanted to reproduce on a larger scale. As usually happened, the first copy was not quite accurate, yet he used it as the basis for a larger one, which is now on the refectory wall of the former monastery at Castellazzo. Everything is executed with great care, but there is the customary arbitrariness in the treatment of detail. And although Bossi does not have much good to say about it, he does admit that it is an important monument and that the treatment of several heads, where the expression was not exaggerated, is commendable. Bossi made tracings of them, and that enables us to compare this copy with the three others and form our own opinion.

A second copy, in fresco—here too we have tracings of the heads—is located on the wall at Ponte Capriasca. It has been dated 1565 and is attributed to Pietro Lovino. We shall discuss its merits later and at this point only mention its distinguishing feature, namely that the names of the figures are added, which will help us to establish the characteristics of the various faces.

We have already described the gradual deterioration of the original in sufficient detail. It was already in poor condition when, in 1612, Cardinal Federigo Borromeo, an avid patron of the arts, sought to prevent the complete loss of the work by commissioning Andrea Bianchi (*Il Vespino*) from Milan, to produce a full-size copy. The artist first merely tested his skill by making copies of a few heads. When these turned out well, he proceeded to do the whole figures individually. Only at the end, and with the utmost care, did he arrange them together as a whole. This copy, at present in the Ambrosian Library in Milan, served as the basis for the copy by Bossi, the most recent one. Its history is as follows.

The Most Recent Copy

Italy had been declared a kingdom, and Prince Eugenio,[13] following Lodovico Sforza's example, wanted to celebrate the beginning of his reign by an act that fostered the arts. Lodovico had commissioned Leonardo to paint the *Last Supper;* Eugenio now decided that the work, which had been thoroughly ruined in the course of three hundred years, was to be recreated, as far as possible, in a new painting. To preserve the recreation for eternity, it was to be done in mosaic,[14] a method for which a local manufacturing facility provided ample materials.

Bossi immediatley received the commission and began work in the beginning of May 1807. He thought it advisable to prepare a preliminary drawing the same size as the picture. He resumed his earlier studies and concentrated completely on Leonardo's artistic remains and particularly his writings, because he was convinced that an artist who had produced such outstanding works must have followed the most well-defined and helpful of principles. In previous years, Bossi had drawn the hands and some other parts of the copy at Ponte Capriasca, also the heads and hands of the copy at Castellazzo and the one by Bianchi. Now he copied all of Leonardo's originals still available, and even works of some of Leonardo's contemporaries. He sought out all existing copies and was able to familiarize himself with twenty-seven to varying degrees. People everywhere were gracious enough to make Leonardo's drawings and manuscripts available to him.

In doing the preliminary drawing, Bossi followed mainly Bianchi's copy at the Ambrosian Library because it was the only one the same size as the original. With the aid of netting and transparent paper, Bianchi had tried to obtain the most accurate copy possible and also worked directly from the original, which had not yet been painted over despite extensive damage.

At the end of October 1807, Bossi's preliminary drawing was finished. The ground was put on a single piece of canvas and the sketch drawn on it. In order to regulate his tints, Bossi first painted the few parts of the sky and landscape that had remained fresh and bright in the original due to the intensity and purity of the colors. Then he did the heads of Christ and of the three apostles on Christ's left. The first garments he painted were those whose colors he was sure of, and subsequently he selected the others according to Leonardo's principles and his own considered judgment. Thus he covered the entire canvas, carefully and thoughtfully, keeping his colors bright and strong.

Unfortunately, the place where Bossi worked was damp and desolate, and he fell ill. Unable to continue his project, he spent his time classifying and cataloguing drawings, engravings and writings as they pertained to the *Last Supper* or other works by Leonardo. A stroke of good fortune put him in the possession of a collection of sketches originally owned by Cardinal Cesare Monti, which, among other treasures, contained excellent items by Leonardo. Bossi even studied writers who were contemporaries of Leonardo to benefit from their opinions and suggestions, and he made note of anything that might prove useful to his project. In this way, he spent his convalescence constructively, and when he finally regained his strength, he resumed work.

Artists and art lovers will find Bossi's description of his methods and procedures fascinating. He gives a detailed account of the thinking behind his portrayal of the facial features and expressions, and even of the hand gestures and how he reproduced them. He also pays close attention to the tableware, the room, the background, and proves that he made no decision without cogent reasons. He describes the painstaking efforts to reconstruct the feet under the table because this area had been treated negligently in the copies.

Up to this point we have reported on Bossi's work in general terms and have provided partial translations and excerpts. We are grateful for the information he has provided, and we have shared his convictions and accepted his opinions. Any additional remarks on our part have been made in agreement with his views. But since we are now going to deal with the principles Bossi adopted as the basis of his copy and the direction he followed in making it, we find reason to differ with him to some extent. We know that he was subject to extensive criticism, that opponents treated him harshly, and that even some friends disagreed with him. All this makes us wonder whether we should accept blindly everything he did. However, since he is no longer with us and cannot defend himself or explain his reasons, it is our duty, even if we cannot justify what he did, at least to present an excuse for his actions. We shall attempt to show that his criteria and approach did not originate with him but were imposed from without.

Artistic projects of this kind, which are intended to be eye-catching showpieces or even sensations, usually have colossal dimensions. Leonardo da Vinci's figures in his *Last Supper* are one and one-half times life-size. If they were standing up they would be nine feet tall, and even though twelve persons are sitting or are behind the table and therefore have to be considered half-figures, the work must have made a tremendous impression when viewed from some distance. Bossi hoped to recapture the impact of the original's overall feeling of power, although not its delicate details.

Something great and miraculous had been heralded to the public at large: A picture, twenty-eight by approximately eighteen feet was to be created by assembling thousands upon thousands of small pieces of glass, but only after a talented artist had carefully studied the original, copied it and, with the aid of all his technical and intellectual resources, had recreated as faithfully as possible the long lost masterpiece. Why should anyone have doubted the feasibility of such an undertaking at the moment of an important national event? Why should the artist not have been carried away by the prospect of performing something extraordinary at the beginning of this new epoch, something that might have seemed utterly impossible in the normal course of life!

Once it had been decided that the mosaic was to be the size of the original and Bossi had accepted the assignment, we find he had sufficient reason to follow Vespino's copy. The old copy at Castellazzo, whose merits certainly are beyond dispute, is considerably smaller than the original, and if Bossi had wanted to use it exclusively, he would have had to enlarge the figures and the heads. But those familiar with art know how difficult enlarging is, particularly heads.

It is generally accepted that only the greatest masters can succeed in painting human faces on a colossal scale. The human figure, and especially the face, is by nature limited to certain dimensions, and only within those dimensions can it appear regular, characteristic, beautiful and expressive. Anyone can test this notion by looking into a concave mirror; he will see a frightening, crude, monstrous shape without a soul, a veritable Medusa! The artist whose hands are to produce a colossal face has a similar experience. Life in a painting derives from details, detail is achieved by particulars, but where can you find particulars when everything is expanded into generalities?

We can no longer tell in how much detail Leonardo painted his heads. Vespino's heads, although respectable and praiseworthy, exhibit a certain vacuity which dilutes and blurs the characteristic features in the oversized faces. Yet at the same time, due to their size, they are imposing and done boldly enought to produce a striking effect at a distance. Vespino's copy was the one available to Bossi. By using it, he was able to avoid the risky task of enlarging, which he would have had to do if he had followed smaller copies. Why should he have been concerned? As a man of enterprising character he had accepted the job at hand and completely rejected all peripheral or contrary considerations. This explains his unjust disregard of the copy at Castellazzo and his unshakable trust in the principles which he derived from Leonardo's works and writings. He became involved in a public controversy over this matter with Count Verri,[15] and even with his best friends he had disagreements, if not quarrels.

Some Remarks About Leonardo

Before going any further we should mention a few things about Leonardo's personality and talents. The many gifts bestowed on him by nature were concentrated mainly in his visual perception. This is why, despite his many other talents, he was at his greatest as a painter. Handsome and with a splendid physique, he seemed a model of human perfection. And since the clarity of man's visual perception is part of the domain of the mind, it follows that our artist was endowed with clarity of apprehension and intelligence to the highest degree. He did not rely on the impulses of his immense innate talent; no arbitrary, random brush stroke was tolerated; everything had to be planned and reflected upon. From the pure, established laws of proportion to the strangest monstrosities consisting of the most contradictory forms—everything had to be based on the principles of nature as well as reason.

This acute and rational way of looking at the world resulted in the painstaking attention to detail in his written portrayals of violent and complex physical events, descriptions that could have just as easily become paintings. His descriptions of a battle or a storm are unequaled in their exactitude.[16] They are subjects that cannot be painted, but they give an indication to the painter of what might be required of him.

Leonardo's posthumous writings show us that his gentle, quiet mind was inclined to absorb vivid impressions of the most varied kind. His approach requires first of all general beauty of form, but at the same time a careful attention to all deviations from this ideal, even ugliness. The visible transformation of a child into an old man, in all its stages, and especially expressions of passion, from joy to rage, must be sketched hastily to reflect the transient quality that they have in life. If one intends to make use of such a sketch later on, one should seek out a similar figure in real life, place it in a similar pose, follow the basic general concept and model it exactly according to life. It is obvious that in spite of all the advantages this method may present, it can only be employed by the greatest talents. Since the artist starts with the particular and proceeds to the general, he will always have a difficult task, especially when he is dealing with several interacting figures.

Let us turn our attention to the *Last Supper,* in which Leonardo portrayed thirteen persons ranging from youthful to old: one quietly resigned, one terrified, eleven stirred and outraged by the thought of a traitor in their midst. Here we see the whole gamut of emotions, from the most restrained demeanor to the most passionate outbursts. If all this were to be taken from nature, how much observation, how much time would be necessary to collect so many details and fashion them into a whole! It is not at all improbable that Leonardo worked on his painting for sixteen years and was still unable to portray successfully either the traitor or the Son of Man because both are concepts and cannot be visualized.

To the Matter at Hand!

To recapitulate: Only an artistic miracle would have made possible the successful completion of the painting. Given Leonardo's approach described above, problems in the portrayal of some of the heads had proved to be insurmountable and became worse in each copy, even the most carefully done. Thus we find ourselves in a predicament; to be sure, the tracings at hand shed some light on the matter, but they cannot help us resolve it satisfactorily.

First of all, we must note that Bossi's treatise, in which he seeks to cast doubt on the quality of all the copies—though we do not question his historical accuracy—seems to have been written for the sole purpose of downgrading the one at Castellazzo. This copy, despite numerous shortcomings, is decidedly superior to Vespino's, the general character of which we discussed above. It is evident that Leonardo's initial intent can be detected in Marco d'Ogionno's heads; indeed, Leonardo may well have had a hand in them and painted Christ's head himself. Is it not also likely that he would have given advice and guidance concerning the other heads and perhaps the rest of the picture as well? Even though the Dominican monks of Milan may have been unkind enough to refuse to let their painting be copied, there were in Leonardo's school several drafts, sketches and preparatory drawings which the master may well have used to help a favorite student in the vicinity who attempted a careful reproduction of the original.

In comparing these two copies (only the eye, not the word, can do justice to the third one!), we must limit ourselves to a brief discussion of just the most basic and striking aspects, since we are not yet fortunate enough to possess reproductions of these interesting works.

Comparison

Bartholomew:[17] In Ogionno's copy he is a vigorous youth with a sharp profile, a composed, harmonious face, lowered eyelids and frowning brow, mouth closed as if he were listening suspiciously; a completely self-contained character. In Vespino's copy there is no trace of individualized facial features: a commonplace face of the kind found in sketchbooks, listening open-mouthed. Bossi approved of and retained the open lips, and in this point we cannot agree with him.

James the Younger: In Ogionno's copy he is likewise shown in profile; there is an undeniable family resemblance with Christ, which is neutralized to some extent by the individuality produced by his protruding, slightly opened lips. In Vespino's copy he has an almost ordinary Christ's face in the art-school tradition; his open mouth seems to express astonishment rather than to ask a question. Our contention that Bartholomew ought to be portrayed with his mouth closed is supported by the fact that his neighbor James has his open. Leonardo would never have permitted himself such a repetition.

Andrew, the apostle next in line has his mouth closed too. He presses his lower lip against his upper lip, as older people are apt to do. In the copy by Ogionno, his head has a peculiar quality that is hard to describe: his eyes seem to look inward, and his mouth, although closed, makes a naive impression. The outline of the left side of his head forms a beautiful silhouette against the background, and so much is visible of the forehead, the left eye, the left side of the nose and beard that the head becomes three-dimensional and thus gains life. Vespino, however, eliminates the left eye completely, but shows so much of the left side of the forehead and beard that a crude, bold expression in the upward-turned face results. To be sure, the effect is striking, but the facial expression is better suited to clenched fists than to extended, open hands.

Judas is reserved, frightened, anxiously looking up and backward. His profile is angular, not exaggerated, by no means ugly; after all, good taste would not have tolerated a veritable monster in the company of such pure and decent people. Vespino, on the other hand, did portray a monster. It cannot be denied that his head, taken out of context, has considerable merit. There is a vivid expression of malicious, bold glee. He would be excellent as a member of a mob jeering at the cry "Ecce Homo!" and shouting "Crucify him! Crucify him!" He would also be appropriate for a Mephistopheles at his most satanic. But there is absolutely no trace of fright and fear coupled with dissimulation, indifference and contempt. His bristly hair fits the general concept; its exaggerated rendering, however, is only acceptable in conjunction with the power and vehemence of Vespino's other heads.

Peter: It is difficult to interpret his features. Even in Ogionno's copy we see merely an expression of pain—no anger at all, no threat. There is also a trace of anxiety, which may reveal a problem Leonardo himself was unable to solve, for it is probably not possible to express in a single face both deep affection for one's beloved master and a threatening attitude toward that master's betrayer. Yet Cardinal Borromeo claims to have seen this miracle in his time. No matter how convincing his words may sound, we have reason to believe that this art-loving Cardinal more likely described his own feelings than what he actually saw; otherwise there would be no excuse for Vespino's lending Peter an unpleasant expression. The disciple looks like a stern Capuchin monk trying to make sinners repent with a Lenten sermon. It is strange that Vespino gave him bristly hair, since Ogionno's Peter has a nice head of short curls.

John: Ogionno painted him completely in Leonardo's spirit. The fine, round, yet slightly oval face and the straight, long hair which ends in gentle curls, especially where it touches Peter's protruding hand, are particularly charming. The partially visible pupils are turned away from Peter—a keenly observed touch! It is indeed natural for someone listening with deep emotion to the furtive words of his neighbor to avert his eyes. In Vespino's copy, John is a youth in a comfortable, relaxed position, almost sleeping, who seems completely disinterested.

Now let us turn to the figures on Christ's left and save the discussion of the Saviour's portrayal till last.

Thomas: Only shown are his head and his right hand with the index finger bent slightly towards his forehead to indicate reflection. This gesture, so appropriate for the suspicious and doubting disciple, has until now been misinterpreted as a threat. In Vespino's copy he is also quite reflective. But because the artist omitted the eye here too, a perpendicular, simple profile results, from which the forward thrust and the inquisitive expression found in the old copy are completely lacking.

James the Elder: Highly agitated facial features, a gaping mouth, horror in the eyes—a bold and original stroke on Leonardo's part! And indeed, we have reason to believe that Ogionno succeeded splendidly in copying this head too. Bossi's tracings are excellent. In Vespino's copy, on the other hand, everything specific is lost: position, bearing, facial expression have disappeared and been allowed to dissolve into something bland and vague.

Philip: Charming and extraordinary, resembles exactly the youths gathering around Bramante on the left side of Raphael's painting, *The School of Athens*.[18] Vespino, unfortunately, omitted the right eye once again; and since he realized that something more than a mere profile was called for, he produced an ambiguous head, bent in an odd way.

Matthew: Young, trusting, with curly hair. His slightly open mouth has an anxious expression. His teeth are visible and indicate a suppressed anger, which is in keeping with the violent movement of the figure. Vespino's copy has nothing at all of that: rigid and blank-faced, Matthew stares into space, not suggesting in the least the violent movement of his body.

Thaddaeus: Ogionno's head is again outstanding; anxiety, suspicion, dismay are expressed in all features. The unity of these varied facial expressions is truly admirable and harmonizes perfectly with the hand gestures which we interpreted above. In Vespino's copy, again everything has been generalized. Also, he made the head less expressive by having it turn too much toward the viewer, while in Ogionno's copy barely one quarter of the left side is visible, which produces so admirably that squinting look of suspicion.

Simon the Elder: He is shown completely in profile, facing young Matthew, who is likewise completely in profile. The protruding lower lip, which Leonardo liked so much in old faces, is very pronounced, but in conjunction with the deep frown it produces an eloquent expression of dismay and reflection, which is in sharp contrast to young Matthew's passionate gesture. In Vespino's copy, Simon is a decrepit, good-natured old man, no longer capable of taking an interest in the momentous event happening before him.

Having now completed our discussion of the apostles, we turn to the figure of Christ himself. We recall the legend that Leonardo was at a loss about how to finish either Christ or Judas, which we tend to believe because, working as he did, it was impossible for him to put the finishing touches on those two extremes of his painting. The appearance of the original must therefore have been very poor, what with the darkening produced by time and with the face of Christ probably not far beyond the sketching stage. We can guess how little Vespino found to copy from the fact that he produced a head of Christ on a colossal scale quite contrary to Leonardo's spirit, without paying the slightest attention to the inclination of the head, which should correspond to John's. We do not wish to say anything about the expression; the features are regular, good-natured and intelligent, the traditional representation of Christ, but without the least trace of sensibility. If we did not know that it was the Last Supper, it would be hard to determine in which episode of the New Testament this head belongs.

However, we are fortunate after all. Scholars maintain that Leonardo himself painted the Saviour's head in Ogionno's copy at Castellazzo, that he dared perform for another artist what he dared not perform for himself. Since we do not have access to this work, we must rely on the tracing. It corresponds totally to the mental picture we form of a noble man burdened by agonizing knowledge, from which he has sought relief by communicating it to intimate friends. Yet, instead of improving the situation, he has made it worse.

Through our comparisons, we trust we have gained an adequate understanding of this extraordinary artist's approach as it emerges in clear detail from his writings and pictures. Fortunately, we are in a position to go one step further. In the Ambrosian Library there is a drawing which has been attributed indisputably to Leonardo. It is sketched on blue paper, a few strokes in white and colored chalk. Bossi made a very accurate facsimile, which we also have before us. It represents the fine face of a youth, drawn from life, apparently a study for the head of Christ in the *Last Supper*. The face has clean-cut, regular features, the hair is straight, the head inclined to the left, eyes lowered, lips half parted; a faint expression of sorrow provides an exquisite unifying harmony. Of course, it represents merely the human side of Jesus, the man who does not conceal his innermost suffering. But how could majesty, independence, strength and divine power be expressed in the same face without obliterating these very characteristics? That was a task which no mortal artist, not even the most ingenious, could perform. In our opinion, this youthful face, a mixture of John and Christ, is the most successful attempt to adhere to nature in the portrayal of the divine.

The older Florentine and Sienese schools departed from the dull stereotypes of Byzantine art by introducing portraits in their pictures. That was easily done because, given the peaceful events depicted in their paintings, the figures could be presented in positions of repose. The meeting of holy men, the listening to a sermon, the collecting of alms, the funeral of a revered man of faith, all these subjects require only that the artist lend each participant the appropriate meditative expression. However, when Leonardo wanted to add liveliness and passion, difficulties became evident, particularly since he was not dealing with similar figures merely standing next to each other, but with very different, contrasting characters. In his writings, Leonardo describes this problem quite clearly and finds it almost insolvable. Perhaps that is the reason subsequent artists of talent made things easier for themselves by vascillating between a particular reality and their own general concept. Thus they moved freely from earth to heaven and back again.

More could be said about the painting's composition, which is both highly complex and highly artistic, and about the spatial relationship of heads, bodies, arms and hands. In particular, we could comment in detail on the hands, since we have the tracings based on Vespino's copy before us. However, we would do better to conclude this preliminary discussion and to await what our friends on the other side of the Alps have to say. They alone are in a position to decide on some points because they have been familiar with each of these works for many years, have access to them and have personally experienced recent events, whereas our knowledge is merely second-hand. We hope that in addition to their reaction regarding the points mentioned above, they will communicate with us concerning the following: Did Bossi make use of the heads in Ogionno's copy at Castellazzo after all? It seems to us quite likely that he did, since the copy was generally regarded very highly. It has also contributed greatly to the value of Morghen's engraving because the latter followed it closely.[19]

Before closing we have to acknowledge with gratitude that our old friend, colleague and contemporary, whom we still like to refer to as Maler Müller[20] in fond memory of years past, has sent us from Rome an excellent essay on Bossi's work, published in the *Heidelberger Jahrbücher,* December issue, 1816. Our discussion, already in progress when the essay arrived, benefited greatly from it because it helped us to express ourselves more concisely in many places. We refer our readers to this essay. They will be delighted to find that our views are close to, indeed often identical with, those of so experienced and knowledgeable an artist. We considered it our duty to concentrate mainly on those points which this expert, for whatever reasons, chose to treat less extensively.

Just as we come to the end, we have received the following work: *Tratato della Pittura di Lionardo da Vinci; tratto da un Codice della Biblioteca Vaticana,* Roma 1817.[21] This large quarto volume contains much material hitherto unknown, from which we expect to gain new insights into Leonardo's art and theory. It is accompanied by a small folio volume of twenty-two engravings of expressive pen sketches, strikingly reminiscent of those which Leonardo customarily used to illustrate his essays. Hence we feel obligated to resume our discussion soon, with the kind assistance on the part of experts in Milan; we trust this will provide some edification to others as well as ourselves.

Giotto's Last Supper[1] (1824)

The Weimar Society of the Friends of Art[2] could easily draw attention to this engraving by merely stating that Mr. Ramboux has copied the work with faithfulness and diligence, and that Mr. Ruscheweyh is likewise to be commended for the great care and competence in his engraving.[3] We could perhaps also suggest that the discriminating art lover should hasten to add these prints to his collection. In this way the matter would no doubt be settled to everyone's satisfaction, and we would not have the least cause to reproach ourselves because we would only offer the truth.

Yet, for some time, grave aberrations in taste have been apparent and are becoming more numerous. That is why we, like any unbiased critic, are obligated to give our considered opinion whenever the opportunity arises. We feel compelled to elaborate more fully on the subject at hand.

Works like the *Last Supper* by Giotto are normally judged from quite divergent, even opposing, points of view. Art lovers with a preference for the old school admire its simplicity, tenderness and naiveté—qualities certainly lacking in the art of our day. But they overlook the artistic inadequacy of fourteenth-century works, and even recommend these as models to imitate, a fate that will presumably also befall Mr. Ruscheweyh's Giotto prints. Others, however, base their opinion on poorly grasped principles of beauty and never settle for anything less than perfection. Whereas the first group lavishes unqualified praise on every good feature, the second seems intent only on finding flaws. They note the difference in length of Apollo's feet, they find fault with the *Laocoon,* insist that in the *Borghese Gladiator* the line of the back barely corresponds with that of the front, and so forth. These strict critics are vexed by honest old Giotto with his long, stiff figures, his imperfections in proportion and design, and his sins against perspective. We now take the liberty of interjecting ourselves into the midst of this dispute with the unceremonious declaration: The first group is in error, and the second spoils our enjoyment of art.

Unless special reasons demand it, truly profitable examination and impartial evaluation must never dwell on flaws, nor disregard them. What we must do is recognize achievement in whatever shape or form it may appear, always remembering not to expect roses in winter and grapes in spring. That is, the fair, discriminating art critic does not praise or find fault with a work according to his personal likes or dislikes. Rather, his judgment is always based on an awareness of the history of art; he carefully considers place and time of origin, the state of the arts at the time and the taste of a particular school and a particular master.

Returning to Giotto's *Last Supper,* we should say at once that it is a remarkable picture, but not in the sense that it is a suitable subject for study for the beginning artist. If he studies it to acquire good taste, to learn about design and other equally important skills, he will be ill-served. But from a historical point of view, the work has great value for the theoretically-minded in that it provides the opportunity of seeing how an excellent artist like Giotto imagined our Lord's last supper as a subject. Yet we also see that the childlike nature of his art was not adequate to the difficult task and inevitably fell short of his intentions and desires.

If we then look at the same subject painted by Leonardo da Vinci, we can make a comparison that provides us with a very clear and instructive view of the progress art had made in the course of almost two centuries. For Giotto and Leonardo, both admirable masters and both unquestionably great in the context of their respective times, chose approximately the same moment as the subject for their works. Leonardo selected the moment when Christ said to his disciples: "One of you shall betray me." (Matt., Ch. 26:21). Giotto seems to have had in mind the passage (Verse 23) which reads: "He that dippeth his hand with me in the dish, the same shall betray me." In Giotto, the Lord's words merely precipitate a discussion. Several of the apostles seem to want to exonerate themselves, others look doleful, one (the fourth on Christ's right) makes a gesture expressing alarm, and Judas calmly helps himself to food. It cannot be denied, however, that the painter made an effort to lend the betrayer a baser character, different from that of other apostles.

In Leonardo da Vinci's painting, artistic skill reigns free, having developed enough to attempt the most difficult task. The Lord's words,

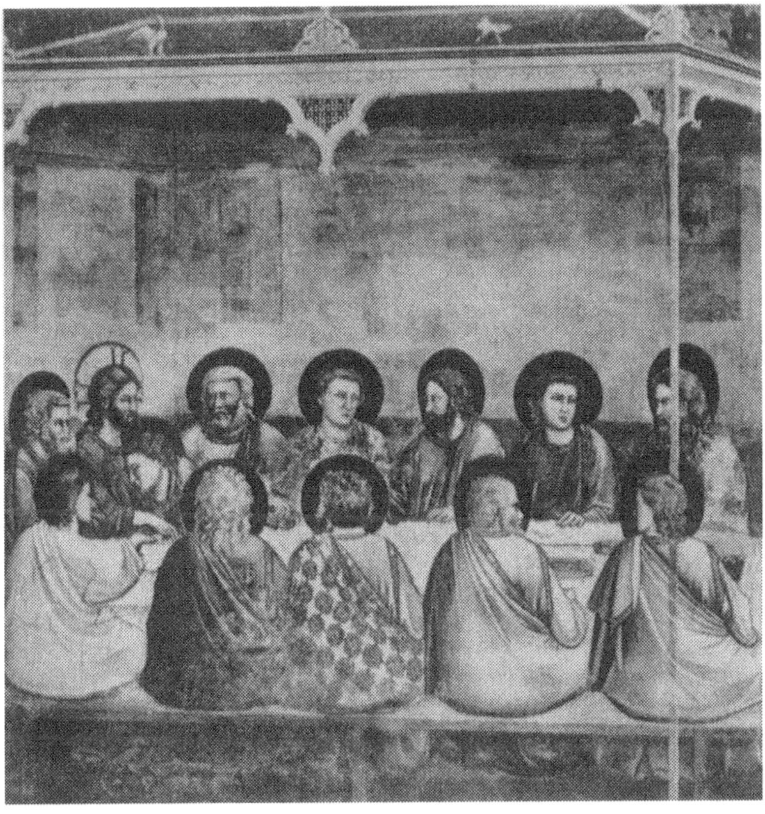

Giotto's *Last Supper*. (Courtesy of the Trustees of the Boston Public Library.)

the prediction that someone at the table would betray him, agitates the whole group with great suddenness and vehemence. All are startled and form highly animated, superbly arranged groups. There is life and movement everywhere. The diversity of emotions and gestures could not be greater. The pose, figure and features of each person reflect perfectly what he has heard and the pain he feels; the rendering is true-to-life and strong. Judas is startled, recoils, and knocks over the salt-cellar in front of him. We could cite several other outstanding features, but we have already furnished sufficient evidence of how profitable and instructive a comparison of these works can be. Probably no other examples could demonstrate so clearly and vividly the beginning stages and later perfection of the art of early modern times.

Ruisdael as Poet[1] (1816)

Jacob van Ruisdael, born in Haarlem in 1635 and active until 1681, is recognized as one of the outstanding landscape painters. His works first of all satisfy every demand that the visual sense can make on a work of art. Hand and brush, working with the greatest freedom, achieve perfect precision. Light, shade, use of color and the overall effect leave nothing to be desired, as art lovers and connoisseurs can see at a glance. We however wish to consider Ruisdael as a thinking artist, even as a poet. And in this respect, too, we must confess that he deserves high praise.

Valuable evidence for this claim is furnished us by three paintings in the Royal Saxon Collection.[2] They depict various periods of human history and habitation with great sensitivity, each one independent, self-contained and well-defined. The artist has grasped with admirable insight the point where creativity converges with intellect to produce a work of art that is in itself pleasant to behold, but which also appeals to the mind, stimulates thought and, finally, expresses a concept without becoming amorphous or, on the other hand, too cerebral. We have good reproductions of these pictures before us and are therefore able to discuss them fully and in detail.

I

The first picture presents successive periods of human history simultaneously. On a cliff overlooking a narrow valley stands an old tower next to well-preserved, newer buildings, and at its foot the stately home of a wealthy landowner. The tall old firs surrounding it indicate that this property has been passed on peacefully from descendant to descendant for many years. A village spread out along the bottom of a mountain slope signifies a fertile and habitable valley. In the foreground, a swiftly moving stream cascades over rocks and the stumps of slender trees, supplying the life-giving element, which one immediately presumes is put to use, upstream or down, in mills and foundries. The movement, clarity and tones of the rushing water enliven in a delightful manner the other objects which are at rest. That is why this painting is named *The Waterfall.* It satisfies even those who have neither time nor inclination to delve more deeply into the meaning of the picture.

II

The second picture, which has become famous as *The Convent,* has a richer, more attractive composition, but a similar intent: the representing of the past in the present. This goal is achieved admirably, with things dead and living juxtaposed most graphically.

On the left side, the viewer sees a dilapidated, almost devastated convent. But behind it there are well-maintained buildings, probably the living quarters of an official or tollkeeper who still collects revenue and tolls, which are, however, no longer the lifeblood of a community as they were in former times.

Facing these buildings is a grove of linden trees, planted long ago but still thriving, which indicate that the works of nature have greater life and endurance than the works of man. For already several centuries ago, during church festivals and fairs, many pilgrims stopped here to refresh themselves after their pious journey.

The remains of bridge foundations in and near the water suggest that people actually thronged here and that there was a constant bustle of activity. At present these ruins serve a picturesque function in that they obstruct the course of the stream, producing small rapids.

But the destruction of the bridge cannot impede the lively flow of traffic which finds its own path everywhere. People and cattle, shepherds and travelers now wade through the shallow water and add to the charm of the gently meandering stream.

Fish must still be plentiful to this day here, as in former times when they were welcome provisions during Lent. For fishermen are still wading in the waters, trying to catch these guileless creatures.

Since the mountains in the background seem to be covered with young bushes, we may conclude that large forests have been cut down and the gentle slopes left to new shoots and brush.

On this side of the water we see a remarkable clump of trees near weather-beaten, crumbling rocks. A splendidly rendered beech tree stands there, dying, leafless, its branches broken off, its bark cracked. In order that the magnificently executed tree trunk lift rather than lower our spirits, live trees nearby are represented covering their barren companion with the rich foliage of their own branches. This lush growth is sustained by the marshy soil close by, of which ample evidence is provided by moss, reeds and marsh plants.

A gentle light spreads from the convent to the linden trees and beyond, and, as if reflected by the white beech trunk, flows back over the gentle stream and the rushing rapids, over the herds and the fishermen, lending life to the whole scene. And in the foreground near the water sits the artist himself, his back turned to the viewer, drawing. We are touched by this motif—elsewhere so often abused—because here it is as fitting as it is significant and effective. The artist sits there as an observer, representing all future viewers of the picture who may wish to join him in contemplating the delightful interaction of past and present.

The work is taken from nature and elevated by thought, and most successfully so. And because it also fulfills all the requirements of art in composition and execution, it will always attract us and maintain its well-deserved reputation through the ages. Even in a reproduction, if it is at all passable, the viewer will be able to sense the great achievement of the original.

III

The third picture is devoted entirely to the past and contains no reflection of life in the present. It is known as *The Cemetery,*[3] and that is what it depicts. Even the gravestones in their ruined state point to something more than the past: they are monuments of themselves.

We see in the background, shrouded by a passing rain shower, the lean ruins of an immense cathedral that once soared heavenwards. A free-standing, spindling gabled wall is threatened by imminent collapse. The area around the convent, surely once cultivated, is now a wilderness, overgrown with shrubs and bushes and dotted here and there with dying and withered trees. The wilderness has invaded the cemetery too, and there is no trace of its former boundaries. Imposing and strange-looking tombs of all kinds, some in the shape of coffins, some marked by large, upright stone slabs, testify to the former prominence of this diocese and to the standing and wealth of the families buried here. The deterioration of the tombs themselves is portrayed with great taste and artistic restraint, inviting the eye to linger on them. But the viewer is then surprised when he sees, or rather surmises, new and more modest monuments far in the background, and mourners gathering around them—as if the past had nothing to bequeath but mortality.

Yet the most important idea in this picture also makes the greatest artistic impression. The collapse of immense walls seems to have filled up or obstructed a gently flowing brook, diverting it from the original course, and now it is rushing past the graves in search of a way in this wilderness. A beam of light struggling through the rain shower illu-

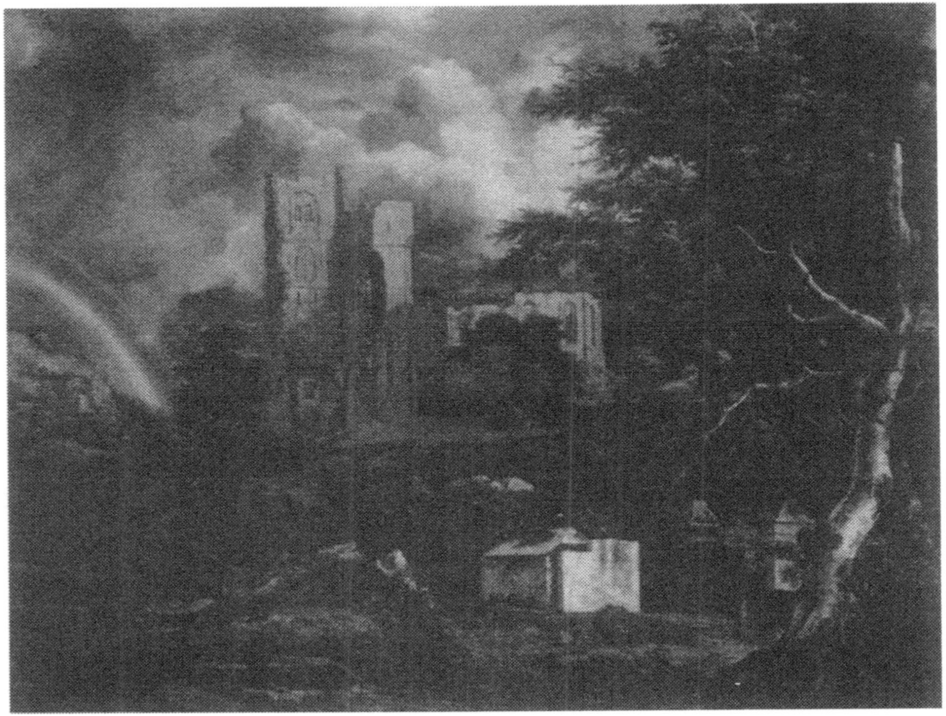

The Jewish Cemetery, by Jacob van Ruisdael. (Courtesy of the Trustees of the Boston Public Library.)

minates a few upright, already damaged tombstones, a gray tree trunk and a stump, but especially the gushing water of the brook cascading over rocks, and finally the foam in the foreground.

Since all these paintings have been copied so often, they are probably familiar to art lovers. Anyone fortunate enough to see the originals cannot but be made deeply aware of how far art can and should go.

In the future we shall try to find more examples where the artist, proving himself a poet in purity of feeling and clarity of thought, achieves perfect symbolism, and at the same time delights, teaches, refreshes and invigorates us through the health of his mind and his senses.

Rembrandt the Thinker[1] (After 1830)

In the picture, *The Good Samaritan,* we see in the foreground a horse almost completely in profile, with a page holding it by the bridle. Behind the horse a servant is in the process of lifting the injured man off the saddle to carry him into the house, which is reached by stairs leading to a balcony. In the doorway stands the well-dressed Samaritan who has just given some money to the innkeeper and is earnestly imploring him to take good care of the unfortunate victim. On the far left side, a young man wearing a hat with a feather looks out of a window. To the right, on level ground, there is a well from which a woman is drawing water.

This print is among the most beautiful of Rembrandt's works. It seems to have been etched with great care, and yet the needle is handled with extraordinary ease.

The old innkeeper in the doorway in particular captured the attention of the redoubtable Longhi,[2] who commented: "I cannot pass over in silence the etching of the Samaritan, in which Rembrandt drew the old man in the doorway in the attitude characteristic of people who have a tendency to tremble. And now, as all the man's memories surge to the surface, he actually appears to tremble, an effect no other painter has even been able to achieve in his art."

But let us continue our remarks on this fine work:

It is striking that the injured man, instead of permitting himself to be carried by the servant, turns laboriously to the left, with folded arms and raised head, and appears to beg the young man with the feathered hat for mercy, who is watching from the window more with disconcern and disinterest than malice. The victim's turning makes the task twice as difficult for the man who has just lifted him onto his shoulder; the servant's facial expression leaves no doubt that he resents the burden.

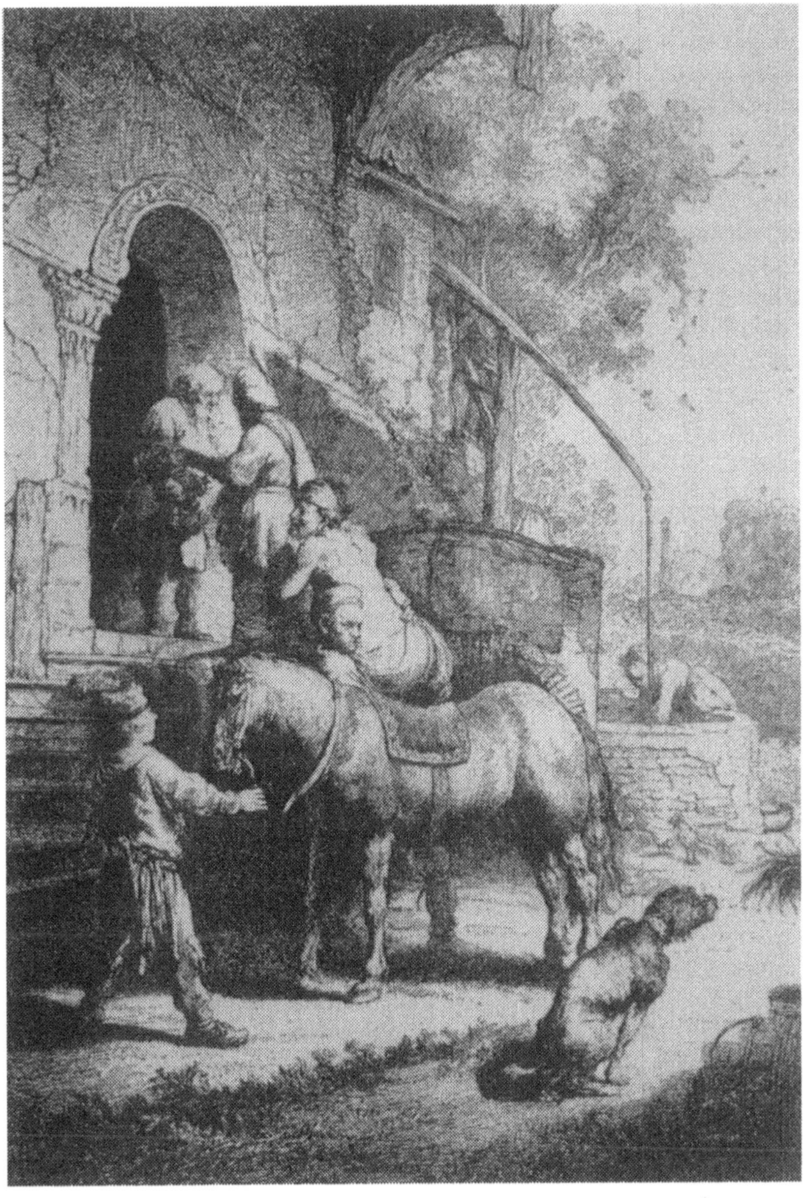

Rembrandt's *The Good Samaritan*. (Courtesy of the Trustees of the Boston Public Library.)

We for our part are convinced that the victim recognizes in the youth at the window the malicious leader of the band of robbers who attacked him a short time before. At this moment the poor man is seized by the fear that he is being taken to a den of thieves and that the Samaritan himself is part of a plot to kill him. In brief, he finds himself in a desparate situation: he is weak and helpless.

As for the faces of the six figures, we see nothing at all of the Samaritan's and only very little of the profile of the page holding the horse. The servant, encumbered with his human load, has a resentful and strained expression, and his mouth is closed. The unfortunate injured man registers utter helplessness. The old man's mien, which characterizes him as a decent person, good-natured and trustworthy, stands in sharp contrast to the taciturn and determined face of our robber chief in the corner.

Two Landscapes by Philipp Hackert[1] (1804)

A few days ago, two paintings arrived in Weimar, landscapes of some size done in oil by Philipp Hackert, which were intended for the castle of the Duke.[2] Their subject matter is interesting and the technique so excellent that we feel obligated to report more fully on them for the benefit of our readers.

One of these pictures is a view from the Villa Madama of part of the Campagna below, in the direction of the Sabine mountains, which are aglow in the evening light. One can see the Tiber meandering through the plain and, in the middle ground, the Ponte Molle and a section of the straight road leading to the former Porta Flaminia, now called Porta del Popolo.[3]

The other painting represents an equally interesting area near Florence. In the hazy blue distance, the mountain peaks of Massa Carrara are visible, as is, closer to the foreground, part of the Apennine mountains sloping towards Pisa and Leghorn. To the right is Fiesole on its cheerful hill, at the left the heights near Florence topped with villas, and in between the fertile plain of the Arno valley towards Prato and Pistoia.

Florence itself is not actually seen in this picture (nor is Rome in the other). The viewer must imagine it behind the trees in the foreground, in which a number of cattle are grazing. Monte Oliveto, on the other hand, situated near the Porta San Frediano, is still visible. It would be difficult to find a more bustling, richer, more pleasant area, or one of greater historical interest. For it was in these charming environs that the arts and sciences of modern times experienced their renascence.

A great injustice would be done to paintings like Hackert's, which represent scenic settings in close imitation of nature, if they were to be judged by the lofty criteria used by the art critic to evaluate landscape paintings. Generally speaking, scenic pictures do belong to that category, but they constitute a subcategory. The landscape painter in the truest sense treats his subject matter freely in order to create his own poetic version of reality, calling upon all the resources of art to arrive at a beautiful whole through tone, color, light, composition, and so forth. The painter of scenic settings, on the other hand, must adhere scrupulously to reality, his only freedom being the choice of vantage point and time of day. Furthermore, he has fulfilled his artistic obligation as soon as he has presented as realistically as possible all objects within his range of vision.

If one makes this doubtlessly fair distinction with respect to Hackert's paintings and regards them as illustrations of areas around Rome and Florence, then one can say they are of exceptional quality. In fact, to the extent that they are merely intended to satisfy the demands of realism, they can be said to represent a near pinnacle of this kind of art. This is especially true of the view near Florence. Here we can identify numerous villas, churches and monasteries; we can follow every path, climb the hill of Fiesole and follow the Arno until it disappears in the distance between the mountains, where only rising mists give evidence of its course. All this is executed with astonishing artistic skill, perfect down to the smallest detail, yet neither cumbersome nor tedious. The most sucessful sections of the painting begin—to use an unusual though fitting expression—approximately a mile into the picture. From this point to the mountains farthest in the distance the execution is so perfect that we indeed doubt that a more realistic representation of such subject matter is conceivable. The foreground, considered by itself, is almost as satisfying. Stones, rocks, grassy soil are all treated in superb detail and presented characteristically. It might have been better for the overall effect if the foreground were dotted with fewer cattle. One might even insist on that point in regard to the picture's literal meaning since the area around Florence is particularly rich in olive oil and wine, not cattle. But Hackert shows neither vines nor olive trees. Yet we just now realize that our objections go beyond what we should expect of paintings of scenic settings, and that we are straying into the higher realm of poetic landscape painting. Let us turn then to the first picture, the area around Rome.

Middle ground and background, as far as the plain extends, can likewise be considered almost faultless. The hills near Acquacetosa are executed beautifully, with well-observed harmony of tone, so that each one is virtually a magnificent painting in itself. The redness of the high mountains in the distance is a shade too bright, and compared to the sun-drenched middle ground, the colors of the adjacent objects are somewhat lacklustre. However, far be it from us to reproach the artist for these shortcomings; we should rather blame his palette, which lacks sufficient means to recreate faithfully the sublime iridescence of such a scene.

IV

THEORY AND HISTORY OF ART

Simple Imitation, Manner, Style[1] (1789)

It seems advisable to give a clear indication of what we mean by these terms, for we will refer to them frequently. They have long been in use, and although they seem to have been sufficiently defined in theoretical works, everyone employs them according to his own understanding. What these terms mean to the individual will depend on the clarity or vagueness of the idea he wishes to express.

Simple Imitation of Nature

Assume that an aspiring artist with some talent begins to paint natural objects after only brief preliminary training in basic techniques. He copies forms with care and diligence and imitates colors as closely as he can, taking pains never to deviate from nature, beginning and completing every picture with an eye to nature. This person will always be an estimable artist because he will necessarily achieve an incredible degree of accuracy, and his works will be assured, vital and diverse.

If we analyze such a course of development carefully, we are led to the conclusion that this method is suitable for a capable but limited talent in treating pleasant but limited subjects.

Such subjects must be easily available at all times. The artist must be able to observe them at his convenience and copy them at his leisure. Whoever engages in such activity must be tranquil, introspective and satisfied with modest rewards.

This type of imitation would, then, be pursued by calm, conscientious persons of moderate talent who paint still-lifes.[2] Within its limits, this procedure does not preclude a high level of excellence.

Manner

However, such a technique is usually too pedantic or inadequate for the artist. He perceives in a multitude of objects a unifying harmony which he can only reproduce in painting by sacrificing details. He is impatient with drawing letter by letter what nature spells out for him. He invents his own method, creates his own language to express in his own way what he has grasped with his soul. As a result he gives a distinctive form to an object that he has often copied, without now actually seeing it before him or even recalling exactly what it looked like in nature.

Now his art has become a language that expresses his spirit directly and characteristically. And just as anyone who thinks for himself will order and formulate his ideas on moral issues differently from others, so any such artist will see, apprehend and imitate the world differently. He will approach the things of the world with a greater or lesser degree of deliberateness or spontaneity and will accordingly recreate them with circumspection or with casualness.

We can see that this kind of imitation is best suited for subjects which constitute a totality made up of many subordinate elements. These elements must be sacrificed if the general character of the whole is to be adequately expressed, as for example in landscapes, where one would miss the point completely by adhering pedantically to detail rather than trying to do justice to the overall concept.[3]

Style

Through imitation of nature, through the effort of creating a general language, through painstaking and thorough study of diverse subject matter, the artist finally reaches the point where he becomes increasingly familiar with the characteristic and essential features of things. He will now be able to see some order in the multiplicity of appearances and learn to juxtapose and recreate distinct and characteristic forms. Then art will have reached its highest possible level, which is style and equal to the highest achievement of mankind.

While simple imitation therefore depends on a tranquil and affectionate view of life, manner is a reflection of the ease and competence with which the subject is treated. Style, however, rests on the most fundamental principle of cognition, on the essence of things—to the extent that it is granted us to perceive this essence in visible and tangible form.

A more detailed discussion of the above would fill volumes. One can already find a number of books on the subject, but the concept itself can be studied only in nature and in works of art. We would like to add a few observations, and we will take an opportunity to refer to this matter in future discussions of the visual arts.[4]

It is quite obvious that the three ways of producing works of art described here as separate categories are closely related and can sometimes overlap imperceptibly.

Imitation of simple subjects such as flowers and fruits can be developed to a high level. It is natural that someone who paints roses will soon be able to distinguish the most beautiful and freshest, and choose only those from among the thousands which summer has to offer. The act of selecting begins at this point, without the artist having formed a definite concept of the beauty of a rose. He is dealing with tangible forms, and everything depends on the varied texture and the color of the surfaces. The fuzzy peach, the finely bloomed plum, the smooth apple, the glossy cherry, the dazzling rose, the bouquet of carnations, the brightly colored tulips—the artist will have perfect specimens of everything he desires available in his studio. He will place his objects in the most favorable light, and without conscious effort his eyes will learn to see the harmony of the brilliant colors. Every year he will be able to find similar objects, and by calmly observing and copying their simple existence, he will recognize and grasp the characteristics of these objects without laborious attempts at abstraction. In this way, the masterpieces of a Huysum and Rachel Ruysch[5] will be produced—artists who we may say achieved the impossible. It is apparent that such an artist will be even more accomplished and self-assured in his work if he is also something of a botanist. Being thoroughly familiar with the structure of plants, he will know the influence of the various parts on the health and growth of the whole as well as the function and interaction of those parts, and he will study and reflect on the successive development of leaves, flowers, pollen, fruit and seed. He will not only show his taste by what he selects but will amaze and instruct us through the correct representation of the characteristic features. Here we could say that he has formed his own style. But it is also obvious that if such a master were not so conscientious and only concerned with the easy expression of the striking and dazzling, he would soon become a mannerist.

Thus simple imitation operates in the vestibule of style. If the artist works faithfully, carefully and purposefully, if his response to what he sees is controlled, if he imitates with deliberateness and develops an awareness of what he his doing, that is, if he learns to distinguish the similar from the dissimilar and to categorize individual objects according to general concepts—then imitation will eventually be worthy of crossing the threshold to the inner sanctum of style.

If we now consider manner, we see that it can be, in the true sense of the word, a composite of simple imitation and style. If a mannerist approaches exact imitation, yet retains some degree of his more casual technique, while at the same time grasping and expressing in tangible form what is characteristic, and if he combines both these approaches and lends the product a distinct, vigorous, active individuality—then his art will be noble, great and admirable. But if such an artist fails to adhere to and respect nature, he will move further away from the foundations of art, and his manner will become the more vacuous and insignificant the further he moves away from simple imitation and from style.

It should be clear that we use the word 'manner' positively and in a respectful sense; therefore, artists whose works in our opinion belong to this category need not feel slighted. Our only concern is to assure the word 'style' a position of the highest honor in order to have available a term to designate the highest level that art has ever reached or can reach. Merely recognizing this level is a great reward, and discussing it with knowledgeable people a rare pleasure which we trust we will have many opportunities to repeat in the future.

On Realism in Art[1] (1798)

For a recent opera performance in a German theater, scenery was designed to represent an oval, amphitheater-like hall, with spectators looking down from their boxes onto the actual stage as though they were watching the action. Some theater-goers in the orchestra and loges were dissatisfied with the scenery and complained about such an unnatural and unrealistic thing being foisted on them. A conversation about this matter took place between an advocate of the scenery and a dissatisfied spectator approximately as follows:

ADVOCATE: Let's see if we can't find some way to reconcile our views.

SPECTATOR: I don't see how you can possibly defend such scenery.

ADVOCATE: When you go to the theater, I'm sure you don't expect everything you see to be true-to-life, do you?

SPECTATOR: No, of course not. But I do expect everything to *appear* true-to-life.

ADVOCATE: Pardon me for contradicting such a firmly held belief, but I maintain that you don't expect that at all!

SPECTATOR: How can you say that! If I didn't expect it, why would the set designer go to so much trouble and draw every line in perspective and paint everything so realistically? Why pay such careful attention to costuming? Why go to all the expense of creating costumes that make me believe I'm back in another time? Why do we most praise the actor who expresses emotions realistically and who is realistic in delivery, posture and gesture? Why do I admire the actor who deludes me into thinking that I am seeing not an imitation, but the real thing?

ADVOCATE: You are very eloquent! But it is perhaps more difficult than you think to determine what one really feels. What would you say if I maintain that theatrical performances do not appear realistic to you at all, but rather give you only an appearance of reality?

SPECTATOR: I would say that you are being overly subtle and are simply playing with words.

ADVOCATE: And my reply would be that words cannot be delicate and subtle enough when we are dealing with the workings of the mind, indeed, that such word play betrays a basic need of the mind. Since we cannot express precisely what we feel, our mind tries to work with contrasts, to answer the question from two sides, and then tries to grasp the matter in the middle, so to speak.

SPECTATOR: True enough. But explain yourself more clearly—and with concrete examples if you don't mind.

ADVOCATE: I can easily oblige you to make my point. For example, when you attend an opera, don't you enjoy it completely?

SPECTATOR: If all aspects of the performance are in harmony, then it is one of the greatest joys I can imagine.

ADVOCATE: But the characters up there on the stage meet and greet each other singing, they sing the letters they receive, they sing their love, their hate and all their passions, they fight singing and die singing. How can you say that the whole performance or even a part of it appears realistic? Or even gives the appearance of reality?

SPECTATOR: I must admit, when I think about it, I can't really say that. You are right, nothing seems true-to-life.

ADVOCATE: But still, you enjoy it thoroughly.

SPECTATOR: Definitely. Of course I have often heard people ridicule opera precisely because it is so far removed from reality. But I myself have always enjoyed it, and I enjoy it even more now that productions have become more elaborate and polished.

ADVOCATE: And don't you feel that you are being completely deluded in the opera?

SPECTATOR: Deluded? No, that's not the word I would use. . .And yet, perhaps I would. . .No, I don't think I would either!

ADVOCATE: Now you are caught in a complete contradiction. I think that's even worse than playing with words.

SPECTATOR: All right! We'll clear this up somehow!

ADVOCATE: When we do, we'll be in agreement. Would you allow me to ask a few questions at this point?

SPECTATOR: I think you should. Since your questions have gotten me into this dilemma, they'll have to get me out.

ADVOCATE: It is true then that you hesitate to call the feeling you get in the opera a delusion?

SPECTATOR: Yes, I do hesitate. And yet, it is a kind of delusion, or something that comes close to one.

ADVOCATE: And isn't it true that during the performance you almost forget yourself?

SPECTATOR: Not almost, but completely. If all or part of it is any good.

ADVOCATE: And you are enraptured?

SPECTATOR: That has happened more than once.

ADVOCATE: Can you tell me under what circumstances?

SPECTATOR: It has happened on so many occasions that it would be difficult to list them all.

ADVOCATE: But you have already answered my question. Doesn't it most often happen when everything is in harmony?

SPECTATOR: No question about it.

ADVOCATE: Is such a perfect performance in harmony with itself, or with some extraneous factor?

SPECTATOR: With itself, I would say.

ADVOCATE: And this particular harmony is no doubt the achievement of art?

SPECTATOR: Certainly.

ADVOCATE: A little while ago we said that opera lacks a certain kind of reality, and that it by no means represents as reality what it imitates. But can we deny the existence of an inner reality which results from the inner logic in the work of art?

SPECTATOR: I grant you, if the opera is good it becomes its own micro-world in which everything follows certain laws—a world which must be experienced on its own terms.

ADVOCATE: Doesn't it follow then that reality in art and reality in nature are two completely different concepts? And that the artist should not and must not try to lend his work the appearance of a work of nature?

SPECTATOR: But so often a work of art does have the appearance of a work of nature.

ADVOCATE: I can't deny that. But may I speak bluntly?

SPECTATOR: Of course. We're not here to flatter each other.

ADVOCATE: Then I take the liberty of saying that a work of art can only appear as a work of nature to the completely unsophisticated spectator. The artist appreciates such a spectator in spite of the fact that he is on the lowest level. But unfortunately this spectator will only be content as long as the artist stoops to his level; he will never be able to share with the true artist the flight to a higher level which genius impels the artist to undertake in order to realize his creative potential to the fullest.

SPECTATOR: That sounds strange, but I can accept it.

ADVOCATE: You would not accept it so readily if you hadn't reached a higher level yourself.

SPECTATOR: Now let me try to lend some order to what we have discussed and proceed from there. Would you mind if I asked the questions?

ADVOCATE: All the better.

SPECTATOR: You say that only the unsophisticated can see a work of art as a work of nature.

ADVOCATE: Yes. Remember the birds who tried to eat the cherries in the great master's painting?[2]

SPECTATOR: Well, doesn't that prove that the cherries were painted to perfection?

ADVOCATE: By no means. To me, it only proves that those connoisseurs were just sparrows and nothing more.

SPECTATOR: It still doesn't convince me that such a painting is not excellent.

ADVOCATE: May I tell you a more modern story?

SPECTATOR: Please. I usually prefer stories to abstract arguments.

ADVOCATE: A famous naturalist had a monkey as a pet. One day the beast was nowhere to be found. After a long search, the man discovered his pet in the library, sitting on the floor, surrounded by prints from an unbound volume on natural history. The man was amazed at his monkey's interest in natural history and even more amazed, and annoyed, when he realized that his snack-loving pet had eaten all the beetles in the illustrations.

SPECTATOR: That's really quite amusing!

ADVOCATE: And appropriate, I hope. I assume you would not say that the colored illustrations can be compared to the painting of the great master.

SPECTATOR: Of course not.

ADVOCATE: But you would say the monkey was an unsophisticated art lover?

SPECTATOR: Definitely, and a greedy one to boot!—Now I think I know what you are getting at! You mean to say, don't you, that the unsophisticated art lover demands that a work of art be natural and true-to-life so that he can enjoy it in his 'natural,' often primitive and unsophisticated way?

ADVOCATE: That's my opinion.

SPECTATOR: And that's why you say an artist demeans himself if he tries for such an effect?

ADVOCATE: That is my firm belief.

SPECTATOR: But I still think there is a contradiction. A few minutes ago, as well as on other occasions, you paid me the compliment of counting me among at least the semisophisticated art lovers.

ADVOCATE: Let's say, among the art lovers who are on the way to becoming true connoisseurs.

SPECTATOR: Well then, tell me, why do I also perceive a great work of art as a work of nature?

ADVOCATE: Because it harmonizes with your better nature, because it is beyond the natural but not outside of nature. A great work of art is a work of the human mind, and thus also a work of nature. But because the work of art treats its diverse subject matter as a unified whole and reveals the significance and dignity of even the most ordinary subjects, it goes beyond nature. A work of art can only be comprehended by a mind that has been formed and developed harmoniously, because only such a mind can relate to what is excellent and complete within itself. The average art lover has no concept of that. He treats the work of art like a piece of merchandise. But the true connoisseur sees not only the realism of what is imitated but also the excellence in the selection of subject matter, the imaginativeness in composition, and the supra-natural spirit of this micro-world of art. He feels that he must rise to the level of the artist in order to enjoy the work, that he must focus his scattered energies on the work of art, that he must live with it, must see it again and again, and thus achieve a higher level of awareness.

SPECTATOR: Well spoken! It is true, I've had similar feelings in art galleries, in the theater, while reading various kinds of literature, and have sensed more or less what you demand of art. From now on I will be more aware of my reactions and be more discerning about works of art. But it seems to me that we have strayed quite far from our original topic: You wanted to persuade me to approve of those painted spectators in our opera. Even though we have come to some agreement, I don't see how those figures fit into your argument and how you could make me accept them.

ADVOCATE: Fortunately, there will be another performance of the opera tonight. You won't miss it, will you?

SPECTATOR: By no means.

ADVOCATE: And the painted spectators?

SPECTATOR: They won't keep me away. After all, I am something more than a sparrow!

ADVOCATE: I do hope that our common interests will bring us together again soon.

Introduction to the *Propylaea*[1] (1798)

A young man who feels attracted to nature and art expects, by striving vigorously, to gain immediate entrance to the inner sanctum. As an adult he discovers that after a long and arduous pilgrimage he is still in the vestibule.

This consideration prompted the selection of a title for our periodical. The place where we will converse with our friends can merely be a stairway, a gate, an entrance, an antechamber, an area between the inside and the outside, between the sacred and the profane.

Should the title *Propylaea* call to mind the gateway through which one had to pass to reach the Athenian citadel, Minerva's temple, we shall not protest. But we hope we will not be accused of presumptuously attempting to compete in these pages with so magnificent a work of art. What we wish to convey by this title is at most something that might have taken place there: discussions and conversations which perhaps would not have been unworthy of those hallowed halls.

Do not thinkers, scholars and artists in their best moments dream of living in that land, among a people whom nature endowed with the perfection we seek and never attain, a people who in the course of time were able to develop a culture that had harmony and continuity, in contrast to our own which seems so fragmented and transitory?

What modern nation does not owe its artistic heritage to the Greeks, and, in certain respects, who owes more than the Germans?

If justification should be deemed necessary for our symbolic title, this should suffice. May it serve to remind us to stray as little as possible from classical ground, and may its brevity and significance attract those art lovers to whom we, a like-minded group of friends, hope to communicate our remarks and observations on nature and art.

Anyone with an artistic calling will show a lively interest in everything around him. Objects and their component parts will attract his attention, and by applying what he learns from his new interest he will gradually become more and more discerning. In the beginning he will work almost exclusively for himself, but later gladly share what he does with others. We, too, want to share with our readers certain things we consider instructive and agreeable, ideas and observations we have collected under various circumstances over the past several years.

One must admit that objective observations are rarer than one thinks. Our feelings, views and judgments become part of our experiences so quickly that we cannot long maintain our position as impartial observer but instead soon begin forming opinions. Yet we should attribute importance to these opinions only to the extent that we can trust the nature and training of our mind as a basis for them.

We have more confidence in our opinions if we have like-minded friends, if we know we are not thinking and working in isolation but in community with others. When views contrary to our convictions are expressed, we quite often succumb to self-doubt and we worry that our opinions are not shared by anyone else. However, our self-confidence is restored and our doubts as good as eliminated when we realize that others agree with us. Only then do we feel secure enough to affirm principles which long experience has gradually shown us and others to be valid.

If several such individuals are close enough that they may call themselves friends, if they share the same interest in a continuous learning process and have similar goals, then they can be sure there will be basic agreement among them. Even if their respective paths seem to lead them apart, there will be a happy reunion sooner or later.

How well conversation serves in communicating ideas! Yet, conversation is transitory, and while the outcome of such an exchange is permanent, the means by which we arrive at it are soon forgotten.

Correspondence better preserves the stages of a continuing exchange of ideas among friends because every step in growth is fixed. What has been achieved gives us a feeling of comfort, while at the same time a look back at how it came about is instructive and provides hope for an indefinite continuation.

Another good means of furthering the intellectual development of oneself and others is the brief essay in which one sets down thoughts, convictions and expectations which may be re-examined later. Aids of this kind must all be used, considering the brevity of life and the many obstacles that stand in the way of every endeavor.

We are of course referring here especially to the exchange of ideas among friends who are interested in expanding their general knowledge of the arts and sciences, although people in politics and business would also benefit from such communication.

In the arts and sciences, however, a limited circle of close friends is not enough. Communicating with the public at large is also desirable, indeed necessary. Everything we think and achieve by right belongs to the world, and any individual effort the world can use, it will bring to fruition. The writer's desire for accclaim is an urge nature has placed in him in order to inspire him to greater heights. The writer may think he has earned his laurels, yet he soon realizes that a more careful development of his innate talents is necessary to retain the public's favor, which he may have captured temporarily through chance.

The relationship between the writer and the public is very important for him early in his career, and even in his mature years. Though it may not be his calling to teach others, he still wishes to communicate with those who share his views but are scattered far and wide. Through his writings he wishes to revive former friendships, strengthen present relationships and find new friends among the younger generation. He wishes to help young writers avoid the mistakes he himself has made. And while noting and utilizing the achievements of the present, he also wants to preserve the memory of the accomplishments of the past.

With these earnest precepts in mind, we have decided to publish our periodical. May it be guided by a positive spirit; where our efforts will take us, only time can tell.

We hope the essays we plan to offer will never be contradictory in essential points, even though the authors' ways of thinking may not be identical. No two persons perceive the world exactly alike, and different minds will often apply differently a principle they otherwise agree on. A person may not even be consistent in his own views and judgments, so that earlier convictions must give way to later ones. Specific thoughts and statements may not withstand challenges, yet what matters is that we remain true to ourselves and others.

Although the authors ardently desire that harmony prevail among ourselves and with the majority of our public, at the same time we must expect dissonant voices from various quarters, especially since we depart from prevailing opinions in more than one point. We do not at all intend to censure or change anyone's way of thinking, but we will express our opinions firmly and will decline or accept a challenge, whichever we deem appropriate. In general, however, we will adhere firmly to principles and reiterate especially those prerequisite conditions that seem to us indispensable in the development of an artist. If you are serious, you must take a stand, otherwise you do not deserve to play an active role.

In promising to present remarks and discussions about "nature," we must point out that they will refer primarily to the visual arts and art theory, but also to the broad education and training of artists.

The foremost requirement for an artist will always be that he follow nature, study it, recreate it and bring forth something which resembles it.

We are not always aware of the great, indeed the enormous scope of this requirement, and the true artist himself realizes it only in the later stages of his development. Nature is separated from art by an enormous chasm, which even genius cannot bridge without resorting to external means.

Everything we see around us is only raw material. It happens rarely enough that an artist, through instinct and taste, practice and experimentation, finally learns how to present the external beauty of things and to select the best from the good, and succeeds in producing at least something agreeable to the eye. It happens even more rarely, especially today, that an artist is able to penetrate the essence of objects as well as the depths of his own soul, which, however, is necessary if he wants to produce something that rises above the merely pleasing and superficially effective, if he wants to rival nature and create a spiritual-organic whole. If the artist is successful, his work will have such content and such form that it appears natural and at the same time seems above nature.

Man is the highest, indeed the only proper subject for the visual arts. In order to understand the human body and to fathom the intricacies of its structure, a general knowledge of organic nature is essential. The artist should also have a theoretical understanding of inorganic bodies and natural phenomena, especially where they have a practical application in art, as do tone and color. Yet, what a laborious process it would be if the artist had to obtain what he is looking for by consulting the anatomist and the natural scientist. It is even questionable if he would find what is really most important to him because their instruction is intended for students of science and cannot deal with the artist's limited, specialized needs. Here is where we would like to step in. And although we do not anticipate being able to complete the necessary work ourselves, we still plan to present a general survey and in addition contribute discussions on specific topics.

The human form cannot be thoroughly understood by merely observing its exterior. We need to expose what is inside, distinguish the parts and note their relation; we must be aware of variations, learn to recognize action and reaction and know the hidden, inert, fundamental elements. Only then can we actually perceive and imitate the beautiful, unified whole which moves before our eyes with the rhythmic grace of waves. Merely looking at the exterior of a living being confuses the viewer. One thinks of the saying, applicable here as in other cases, that we truly see only what we know. A nearsighted person approaching an unfamiliar object sees it less clearly than if it were one familiar to him, because then his mental vision would come to his aid. Thus, observation reaches perfection in knowledge.

An artist knowledgeable in natural history will draw objects masterfully because he is able to recognize and emphasize the important and significant parts which give the whole its character.

Accurate knowledge of the individual parts of the human body and the ability ultimately to perceive them as a whole are of the greatest advantage to the artist. He will also find it most useful to take note generally and specifically of related objects, assuming he is capable of conceptualizing and grasping the close relationship of seemingly dissimilar things.

Comparative anatomy provides a general understanding of organic structures. It leads us from a single form to many, and as we observe closely or remotely related organisms, we gain intellectual distance and see their individual characteristics as components of an ideal whole.

If we keep this in mind, we realize that our attention follows a specific direction when we observe objects, and that isolated facts are easier to learn and retain through comparison. And finally, we realize in regard to art that we can compete with nature only if we have learned, at least to some degree, how she goes about creating her works.

When we encourage the artist to acquaint himself with inorganic nature too, we do so because detailed knowledge of the mineral kingdom is so easily and conveniently obtained today. The painter needs some familiarity with stones to present their characteristic features, as do the sculptor and architect to put them to practical use. The gem engraver must know precious stones, as should the connoisseur and collector.

In general terms, our advice to the artist is to familiarize himself with the manifestations of nature in order to find those of special interest to him, which will help broaden his education and give him a better understanding of what applies to his field. We would like to add something further about this important point.

Until now the painter has only been able to marvel at the physicist's theory of colors, without deriving any practical advantage for himself.[2] Yet artistic instinct, constant effort and practical necessity helped him to find his own way. He intuitively knew which strong contrasts should be juxtaposed to produce the harmony of colors. He described certain characteristics of colors in terms of physical sensation: warm and cold, colors suggesting proximity, others distance, and the like, so that his descriptions reflected the basic laws of nature. Perhaps the supposition will be proven that all color effects in nature—like magnetic, electric or other effects—are based on reciprocity, on polarity, or whatever name we may give to the phenomena of duality or indeed multiplicity within one distinct unit.

We shall take it upon ourselves to present this subject for the artist intelligibly and in detail. We are confident he will welcome our efforts, as we will only try to explain and reduce to general principles what he has been doing instinctively.

So much for what we hope to offer on the subject of nature. Now briefly our thoughts on art.

The format of our journal is such that we will publish individual essays, and most of those in installments. However, we have no desire to fragmentize, but rather ultimately to create a whole from these many parts. It is therefore necessary to inform our readers in advance and in general outline of what we intend to present in specific articles. The first piece will be an essay on the visual arts, in which the well-known principles will be presented according to our own interpretation and method.[3] Our main concern is to demonstrate the importance of each aspect of art, and to show that the artist must not neglect any one of them, as still happens so often today.

We maintained above that nature is an abundant source of raw material for the artist. Now let us turn our attention to the important question of how he should prepare this material.

As soon as the artist selects a natural object, it no longer belongs to nature. We may even say that he creates it at this very moment, when he perceives in the object what is significant, characteristic and interesting, or better, when he imbues it with a higher value.

In this way, more beautiful proportions, nobler forms and higher characteristics are, as it were, imposed on the human body. The boundaries of harmony, greatness, significance and completeness are drawn, within which nature offers its best. Normally, owing to its immense range, nature can easily degenerate into ugliness or create the impression of blandness.

The same is true for more elaborate works, their subjects and content, whether they are based on legend or history.

Happy the artist who makes the right choice, who knows how to select, or rather determine, what is appropriate to art!

If he gropes anxiously for a subject among unrelated myths or in the vast realm of history, if he aims for scholarly significance or allegorical interest, he will encounter unexpected obstacles halfway through his endeavors, or find when finished that he has missed his objective altogether. If he does not speak clearly to the senses, he will not clearly address the mind. We consider this point so important that we include a detailed discussion of it in our first issue.[4]

Once a suitable object has been found or invented, the next step is artistic treatment, which can be divided into three categories: intellectual, sensuous and technical.

Intellectual treatment develops the inner structure and identifies the subordinate motifs. If choice of subject is a guide in judging the depth of artistic talent, the selection of motifs reveals its breadth, richness, scope and attractiveness.

Sensuous treatment is what makes the work totally accessible and pleasantly gratifying to the senses, and lends it an irresistible charm.

And finally, the technical treatment is that through which physical means, acting on certain materials, bring the work into existence.

While we wish to prove useful to the artist with our observations, and fervently hope he will make use of some of our advice and suggestions, we are at the same time quite aware that for better or for worse all projects, like human beings, are at the mercy of their age. For this reason we cannot help but wonder what reception we will find.

Everything is subject to constant change, and because certain things cannot co-exist, they try to displace each other. This is true of knowledge, of technique, of ideas and principles. Man's goals do not change much. One still wants to be a good artist or poet or become one, just as in centuries past; however, the means to realize this goal are not always clear to everyone. And yet, why deny that nothing would be more desirable than being able to achieve a great goal without much effort?

The public, of course, has great influence on art. In return for its applause and its money, it demands a work to its taste, a work which provides immediate gratification. Usually the artist is glad to comply because he too is part of the public, because he has developed during the same period, feels the same needs and shares the same general aims and desires. So he willingly subordinates himself to the crowd, which supports him and that he in turn animates.

As a result, whole nations, whole eras are delighted with their artists, and the artists savor the response they find in their nations, their eras. And neither side has even the slightest suspicion that their path might be wrong, their taste at least onesided, their art in decline, or their efforts perhaps misguided.

Instead of generalizing further, we would like to elaborate on a matter particularly relevant to the visual arts.

The German artist, and any modern northern artist, finds it difficult if not impossible to make the transition from shapeless mass to form, or if he succeeds, to maintain it.

Any artist who has spent some time in Italy should ask himself whether it was not the contact with the best works of ancient and modern times that aroused in him the incessant desire to study and copy the human body, its proportions, forms and characteristics? Did he not wish to be exact and painstaking so that he might approximate those classic, self-contained works and produce one of his own which would both satisfy the senses and elevate the mind to the highest? He also has to admit to a gradual slackening of his efforts after his return because he found few people who are inclined to see, enjoy and reflect on art. Most viewers will only look at a work casually, thinking random thoughts and enjoying their own feelings.

Even the worst picture can speak to our emotions and imagination by setting them in motion, releasing them and letting them run free. The best work of art also addresses the emotions, but it speaks a more refined language, one that not everyone understands. The great work of art restrains feelings and imagination, it robs us of our free choice, and so we cannot deal with it as we please. We are compelled to submit to it so that it can give us back to ourselves, elevated and enhanced.

We shall seek to show as clearly as possible and in detail that such considerations are not idle fantasies. We will especially draw attention to a contradiction of which the moderns are so often guilty. They call the ancients their teachers, they admit to the unsurpassable excellence of works of antiquity, and yet, in theory and practice, they abandon the principles to which the ancients adhered.

This important issue will be our point of departure, and we shall return to it frequently. But there are others of which some mention must be made.

One of the most striking signs of decline in art is the intermingling of the various forms of art.

To be sure, the arts themselves and the various art forms are intimately related and have a certain tendency to unite, if not merge completely. However, the duty, task and worth of the true artist lie precisely in keeping one particular art form separate from others. He should give autonomy to each branch and form of the arts and isolate them as far as possible.

It has been argued that all visual art tends toward painting, and all poetry toward drama.[5] This notion may give us occasion for important discussions in the future.

A true artist who works according to principles strives for artistic truth. An artist without principles, following a blind instinct, seeks only realism. The former leads art to its highest peak, the latter to its lowest level.

What is true of art in general also applies to individual art forms. The sculptor must think and feel differently from the painter, and must use different techniques for relief and for statues. Art began to decline when low relief became increasingly three-dimensional, when individual parts, then whole figures were raised, and finally buildings and landscapes were added, with an end result that was half painting, half puppet show. Unfortunately, some excellent artists of more recent times have followed this course.

When in future we suggest principles we consider true, we would welcome it if these principles, themselves derived from works of art, were tested by artists in practice. How rarely people can agree on a theory! On the other hand, it is much easier to decide what is practical and useful. How often we see artists at a loss in choosing subjects, in devising artistically appropriate compositions, or a painter hesitating when selecting his colors. That is the time to test a principle; then it is easier to determine if it brings us closer to the great models and everything we so cherish about them, or if it simply produces the confusion of an experience not sufficiently thought through.

Not only are such principles helpful in the training of artists and as a guide in difficult decisions, they will also prove useful in the understanding, appreciation and criticism of ancient and modern works of art—and these are the very principles that can be deduced from the works of art themselves. Indeed, it is all the more necessary to adhere to principles because individuals as well as whole nations in our modern era often fail to recognize the very nature of the excellence of ancient works of art, which nonetheless enjoy universal praise.

Examining these works closely will usually prevent this failure. One example of an experience with sculpture should suffice to show that scrutiny of ancient and modern art must be exact if it is to be of use.

Even a rough, imperfect plaster cast of a fine ancient work will have a strong effect on the viewer who, although inexperienced, is receptive to beauty. For even in an inferior reproduction we still perceive the idea, the simplicity and grandeur of form, in short, the general concept—

as much as one with poor eyesight would see when looking at the original from a distance.

As we know, such imperfect reproductions often arouse a strong interest in art; yet the effect is commensurate with the object. What the novice art lover experiences is more an undefined, muddled feeling than the real worth and greatness of the original work. Such people usually claim that too close a critical examination destroys pleasure, and they are the ones who tend to oppose and resist evaluating details.

However, if after more experience and practice they see a finished rather than a rough cast, or even an original work, their enjoyment together with their insight grows, and increases as they become acquainted with originals, and finally with originals of the highest order.

We gladly follow the labyrinthine paths of close scrutiny if the component parts as well as the whole are superior. In fact, only to the extent that we can learn to recognize inadequacy, can we recognize excellence. To be able to tell the difference between restored and original parts, between copy and model, to be able to perceive in the smallest fragment the vanished splendor of the whole—that is the joy of the true connoisseur. It is one thing to view an inexpressive work with muddled perception and quite another to grasp a great work with clear perception.

We should all strive for the highest in our intellectual pursuits. Insight is a very different matter from practical application, for in the latter we must soon resign ourselves to the limitations of our skill. On the other hand, far more people are capable of acquiring knowledge and insight; in fact, we may say that anyone can who will subordinate himself to his subject matter, and who does not try, with narrow-minded stubbornness, to interject himself with his petty one-sidedness into the highest works of nature and art.

If a discussion of works of art is to be meaningful and useful for ourselves and others, it should of course be conducted only in the presence of those works, for everything depends on the visual perception. It is important that the words which are to elucidate a work of art convey very precise thoughts—otherwise nothing is conveyed at all.

This is why written commentaries on works of art so often deal only in generalities. They no doubt stir thoughts and emotions in readers, but they do not help the viewer who examines the work in question with book in hand.

For this very reason, some of our own essays may stimulate perhaps more than they will satisfy. When we read an analysis of a fine work of art, we quite naturally wish to have it immediately before us so as to enjoy the total effect and evaluate for ourselves what is said regarding details.

Although the authors of the projected periodical intend to write mainly for people who either have already seen or are planning to see the works discussed, those who fall into neither category will also derive some benefit. We will mention reproductions and announce where casts of works or even originals from antiquity are located, to make them more accessible, especially to Germans. We shall do our best to meet the needs of true art lovers and connoisseurs.

A history of art can only be based on the highest and most precisely defined concept of art. Only when we know the best that man has been able to produce, can we describe the stages of his psychological development as reflected in art or in other areas. The first limited artistic efforts were concentrated on tedious, even inept imitation, with no distinction between significant and insignificant subjects. Then a closer and more agreeable relationship with nature developed, and when it was complemented by knowledge, order, seriousness and discipline, and favorable conditions prevailed, art reached the pinnacle where finally the fortunate genius, finding himself in this auspicious environment, was able to produce works of delight and perfection.

Unfortunately, works of art that communicate so easily and give man such a feeling of confidence and instill in him such a sense of serenity and freedom, lead the novice to believe that their creation is also easy. He is tempted to take the easy way and aim merely at semblance, since the ultimate achievement of art and artistic genius seems to have been accomplished without effort.

And so art gradually declines from its peak, in general and in particular works. To gain a clear understanding of this process, we will have to look at the details of details. This is not always a pleasant or exciting undertaking, but in due time it leads to a solid grasp of the whole, which more than compensates us.

Although experience has confirmed the usefulness of certain principles for evaluating ancient and early modern art, we need these principles most in judging modern, especially contemporary works. In discussing living and recently deceased artists there is always the risk that personal relationships, individual admiration or dislike, and public favor or disfavor may influence what we say. Consequently, standards are all the more necessary in arriving at a fair judgment of our contemporaries, and they ensure that the investigation will be equitable and impartial. The role or arbitrariness is diminished by referring the matter to a higher authority, and the validity of the principle itself and its application can be examined. Even if the parties cannot agree, at least moot points can be clearly defined.

We especially hope that living artists whose works we might criticize will weigh our opinion in this spirit. For anyone deserving the name of artist is obligated today to form, if not a theory based on his work and thoughts, then at least a set of theoretical rules of thumb which he finds useful. Experience tells us that the artist often accepts as guidelines only those principles which suit his talent, inclination and convenience. An artist is human, too, and acts like those in other fields. But we do not develop if we merely activate the talent we already have and avoid effort and inconvenience. The artist, like any human being, is by nature one-sided and will always gravitate in a particular direction. That is why every human being must assimilate, as far as he can, what is contrary to his nature, in thought and in action. The easygoing should look for seriousness and strictness, the strict for ease and casualness, the vigorous for gentleness, the gentle for vigor. Then each will develop his own nature the more he seems to stray from it. Every art demands the whole man, the highest form of art the whole of humanity.

Producing visual art requires technique, and the artist begins in his earliest years with the acquisition of technical skills, and rightly so. His general education, on the other hand, is often neglected, whereas it should be more thorough than that enjoyed by others, who have the opportunity to learn from life, where society soon teaches the crude person manners, and experience in the active world makes the most trusting cautious. Literary works are accessible to a wide public and therefore subject to opposition and criticism from all sides, while the artist, the only one confined to a lonely studio, finds his contact with the outside world limited almost exclusively to those who order and pay for his work, to a public often obsessed with peculiar whims, to experts who make him uneasy, and shady art dealers who greet everything new with words of praise which would more than honor a masterpiece.

But it is time to conclude this introduction, lest it prejudge and preempt rather than simply preface our work. At least we have defined the proposed point of departure for our journal. What its limits will or must be, only time will tell. In the near future we hope to deal with the theory and criticism of literature.[6] Anything that life, travel or events of the day have to offer shall not be excluded. In this last regard, we wish, finally, to discuss an important matter of some present concern.

The location of works of art has always been of utmost importance in the training of artists no less than for the enjoyment of art lovers. In the past, art works had permanent locations, with only minor exceptions. But now a great change has taken place which will have major consequences for both art in general and individual works.

Now more than ever we should regard Italy as what until recently it has always been, as one vast repository of art. Only if we make a catalogue of all its holdings, will it become clear what the world lost when so many sections of this great museum of antiquity were dismantled.[7]

How much has been destroyed in the process will probably never be known. A description of the new repository being created in Paris will be possible in a few years, and a guide for artists and art lovers to profit both from the art works of France and Italy can possibly be developed. In this context, an important and worthy issue requires attention: what other nations might do, especially Germany and England, to make the widely scattered art treasures generally accessible in this time of dispersal and loss; how they should approach this task in that true cosmopolitan spirit which is probably most effectively expressed in the arts and sciences; how they can help form an ideal art repository which, in time, would perhaps indemnify all for what is scattered for the moment, if not permanently lost.

So much for the general intent of our publication, which we hope will be granted a serious and kind reception.

Ancient versus Modern[1] (1818)

In an earlier essay I felt obligated to be lavish in my praise of antiquity and especially of the artists of that time. I am most anxious to avoid any misunderstanding, since it happens unfortunately all too often that the reader feels inclined to assume a contrary position rather than compromise and arrive at a balanced view. I am therefore glad to take this opportunity to clarify my statements and refer to examples from the visual arts which at the same time serve as symbols of the eternal life of human endeavors.

I would like to quote from an essay by a young friend, Karl Ernst Schubarth,[2] 'Goethe: A Critical Evaluation,' which in every regard merits my respect and gratitude. He says at one point: "I do not agree with most admirers of the ancients—Goethe himself among them—that nowhere in the world have there ever existed more favorable conditions for a superior and full development of humanity than among the Greeks." Fortunately, I can settle this disagreement by quoting Schubart again: "But with reference to Goethe I must say that I prefer Shakespeare to him because I see in Shakespeare such an excellent writer, one so unselfconscious, who with the utmost confidence can always identify precisely and intuitively what is authentic or false in man. And he does so without arguing, pondering, hairsplitting, analyzing and overemphasizing. To be sure, when I read Goethe, I always recognize the same goal in the end; but from the very beginning I have to struggle with opposing views and overcome them and be on guard, lest I take for plain truth what is meant to be rejected as totally erroneous."

Here our friend hits the nail on the head. For in that very point where he finds me at a disadvantage compared to Shakespeare, we all are at a disadvantage in relation to the ancients. But why speak of the ancients? Any talent whose development is not favored by time and circumstances but who must struggle to surmount obstacles and rid himself of errors—such a talent is at an immense disadvantage compared to a contemporary who has the opportunity to develop unencumbered and create freely to the utmost of his ability.

An older person with his wealth of experience often can recall some incident which may serve as an example to clarify and support an assertion he has made. That is why I beg the reader's indulgence when I relate the following anecdote. A seasoned diplomat once wanted to make my acquaintance. After we had exchanged only a few words, he turned to his friends and said: "Voilà un homme qui a eu de grands chagrins!" This remark gave me pause. The experienced physiognomist had made a correct observation, but had interpreted his finding as being merely the result of endurance, whereas he should have attributed to it resistance as well. An observant straightforward German would have said: "Here is someone who has had a hard time!"

Since the suffering we have endured and the actions we have performed leave an indelible imprint on our face, it is not surprising if every work or achievement which may result from our struggling bears the same imprint. To the attentive observer it reveals a human being whose aim has been to remain true to himself whether circumstances permitted him free development or restricted him, a human being who sought to maintain, if not always his dignity, then at least the perseverance that is characteristic of man.

So let us leave behind us the issue of old versus new, past versus present, and say: Every artistic work puts us into the state of mind of the artist; if he felt serene and at ease, we feel free; if he felt constrained, anxious and doubtful, we feel just as restricted.

But we should note that we are here concerned solely with technique, not subject or content. If we bear this in mind when we examine works of art, we must admit that we take pleasure in any work which the artist accomplished with ease and confidence. What art lover does not enjoy a good drawing or etching by Chodowiecki?[3] In his works we see such a clear perception of nature as we know it that nothing remains to be desired. However, when he tries to go beyond his area of competence and abandons his usual format, all the qualities which derive from his individuality are lost.

I would further maintain that even mannerists, if they do not go too far, can be very enjoyable, and that I very much like the originals I own. Artists known by this designation have a considerable innate talent. However, due to the conditions of the time or the school to which they happen to belong, they are soon made to feel that leisurely development is frowned upon and that they must make up their minds and strike out on their own. They therefore develop a kind of pictorial language which enables them to represent the visible world, more or less successfully, with dexterous and easy strokes. Thus they bedazzle us with all kinds of scenes, so that sometimes whole nations are pleasantly entertained and beguiled for decades on end, until at last one or the other artist returns to nature and a higher concept of art.

Antiquities of Herculaneum[4] offer proof that even the ancients finally declined into a sort of mannerism. But the models they learned from were too grand, too imposing and still well-preserved and accessible for ordinary painters to lose themselves completely in insignificance.

In order to examine the issue from a higher and more rewarding vantage point, let us turn to Raphael's unique talent. He was born with the most promising natural gifts and grew up in a time when art was pursued with utmost dedication and interest, hard work and perseverance. Masters showed the way and led the novice to the threshold, and he only had to take a final step to enter the temple of art. Guided by Pietro Perugino[5] in the acquisition of a most painstaking technique, Raphael developed his remarkable talent using Leonardo da Vinci and Michelangelo as models. Despite the heights their genius attained, both these masters seem to have derived little genuine satisfaction from their artistic endeavors during their long lives. Leonardo literally thought himself into exhaustion and labored too long on technical matters. Instead of adding extraordinary works of sculpture to his list of artistic achievements as he intended, Michelangelo toiled in quarries during the last years of his life selecting marble blocks and slabs. As a result, of all the planned sculptures of major figures from the Old and New Testaments, only Moses was completed—an example of what he could and should have accomplished.[6] Raphael on the other hand worked all his life with constant and ever growing ease. His mental vigor and his physical energies were in such complete harmony that we feel safe in saying that no modern artist has conceived his works so purely and effectively, and expressed himself so lucidly as did Raphael. He was one of those talents who present us with the freshest water from the purest source. He did not work at all in a Greek manner or style, but he felt and thought and acted very much like a Greek. We see here a superlative artist who developed during a time which was as favorable to the arts as the time of Pericles when similar conditions and circumstances prevailed.

Therefore, it cannot be emphasized enough: The born talent is required to produce, but in turn he must be provided the opportunity to develop as an individual and as an artist; the artist cannot renounce his talent, but he will not be able to perfect it without the benefit of favorable conditions during his lifetime.

A case in point was the Carracci school.[7] There the basic requirements were talent, dedication, hard work and perseverance. What was offered was an environment where fine talent could develop individually and artistically. The school produced a good dozen artists of such excellence—every one of them practicing and developing his special talent according to the same general idea—that it seems hardly possible that later periods could produce their equal.

Let us also look at the immense impact the highly talented Rubens had on the art world! He was no normal mortal either;[8] we must not forget that he was heir to a great inheritance left by the old masters of the fourteenth and fifteenth centuries and by all the outstanding artists of the sixteenth, towards the end of which Rubens was born.

Or consider the great number of seventeenth-century Dutch masters, Rubens' contemporaries and successors, who developed their talents at home, in the south or the north. Can anyone deny finding great delight in the incredible acumen with which they observed nature and the ease with which they expressed their own serene enjoyment? Indeed, one understands why those who are fortunate enough to own such works spend hours of their time contemplating and admiring them. Nor can one blame art lovers for devoting themselves exclusively to collecting and treasuring works from that era.

We could go on and cite a hundred examples in support of what we have said. The clarity of the view, the serenity of the perception, the ease of communication—that is what delights us! And if we now say that we find all that in genuine Greek works which represent the noblest subjects, have the most worthy content and are executed to utmost perfection—then it will be understood why we always begin with them and end with them. Let everyone be a Greek in his own way, but let him be a Greek!

A Challenge for a Modern Sculptor[1] (1817)

Of late there has been some discussion as to how the artist, especially the sculptor, should go about honoring a conqueror. How should he portray the victor and his defeated enemies as architectural adornment on pediments, friezes or other types of ornamentation, as was frequently done in antiquity? Finding an answer is more difficult today when civilized nations fight than in the mythical past when men of superior qualities contended with primitive brutes or animal-like creatures.

The Greeks, whom we must always revere as our masters, were able to lend such representations immediate interest by the very contrast between the opponents. Here were Gods fighting Titans, and the viewer immediately sympathized with the nobler figures. The same holds true for Hercules battling monsters or the Lapithae[2] struggling with the centaurs. In the latter case the artist usually made the scales of victory tip one way, then the other, letting victors and the vanquished change roles, and yet we are always inclined to side with the vigorous race of heroes. A very different feeling is aroused when men fight with Amazons. Although these heroic women are strong and daring, they are still seen as the weaker sex and arouse our compassion as soon as they appear defeated, wounded or dead. The best example of such a theme—one that merits high praise for its lighthearted spirit—is still the battle of the Bacchantes and Fauns against the Tyrrhenians. The former, like the true mountain dwellers they are, fight off the pirating seafarers in the manner of deer and goats, and succeed so well that the intruders are forced to leap from a sea cliff, and in falling are transformed into dolphins by a merciful god, who thus assures them of remaining in their own element, the sea. Surely nothing can be more imaginatively conceived, more charmingly presented.[3]

Roman art handled the problem somewhat less elegantly. On their victory columns, for example, they depicted the defeated and captured Thracians dressed in pleated garments, as subordinate to their own armored and well-armed warriors.[4] In later times, however, Polidoro Caravaggio[5] and his contemporaries had the contending factions in the Florentine civil war fight each other as equals. To give the corbels in the hall of Alexander Fava's palace in Bologna some meaningful decoration, Annibale Carraci chose to portray vigorous masculine forms in a brawl with sphinxes and harpies, in which the latter are always totally crushed.[6] It is difficult to evaluate the effect of this motif. The painter drew great artistic advantages from the contrast; however, the viewer who finally perceives that the one-sidedness of the battle has become mere routine feels quite uneasy. For even monsters we wish to see simply as defeated opponents, not as totally crushed.

All this points up the basic difficulty of contrasting people characteristically, first as combatants and then as the victorious and the vanquished, so that a balance is maintained and the emotional concern for both sides remains intact.

There are not many modern works that appeal to us in such a way. Seeing armed Spaniards in battle with naked American Indians is unbearable because the contrast of violence and defenselessness is too extreme and too reminiscent of the Massacre of the Innocents.[7] Seeing Christians victorious over Turks is more acceptable, especially if the Christian warriors appear in seventeenth-century dress. The Moslems' contempt for adherents of all other faiths and their cruelty against enslaved members of our people justify hating them and killing them.[8]

Christians fighting Christians, especially in our time, is not a good subject. There are some beautiful engravings representing scenes from the American war,[9] and yet, viewed purely emotionally, they are unbearable. Properly uniformed, well-armed regular troups in the heat of battle with a motley group of civilians, among them priests as leaders and children as flag bearers, cannot please the eye, even less the mind, although the mind tells us the weaker side will prevail in the end. And if we also see half-naked savages involved in the battle, we cannot help realizing that this motif is merely based on newspaper reports. A panorama of Tippoo Sahib's[10] horrible downfall can only be relished by those who participated in the plunder of his treasures.

If we contemplate the situation in the modern world we realize that all Christians are related to one another through religion and customs and are really brothers, and that we are not at odds because of our philisophies and opinons, but rather because of trade and commerce. The German landowner welcomes it when the Englishman raises the price of wool, and for the very same reason the Mediterranean manufacturer curses him.

Germans and French, although constantly at odds politically and socially, can no longer be presented pictorially in combat. We have adopted too many of their customs, too much of their military attire, for us to be able to see a clear difference between almost identically uniformed members of the two nations. But to return to our point of departure: If a sculptor found it expedient to divest his figures of all uniforms and decorations, then every characteristic difference would be lost and the opponents would look identical. We would only see handsome people murdering each other. The tragic destiny of Eteocles and Polynices would have to be repeated again and again, without the existence of the Furies which alone lent the motif its significance.[11]

Russians battling foreigners is a more suitable subject. They have distinctive traditional helmets and weapons, and the numerous nationalities in their immense empire also offer a variety of costumes which an ingenious artist could use to his advantage.

To such artists we dedicate these remarks. Our intent has been to call attention once again to suitable and unsuitable subjects. The former have a natural buoyancy and float by themselves; the latter can be kept afloat only with cumbersome artistic contrivances.

Christ and Twelve Figures from the Old and New Testaments: A Suggestion for Sculptors[1] (1830)

Although we have advised painters against concentrating on biblical themes, we turn to sculptors with that very suggestion,[2] for we wish to find an outlet for the great reverence we feel for biblical cycles. We envision here just such a cycle done on a large scale.

We are always distressed when we hear that a sculptor should portray Christ and the apostles separately. Raphael once painted them as individual figures,[3] expressively and yet serenely, and we should be satisfied with that. But where would the sculptor find the characteristics necessary to differentiate them sufficiently? Since indications of martyrdom are not considered in good taste in modern times, the artist, not wanting to reject a commission, has no choice but to drape simple, well-built men with yards and yards of cloth, more than they probably ever used in all their lives.

In the kind of despair which always seizes us when we see fine talent misguided or exploited, we hit upon the idea of creating thirteen figures that comprise the entire biblical cycle, an idea which we herewith present with good conscience, and confidence in its soundness.

1. Adam,
full of human vigor and beauty; to be pictured as prototype of the average man, not heroic, but rather the successful, gentle yet strong father of mankind, clad in the animal skin given him from above to cover his nakedness. Portraying his face would be the task of the greatest master. Serious, with a half-sad smile, the first ancestor is looking at a sturdy, vigorous boy while placing his right hand on the child's head, and lowering his spade indolently with his left as if to rest from work.

His first-born son is a robust boy who, wild-eyed and with powerful hands, crushes dragons about to attack him. His father watches him, consoled as it were at the loss of paradise. We suggest to the artist merely the idea, which in itself is clear and complete and requires little more.

2. Noah,
a vintner, lightly dressed in a tucked-up tunic, providing a charming contrast to Adam in the animal skin. In his left hand he is holding a vine heavy with grapes, in his right a cup which he proffers invitingly. His face is noble and serene, slightly animated by the wine. He must suggest contentment and his reassuring awareness that while unable to free human beings from serious ills, he is fortunate enough to be able to provide them with a means of alleviating worry and sorrow, if only temporarily.

3. Moses

I must admit, I cannot imagine this major figure in any position but seated, a notion I find not at all objectionable, since for the sake of variety I would prefer one male figure represented as sitting and resting. It is quite likely that the overpowering statue by Michelangelo at the tomb of Julius II has taken such a hold on my imagination that I cannot free myself from the memory. For this reason I leave further considerations and suggestions to artists and experts.

4. David
must not be omitted, although it seems to me that he presents a difficulty. To portray the son of a shepherd as an adventurer, a hero, bard, king and lover, all in one person, or to emphasize one major characteristic—that is a challenge for the most ingenious artist.

5. Isaiah
Son of a prince, the patriot and prophet, to be characterized as a dignified, admonishing figure. If there were some source to determine the costume of those times, it would be most helpful here.

6. Daniel
This figure I dare describe in more detail. A serene, oval, well-formed face, appropriate clothing, long curly hair, a slender and graceful body lively in facial expression and movement. Because he will be positioned next to Christ in the sequence of sculptures, I would suggest that he face him, as if anticipating in spirit the promised messiah.

If we imagine having entered a basilica and, while moving along the aisle on the left, having viewed the figures described above, we now arrive at the center where we see

7. Christ Himself,
who is portrayed as stepping from the tomb. If he is represented with the shrouds falling from his body, it will provide an opportunity to depict the resurrected Christ with an idealized body and with a proper degree of nakedness to compensate for the many inappropriate portrayals of him as tortured, naked on the cross, and as a corpse. This will be one of the most gratifying tasks for an artist, and one which to our knowledge has never been successfully accomplished.

If we now walk back along the other side of the basilica and view the six figures from the New Testament, we find first

8. The Disciple John
We would give him a round face, curly hair, and certainly a more robust build than Daniel's. The latter would express love yearning for the highest, the former love fulfilled in the presence of the most magnificent being. In such contrasts we can present in a subdued way, hardly noticeable to the eye, the idea which we see as central.

9. Matthew the Evangelist
We would represent him as a serious, quiet man of decisive though calm character. The angel traditionally associated with him would here assume the form of a boy who is chiseling a bas-relief on a stone slab. On its visible part we would see a king adoring the infant Jesus sitting on his mother's lap, in the distance a shepherd adoring Christ, and others faintly indicated. The Evangelist, a tablet in his left and a stylus in his right, is looking calmly and attentively at the slab, like one who

is about to commence writing. We imagine this figure as being in felicitous harmony with its surroundings, and in an interesting way.

In essence we see Matthew as the counterpart to Moses, and we wish that an artist of profound insight would here contrast the Law and the Gospel. Moses is in possession of the rigid commandments which are already inscribed in ancient stone; Matthew is about to record events of living history. I would not give a companion figure to Moses because he received his tablets directly from the hand of God. In Matthew's case, however, if we want to allegorize, the angel may signify the means by which the good tidings have reached the Evangelist.

10.

This spot we would dedicate to the Centurion of Capernaum. He is one of the first believers; he asks the Miracle Worker for help, not for himself or a relative, but for his most faithful and dedicated servant. There is such a tender quality in this story that we wish it could be conveyed.[4]

Because variety is part of the overall intent of this project, a Roman centurion in uniform would make a splendid addition. We do not insist that the nature of his request be absolutely discernible from his appearance; it would suffice if the artist represented a thoroughly sensible and kindhearted man.

11. Mary Magdalene

I would like to see her represented sitting or half reclining, but holding neither a skull nor a book. An angel at her side would show her the flask with the ointment she used to anoint the Lord's feet, and she would look at it with pious, contented joy. We have seen this motif in a lovely drawing, and we cannot imagine anything more devout and charming.

12. Paul

The first, mighty teacher! He is traditionally represented with a sword, which, however, we must reject as we would any instrument of torture. We would rather see him in the animated pose of one wanting to lend emphasis to his words and convince his listeners through facial expression and gesture. As a counterpart to Isaiah, he need not stand directly opposite that admonishing figure, that prophet of doom, but their relationship should be suggested.

13. Peter

This figure I would like to see treated most imaginatively and realistically.

When we entered the basilica, we first took general note of our twelve figures between the columns on both sides; in the center, in the most sacred place, we noted the unique, incomparable One. Then, starting on the left, we proceeded to view the statues individually in historical sequence.

In St. Peter's figure, face and movements, I would like to see the following expressed. In his left hand he is holding a colossal key and in his right its companion, like a person about to open or lock a door. To portray this attitude and expression with veracity should bring the greatest joy to a true artist. Peter's earnest, searching glance would be directed at the visitor entering the basilica, as though asking him if he is entitled to set foot here, and then warning him at his departure to take care, lest the door be closed behind him forever.

Summary

Before we leave we must add one more observation. Here we have statues from the Old Testament pointing figuratively to Christ, then the Lord himself appearing in his glory, and finally New Testament figures connected with him in every respect. Despite their great variety, the characters can be divided easily and without artificiality into relatively close pairs: Adam and Noah, Moses and Matthew, Isaiah and Paul, Daniel and John. David and Magdalene could be seen as relating directly to Christ himself: David in that he is proud of such a descendant, and Magdalene because she is suffused with the sublime feeling of having found a deserving recipient for her loving heart. Christ stands alone on his spiritual relationship to his heavenly father. The idea of portraying him as his shrouds fall is not original. However, it is not a question of suggesting something new but rather of finding what is appropriate, and, once it has been found, of utilizing it.

It is obvious that sculptors, for all their productivity, are not always fortunate in their choice of subject matter. Here we offer them many figures, each worthy of portrayal. And even if creating the whole group on a large scale should prove possible only in the imagination, sculptures of reduced size[5] would provide many an exhibition with charming diversity. The sponsors would no doubt find approval and satisfaction.

If several sculptors were invited to divide up the characters among themselves according to interest and ability and do them on the same scale, one could create an exhibition which in a city of some size and importance would certainly attract many viewers.

Winckelmann and His Age[1] (1805)

Introduction

The memory of remarkable men, no less than the presence of significant works of art, causes us from time to time to reflect. Both represent a legacy for every generation, the former by virtue of immortal deeds, the latter as ineffable but tangible presences. The perceptive person knows full well that only contemplating their uniqueness is of real value; yet, we keep on trying to deepen our understanding through thoughts and words.

We are especially encouraged to do so if new information concerning such eminent men or their works is discovered and publicized. Thus, we trust that our present consideration of Winckelmann, his character and his accomplishments, will be found appropriate at a time when newly published letters should shed further light on his thinking and the circumstances of his life.

Early Years[2]

Nature presents human beings at birth with a precious gift: the strong urge to take hold of the world and experience it, find a place in it and become a harmonious part of it. Some excellent minds, on the other hand, tend to shy away from real life, withdraw into themselves, create a special world within and achieve excellence which is inwardly directed.

However, if a highly gifted human being is capable of combining both tendencies, that is, if he seeks to complement his natural abilities with corresponding experiences in the outer world and hence develop his gifts to their utmost potential, then we can be assured that his existence will delight his contemporaries and generations to come.

Winckelmann was such a person. Already richly endowed by nature, he nevertheless spent his life seeking in man and in art—which is primarily concerned with man—those qualities of excellence and nobility he most admired.

As did others, Winckelmann endured a humble childhood, insufficient schooling as a youth, an irregular and unsystematic course of studies as a young man, and the burden of a schoolmaster's job with the familiar difficulties and worries that go with such a career. He turned thirty without fate having once smiled on him; but within him he carried the seed of his future happiness.

Even during those sad years we detect a desire to get firsthand experience of life and the world. Although his urge was unfocused and confused, it was strongly expressed. A few ill-planned attempts to visit foreign countries failed. He dreamed of a journey to Egypt, and he did set out to visit France, but unforeseen obstacles forced him to return. Better counseled by an inner voice, he finally decided that he must get to Rome at all costs. He felt that Rome was his true destination. This was more than a whim or mere idea, it was a definite plan which he sought to realize with shrewdness and perseverance.

Spirit of Antiquity

Man can achieve much through the appropriate use of his individual abilities, and can achieve extraordinary things if several of his talents are combined. But he can only accomplish the unique, the wholly unexpected, if all his qualities unite within him and work together as one. This was the happy lot of the ancients, especially the Greeks in their golden age. We moderns are forced by fate to content ourselves with the first two possibilities.

When man's nature functions soundly as a whole, when he feels that the world of which he is part is a huge, beautiful, admirable and worthy whole, when this harmony gives him pure and uninhibited delight, then the universe, if it were capable of emotion, would rejoice at having reached its goal and admire the crowning glory of its own evolution. For, what purpose would those countless suns and planets and moons serve, those stars and milky ways, comets and nebulae, those created and evolving worlds, if a happy human being did not ultimately emerge to enjoy existence?

Modern man often loses himself in the infinite before finally returning if possible to a limited point of reference—as we seem just now to have demonstrated. The ancients, however, immediately felt completely at home within the pleasant boundaries of this beautiful world. Here was their natural habitat, here was the setting for their activities and here the focal point of their passions.

Why are their poets and historians the object of admiration to the discerning and a cause of despair to their emulators? Because the figures they put before us restrict themselves in the range of their interest to such subjects as themselves, their nation, their own lives and those of their fellow citizens. Because they concentrate all their thoughts and desires and energy on immediate reality. Hence it was not difficult for the like-minded poet to immortalize this reality.

For them, actuality had the unique significance that the imagination and emotions have for us today.

The ancient poet lived in his imagination, just as the ancient historian lived in the political world, and the ancient scientist in the world of nature. They all adhered to the immediate, the true, the real; even the products of their imagination have bones and marrow. Among all things, man and human nature enjoyed the highest respect, and man's inner and outer relationship to the world was observed and represented with profound understanding. Emotions and thinking were not yet fragmented, and the all but irreparable rift in the healthy oneness of man had not yet occurred.

The ancients knew as well how to savor happiness as to endure misfortunes. Just as a healthy organism resists sickness and recovers quickly after an attack, their soundness of mind was easily restored after emotional or physical distress. Winckelmann was the reincarnation of ancient man—insofar as that may be said of anyone in our time. The first thirty years of his life provide overwhelming evidence, for neither his lowly existence, nor discomfort, nor worries could subdue, defeat or wear him down, and as soon as he obtained the necessary freedom, he became, in the sense of the ancients, a whole and complete human being. He was compelled to work, and he experienced joy and deprivation, happiness and sorrow, gain and loss, honor and humiliation in the course of his life. Although tossed between extremes, he was content on this beautiful earth where we are all at the mercy of fate.

The spirit of antiquity which accompanied him in life did not abandon him in his studies. To be sure, even the ancients were in a somewhat difficult situation in those branches of knowledge where the comprehension of the various subjects not pertaining to man required a division of strengths and capabilities that meant an almost unavoidable fracturing of the whole. Modern man runs the even greater risk of losing his focus by his specialized studies in the many fields of knowledge, of becoming lost in disconnected expertise, and, unlike the ancients, he does not have the resources of a unified personality to compensate for the shortcoming.

Motivated partly by inclination, partly by necessity, Winckelman broadly explored various areas of knowledge. But sooner or later he inevitably returned to the study of antiquity, especially Greek antiquity, as the subject for which he felt so close an affinity, and to which he was to devote himself so completely in the happiest period of his life.

Pagan Spirit

Our description of the spirit of antiquity, a spirit focused on the world and what it has to offer, leads us directly to the consideration that such features are only compatible with a pagan spirit. Trust in oneself, concentration on immediate reality, worship of gods purely as ancestors, admiration of them only as works of art as it were, submission to a supreme fate, and the concept that the future, due to the high value placed on fame after death, is dependent on the here and now—those elements are so interconnected, constitute such an indivisible whole, form a human condition so obviously intended by nature herself, that we perceive in ancient man an imperishable state of health, in moments of sublime joy no less than in abject misery and even death.

This pagan spirit permeates Winckelmann's activities and writings and is most obvious in his early letters, where he is still struggling to come to grips with modern religious views. If we want to understand his so-called conversion, we must remember this attitude of his, this incompatibility of his thinking with, even his aversion to, Christianity. The various factions into which the Christian faith is divided were a matter of total indifference to him, so that, in spirit, he never really belonged to any of its denominations.

Friendship

Since the ancients, as we claim, were truly complete personalities in harmony with themselves and the world, they also had to experience the full scope of human relationships. They did not want to deny themselves the delight that results from the bond between people of similar temperament.

Even in this respect there is a remarkable difference between ancient and modern times. The relationship to women, which in our time has become so tender and spiritual, scarcely rose above the level of physical need. The relationship of parent and child seems to have been somewhat more loving. But friendship among men was for them the only genuine emotional relationship—although two women, Chloris and Thyia,[3] remained inseparable friends even in Hades.

We react with astonishment when, with regard to two young men, we hear of passionate fulfillment of love's desire, the bliss of being inseparable, lifelong devotion, or the need to follow the other into death. Indeed, we feel embarrassed when poets, historians, philosophers, orators inundate us with stories, events, sentiments and opinions pertaining to the subject.

Winckelmann felt born for friendship of that kind. He felt not only capable, but greatly in need of it. He experienced his real self only in the context of friendship and could perceive himself as a whole only if he was complemented by another. Early in life he found a perhaps unworthy object of his feelings.[4] He was utterly devoted to him, and even in his poverty he found the means to be generous, to give, to sacrifice for the friend; indeed, he did not hesitate to mortgage his existence, his life. It is here that Winckelmann, himself in great need, felt noble, rich, magnanimous and happy because he could be of service to the one he loved most, the one for whom he could make the greatest sacrifice, that of forgiving ingratitude.

No matter how times and circumstances changed, Winckelmann modeled all his friendships on the pattern of the first. And although many of these idealized relationships faded, his idealistic attitude nevertheless ensured him the affection of many a good man. Thus he had the good fortune to establish excellent relations with some of the best people of his time.

Beauty

Granted that a latter-day Greek in his intense need for friendship actually creates the object of his affections, he would still gain only a one-sided, an emotional benefit from it and little from the external world, unless there emerged a different, yet related and similar need and a satisfactory object for this need. We are referring to the need for physical beauty, and the incarnation of beauty itself. For the ultimate goal of evolving nature is the beautiful human being. To be sure, nature only rarely succeeds in producing him because there are numerous obstacles to her plans, and even her omnipotence cannot linger long with perfection and lend permanence to the beauty she produces. We are justified in saying that a beautiful human being is beautiful only for one brief moment.

At this point, art enters. Since man represents the pinnacle of nature, he sees himself as a complete being who in turn has to produce a pinnacle. To that end, he strives upward, imbuing himself with all perfection and virtue, and calls to his aid his ability to select, to create order and harmony, to lend significance. Finally he reaches the level where he can produce art, which will now occupy a preeminent place next to his other deeds and works. Once produced, the work of art stands before the world as an ideal reality, producing a lasting, indeed, the ultimate effect. For by developing from a totality of strengths, it absorbs everything magnificent, admirable and agreeable, and, by giving life to the human figure, it elevates man above himself, rounds out the circle of life and deeds, deifies him for a present which comprises past and future. Those who saw the *Olympian Jupiter*[5] were seized by such feelings, as we can gather from ancient descriptions, reports and testimony. A god had become man in order to make man into a god. They saw supreme majesty and were inspired by supreme beauty. In this sense we can agree with those ancients who were fully convinced that it was a misfortune to die without having seen this work.

Winckelmann, by nature, was receptive to such beauty. He first became acquainted with it in ancient literature, but he encountered beauty more intimately in the visual arts, where one learns to recognize it before perceiving and appreciating its manifestations in nature.

If the need for friendship and for beauty are both satisfied by the same object, then man's happiness and gratitude seem to know no limit. He will gladly give all he owns as a token of his devotion and admiration.

Hence we often find Winckelmann in the company of beautiful young men. He never seems more alive and likable than in these often only fleeting moments.

Catholicism

With such a disposition, such needs and desires, Winckelmann was for a long time a slave to the interests of others. Nowhere around him did he see the slightest hope for aid and support.

If Count Bünau, a man of independent means, had bought one important book less,[6] it would have been possible for Winckelmann to go to Rome. As secretary to the court, Bünau also had enough influence to help this deserving man out of any difficulty. Yet he may not have wanted to lose such an efficient assistant or simply did not realize how great a service he would have rendered by relinquishing so capable a man to the world. Furthermore, the court at Dresden, where Winckelmann had some hope for receiving adequate support, was of the Catholic faith. There was only one way of obtaining the court's favor, and that was through father confessors and other clergy.

The example of a prince in manner and morals has immense influence and tacitly requires all his subjects to conduct themselves in a similar way in their private lives. The prince's religion is almost always the predominant one, and Catholicism, like an eternal whirlpool, pulls the calmly passing ripple into its eddy.

So Winckelmann came to the conclusion that in order to be a Roman among the Romans, to become an integral part of that community and enjoy the confidence of its members, he had to adapt to the community, adopt its faith and its customs.[7] His later success proved that he would not have realized his ambition so completely, had it not been for this earlier decision, which was made immeasurably easier by the fact that, being a pagan at heart, his Protestant baptism had not been able to turn him into a true Christian.

Yet his conversion did not come about without intense struggle. A person may, in accordance with his conviction and after due thought, finally make a decision which is in complete harmony with his intentions, desires and needs, which indeed seems so essential for the maintaining and furthering of his very existence that he has no reservations at all about such a step. However, the decision can be in opposition to the general attitude and conviction of many others. Then begins a new conflict which, to be sure, does not cause him uncertainty, but does cause discomfort, impatience and annoyance, because he finds himself in disharmony with the world while he believes he is in harmony with himself.

Hence Winckelmann was torn when he contemplated his conversion. He was anxious, depressed and emotionally wrought when he thought of the effect it would have, especially on the Count, his first patron. How beautiful, profound and candid are the remarks in his letters regarding this matter!

As we know, everyone who changes his religion remains somehow tainted, and it seems impossible to cleanse him. This suggests that people value constancy above all else, not least because, divided into factions as they are, they must forever be concerned with the security and permanence of their group. Neither feelings nor convictions are the issue here. We must endure where fate, rather than choice, has placed us. To remain loyal to a nation, a city, a prince, a friend, a woman, and to focus everything on that relationship, to work and sacrifice and suffer for it—that is valued. Disloyalty, on the other hand, remains odious, and fickleness is ridiculed.

This is a harsh, very serious view of the matter; but we can look at it from another perspective which permits a more kindly and lenient view. Certain character traits we by no means approve of, certain moral blemishes in others we find especially titillating. If we may be allowed an analogy, we would say that it is the same as with venison roast which the gourmet much prefers slightly gamy. We find a divorced woman or a renegade especially fascinating. Persons who otherwise would perhaps seem merely interesting and charming suddenly appear wondrous. It cannot be denied that Winckelmann's conversion heightens the romantic aspects of his life and character in our imagination.

As for Winckelmann himself, the Catholic faith had no profound meaning. He saw it only as a disguise to be worn, and his remarks in this regard are frank enough. It seems that later on he did not observe the practices of his new faith closely enough, and perhaps even aroused the suspicions of zealots through his loose remarks. At least here and there we detect a slight fear of the Inquisition.

Interest in Greek Art

It is difficult, if not impossible, to make the transition from the purely literary, even in its most highly evolved forms of poetry and rhetoric, to the visual arts. Literature and art are separated by a wide chasm which only a very special talent can help bridge. We now have sufficient documentation to judge how well Winckelmann succeeded in this regard.

His love of pleasure first drew him to art treasures. However, for understanding and critical judgment he still needed artists as intermediaries, whose more or less professional opinions he was able to absorb, revise and put into writing. This practice led to the essay he published while still in Dresden, 'Reflections on the Imitation of Greek Works in Painting and Sculpture,'[8] and two supplements.

In this work Winckelmann certainly seems on the right path. The essay contains some superb passages of fundamental importance, and the ultimate goal of art is correctly indicated. However, in subject matter and form, the discussion is so baroque and strange that it would seem impossible to make sense of it without knowing the personalities of the art experts and critics in Saxony at the time and without being aware of their expertise, opinions, inclinations and whims. The work will be incomprehensible to later generations, unless older art lovers who lived closer to the period soon decide to write a description of the conditions which then prevailed, to the extent that such an undertaking is still feasible.

Men like Lippert, Hagedorn, Oeser, Dietrich, Heinecken and Österreich[9] loved, practiced and promoted art, each in his own way. Their goals were limited, their principles one-sided, and quite often peculiar. Their writings abounded with stories and anecdotes that were meant to be entertaining as well as instructive. Winckelmann adopted this method and style, but he himself soon found what he wrote inadequate, a fact he readily admitted to his friends.

Finally, though insufficiently prepared but with some practical experience, he made his way to Italy, the land where true education begins for the truly receptive. It is an experience which suffuses one's entire being and produces effects that are not only harmonizing but tangible as well, because subsequently it can form a strong common bond among people of quite different character.[10]

Rome

Now Winckelmann was in Rome,[11] and who could have been more receptive to the impact of that great experience! His wishes were fulfilled, his happiness established, his hopes more than realized. He saw his ideas embodied in the sculptures around him. In amazement he walked among the remains of an age of splendor. Here the most magnificent works of art of all time stood in the open, and he beheld these miracles as if gazing at the stars, free of charge. And for a token fee every private treasure opened up for him. Like a pilgrim, the new arrival walked around quietly and unnoticed; humbly dressed, he approached the most magnificent and most sacred works. He did not yet pay attention to the impact of individual objects, but their overall effect was endlessly varied, and he already anticipated the harmony that would ultimately and inevitably grow out of their many, often seemingly incompatible elements. He examined and contemplated everything, and was taken for an artist, an error which made his enjoyment even greater and which, after all, flatters anyone.[12]

Instead of continuing our observations, we would like to share with our readers the impressive words which a friend[13] used to describe the powerful effect of his own experience in Rome:

"Rome is the place where all of antiquity converges into one, for us to see. What we feel when we read ancient literature or hear about ancient forms of government, we believe, in Rome, not merely to sense but to experience directly. Just as Homer cannot be compared to other poets, so Rome cannot be compared to any other city, the Roman countryside to any other landscape. For the most part, however, this impression is subjective, not objective. And yet it is more than the sentimental notion of standing at the spot where some great man stood. A powerful force is pulling us into the past which we perceive as nobler and more sublime, though that might simply be a necessary delusion. Even if we wanted, we could not resist this force because the desolation, which the present inhabitants do nothing to prevent, and the unbelievable amount of rubble make us take refuge in imagination. In these surroundings the past appears to our mind with a greatness that makes envy impossible and which we are overjoyed at perceiving, in the only way we can, in our imagination. At the same time, our eyes actually see with absolute clarity the lovely forms, the grandeur and simplicity of the figures, the rich vegetation (though not as luxuriant as further south), the clean outlines in the clear air, and the beauty of the colors. Thus enjoyment of nature is here pure enjoyment of art, perfect and complete. Anywhere else, modern associations interfere with this enjoyment, and it becomes sentimental or intellectual. To be sure, this impression is also subjective. Horace thought Tibur[14] more modern than we find Tivoli today, as is shown by his words: 'Happy he who is far from the throng.' But it is only a delusion to want to be inhabitants of Athens and Rome. We should experience antiquity only from a distance, as isolated from everything ordinary and as something irrevocably past—a feeling a friend and I have when we see ruins. We are always annoyed when a half-buried ruin is excavated. At most, that may benefit scholarship, but at the expense of imagination. There are only two things I dread: if they cultivate the Campagna di Roma, and if they make Rome into an orderly city where no one would carry a knife anymore. If ever such a strict pope comes along (which, I pray, the seventy-two cardinals will prevent!), I shall leave. Only if Rome remains a city of divine anarchy and the area around it such a heavenly wilderness will there be room for the shadows of the past, one of which is worth more than this whole present generation."

Mengs[15]

If Winckelmann had not had the good fortune to meet Mengs so soon, he would have groped for a long time among the ancient remnants in search of works most worthy of study. Mengs' great talent was concentrated on ancient works, and especially those of great beauty, and he immediately acquainted his friend with outstanding examples meriting particular attention. From them Winckelmann learned about beauty of form and style and was immediately inspired to write a treatise, 'On the Taste of Greek Artists.'[16]

If we are at all seriously concerned with works of art, we soon become aware that they are not only produced by different artists, but also in different periods, and that we have to study location, age and the individual talent simultaneously. Hence Winckelmann with his direct way of thinking came immediately to the conclusion that here was the crucial point in the consideration of all art. At first, he addressed works of the highest order, examples of which he intended to present in a study, "On the Style of Sculpture During the Age of Phidias." But he soon went beyond the particular and developed the concept of a history of art. Like a new Columbus, he discovered a new world, long surmised, interpreted and discussed—a world, we can say, which was previously known and had been lost.

It is always saddening to realize that the disorder caused first by the Romans and later by the invasion of peoples from the north, brought the human race to such a pass that the growth of genuine culture was long stunted and even came close to being destroyed for all time.

No matter which branch of art or knowledge we look at, we find that the logical, right perception of the ancient mind had already discovered many things which were later lost because of barbarism and the barbaric means used to free oneself from this barbarism. The things thus lost will remain so to most people for years to come, since high culture in the modern age needs time to make its impact generally felt.

We are not speaking of skills, which mankind fortunately uses without asking where they came from or where they lead.

Our observations are prompted by passages in some ancient authors, where we find preliminary thinking about, and even suggestions for, a history of art which they evidently considered possible and necessary.

Velleius Paterculus[17] noted with great interest a similar pattern of rise and fall in all the arts. As a man who knew about life he was especially intrigued by the observation that the arts are able to remain only a short time at the peak of their development. From the perspective of his time he was not able to see art as a living organism *(zõon)* which has imperceptible beginnings, slow growth, a brilliant moment of perfection, and gradual decline, and that in this respect, art as a whole is like any other being, except that its various stages can only be found separately. Hence Paterculus cites just human factors as a cause in the process, which of course cannot be excluded, but which did not satisfy his keen intelligence because he was quite aware that a pattern was involved which could not be assembled from random pieces.

"That grammarians, painters and sculptors have shared the fate of orators will be discovered by anyone who examines the evidence through the ages. Excellence in any branch of art is found within a very short span of time. I have often wondered why a number of similar-minded, talented artists appear during the same period and gravitate towards the same type of art. I can find no reasons that I consider convincing, but among likely reasons the following are the most important. Emulation serves as nourishment for artists; envy or admiration induces them to imitate; soon what they have produced with such diligence attains the highest level. Yet it is difficult to remain there for long, and whatever cannot progress, must regress. Thus in the beginning we try to catch up with those ahead of us; but when we give up hope of surpassing or even catching up with them, effort fades together with hope. What we cannot obtain we no longer want to pursue, nor do we strive to possess what others have already laid hold of. We look for something new, we abandon what we cannot excel in and seek a different goal. This vascillation, it seems to me, is the greatest obstacle to producing great works."

A passage in Quintilian[18] containing a succinct outline for a history of ancient art also deserves to be singled out as an important contribution to the subject.

Quintilian too, from his conversations with Roman art lovers, may very well have discovered that there was a striking resemblance between the character of Greek artists and of Roman orators, and he may, therefore, have sought more information from experts and connoisseurs. As a result of his studies, and given his comparative approach which made clear that the character of an art coincided with the character of its time, he ended up outlining a history of art, but without knowing or planning to do so.

"It is said that the first painters whose works were admired not solely for their antiquity were Polygnotos and Aglaphon. Their simple colors are still much valued by some who prefer primitive works and the rudimentary stages of a developing art to the greatest masters of the following period—a curious preference, in my opinion.

"Later, Zeuxis and Parrhasius, near contemporaries at the time of the Peloponesian War, did much for the progress of art. Zeuxis is said to have introduced the use of highlights and shading, Parrhasius to have undertaken an intensive study of line. In addition, Zeuxis gave the limbs more substance, made them fuller and more distinctive. It is believed that he followed Homer's example in this, who liked ample forms in women. Parrhasius defined everything meticulously: they call him the lawmaker because his gods and heroes are considered models to be followed now and in the future.

"Painting flourished from the time of Philip of Macedon to the time of Alexander's successors, but was practiced by artists with varied talents. Protogenes excelled in meticulousness, Pamphilus and Melanthius in organization, Antiphilus in lightness of touch, Theon the Samian in strange creations called phantasies, and Apelles in wit and grace. Euphranor is still highly regarded because he was among the best in general artistic ability and was outstanding in painting as well as sculpture.

"We find the same differences in sculpture. Kalon and Hegesias worked with harder lines, similar to the Tuscans; Kalamis had less severe lines, and Myron's were even softer.

"Polyclitus surpasses others in diligence and elegance. Many consider him the best, although some detractors claim that he lacks substance, for by portraying the human form more delicately than it is in reality, he does not seem to do complete justice to the dignity of the gods. He is even said to have avoided depicting old people and not to have ventured beyond smooth cheeks.

"What Polyclitus lacks, Phidias and Alcamenes purportedly possess. Phidias is supposed to have formed gods and humans superbly and, especially in ivory, to have far surpassed his rival. This would be the opinion had he created nothing but his *Minerva* at Athens or his *Olympian Jupiter* in Elis, a statue whose beauty is said to have benefited the adopted religion, so closely did the majesty of the work approximate that of the god it portrayed.

"It is generally held that Lysippus and Praxiteles reached a high degree of verisimilitude in their works. Demetrius, however, is criticized for going too far and preferring likeness to beauty."

Librarian

It happens rarely that a man is fortunate enough to find selfless patrons who are willing to provide the means to further his education. Even those who believe they want the best can only promote what they themselves love and know or, more often, what is useful to them. And so it was Winckelmann's competence in the literary-bibliographical field which drew first Count Bünau's and later Cardinal Passionei's[19] attention to him.

A bibliophile is welcome anywhere, and was so even more at that time, when the desire to collect unusual or rare books was keener and library science not yet a common pursuit. A large German library resembled a large Roman library and was comparable in the size of its holdings. The librarian of a German count was a welcome companion for a cardinal, and the companion in turn felt at ease with his host. Libraries then were veritable treasure troves, whereas today, with the rapid advance of the sciences and the both purposeful and purposeless piling up of material, they are more in the nature of useful storerooms or useless attics. As a result, a librarian, much more than formerly, has reason to stay abreast of developments in the sciences and be aware of the relative value of what is published. Furthermore, a German librarian has to have knowledge that would be of no use in a foreign country.

But only for a short time, and only as long as it was necessary to earn a modest living, did Winckelmann pursue his occupation in the world of books. He also soon lost interest in doing research projects and no longer wanted to compare manuscripts or give information to German scholars who turned to him for advice.

However, his store of knowledge had already earlier helped open up opportunities for him. In their private lives, most Italians, and especially those living in Rome, are for various reasons quite secretive. This secretiveness, this fondness for seclusion, if we may call it that, also prevailed in their literary activities. Unbeknownst to others, many a scholar devoted his life to the study of an important work, without wanting or being able to make his findings public. Also, more frequently than in any other country, there were men who could not be persuaded to commit their opinions and considerable knowledge to writing, much less to publish them. Winckelmann soon found access to such men. Among them he mentions especially Giacomelli and Baldani, and he expresses his pleasure about his ever-widening circle of acquaintances and his growing influence.

Cardinal Albani

Winckelmann was especially fortunate to become companion to Cardinal Albani who, because of his considerable wealth and influence, was in a position to satisfy his great love for collecting art, a passion he had acquired early in life and which, together with almost miraculous good fortune as a collector, had resulted in an outstanding collection. In his later years he took great pleasure in arranging it for exhibition, hoping to emulate those Roman families who in former times had been aware of the worth of such treasures. He even followed the ancient custom of filling the exhibition area with a superabundance of art works. In building after building, wing after wing and hall after hall there were fountains and obelisks, caryatids and bas-reliefs; statues and vessels filled every corner in court and garden, and small and large rooms, galleries and cabinets contained the most unusual artifacts from all periods.

We mentioned that the ancients filled their public places in much the same way. For example, the Romans overloaded the Capitol in a manner we find hard to believe, and the Via Sacra,[20] the Forum, the Palatine were so overcrowded with buildings and monuments that it is difficult to imagine how great numbers of people also found room to live there. But the excavated cities make the true picture clear and let us see with our own eyes how narrow, small, almost model-sized the buildings were. This applies as well to Hadrian's[21] villa, although he had enough space and means to build something on a larger scale.

When Winckelmann left the Cardinal's villa, the place which furthered his education in a most gratifying manner, it displayed similar superabundance. It remained this way long after the Cardinal's death, an object of pleasure and admiration until it was robbed of every treasure during that time of upheaval and disruption.[22] The statues were taken from their niches and pedestals, the bas-reliefs were torn from the walls, and the huge collection was packed for transport. Due to some unexpected change of fortune, these treasures only got as far as the Tiber. After a short while they were returned to the owner, and most of them, except for a few jewels, are again at the original site. Had he lived, Winckelmann might have witnessed this dismantling of an art paradise and its restoration caused by a strange turn of events. But fortunately he was already beyond earthly suffering, and earthly joy, which is not always sufficient compensation.

Good Fortune

Winckelmann met with much good fortune during his life. Not only was he in Rome when the excavation of ancient artifacts was at its height, but there were also the discoveries at Herculaneum and Pompeii,[23] some of which were new, some of which did not become known until then because of professional envy, secrecy and delay. Thus

Winckelmann benefitted from a rich harvest which challenged him intellectually and provided an outlet for his scholarly interests.

It is sad to have to think of anything as final and complete. Old armories, galleries and museums to which nothing is added are like mausoleums haunted by ghosts. Such a limited circle of art limits our thinking. We get accustomed to regarding such collections as complete, instead of being reminded through ever new additions that in art, as in life, we have nothing that remains finished and at rest, but rather something infinite in constant motion.

Winckelmann found himself in such a fortunate situation. The earth relinquished its treasures, and a lively trade in art objects brought many old possessions to light which aroused his interest, excited his mind and increased his knowledge as they filed past his eyes.

Of no small advantage to him was his relationship with the heir to the great Stosch[24] estate. Only after Stosch's death did Winckelmann get to know this little empire of art, and he ruled there according to his wisdom and convictions. To be sure, not the same degree of concern was shown for all parts of this extremely valuable collection, the whole of which deserved to be catalogued for the enjoyment and use of later generations. Some items were sold off cheaply. However, in order to publicize the superb collection of engraved gems and attract potential buyers, Winckelmann and the Stosch heir started cataloguing that part. The letters pertaining to this undertaking give interesting testimony of the hasty and yet always intelligent way the project was handled.

Our friend took an active part in breaking up this collection, just as he had done in increasing and assembling the Albani collection. Whether his task was to gather or dispose of works of art, everything passing through his hands expanded the treasure accumulating in his mind.

Writings

At that time in Dresden when Winckelmann first came into contact with art and artists and was a novice in this field, he was already an accomplished writer. He had a good grasp of history and the sciences in many respects. Even in his lowly position, he had a sense and understanding of antiquity and recognized what was of value in his own time, in life and in the individual. He had developed his own style, and when he entered the domain of art he was not merely an eager student but already a learned disciple of his masters. He absorbed their special knowledge quickly and soon found ways of putting it to practical use.

Even later, in a setting artistically richer than in Dresden, when a higher intellectual plane had become accessible to him, he did not change. The things he heard from Mengs, or learned from his new environment, he did not keep to himself for long, did not let the new wine ferment and become clear. He exemplified the saying that you learn by doing, and learned by drafting projects and by writing. How many titles has he left for us, how many subjects he named about which he intended to write![25] His whole antiquarian career resembled this beginning. We always find him active, occupied with the moment, seizing and holding on to it, as if to something complete and satisfying. And he approached the next moment in a similar way. Knowing this, we are in a better position to evaluate his works.

That they appear in the form we have them today,[26] either in manuscript or fixed in print for posterity, is due to numerous minor circumstances. Had Winckelmann been able to work one month longer on any one of them, we would have a somewhat different work, more correct in content, more definite in form, perhaps something altogether different. For this very reason we regret his premature death, since he would always have revised his writings, incorporating his most recent experiences.

And so, everything he wrote is alive and meant for the living, not for worshippers of the written word. His works, in conjunction with his letters, are a portrayal of life, a living thing. Like the lives of most people, they resemble a first draft, not a finished work. They fill us with hopes, wishes, presentiments. If we attempt to improve them we realize that we ourselves have to improve. If we attempt to criticize them we realize that the same criticism, perhaps on a different level, might apply to us. For limitation is our lot everywhere.

Philosophy

As culture progresses, not all human endeavors and activities concerned with the various fields of learning thrive equally. Rather, depending on a favorable disposition of individuals and on circumstances, one discipline may outpace the other and stimulate more general interest, which causes a certain displeasure among the members of this elaborate family who often get on less well the more closely related they are.

It is usually a baseless complaint of scholars in this or that discipline who bemoan the fact that their field is neglected by their contemporaries. For a capable master need only show himself to attract attention. If Raphael were to appear today he would be assured an abundance of honors and wealth. A capable master draws good students, and their activities in turn branch out indefinitely.

Yet philosophers have always been the special object of hatred, not only of their fellow scholars but also of the more practical people of the world, a hatred for which their situation is perhaps more to blame than they are themselves. For since philosophy by nature addresses itself to the ordinary as well as the sublime, it has to treat worldly things as part of, indeed as subordinate to, itself.

One does not explicitly deny philosophy this presumptuous claim, but everyone believes himself entitled to share in its discoveries, to apply its principles and use whatever else it may have to offer. However, in order to become universal, philosophy has to employ its own terms, strange correlations and peculiar preambles, which do not quite coincide with the current circumstances of people in general or their needs of the moment. Philosophy is then reviled by those who cannot immediately find a means of grasping it.

On the other hand, if one were inclined to make a case against philosophers, one could say that they are themselves unsure of finding the transition to life, and that precisely where they wish to put their convictions into practice they are most prone to error, thereby diminishing their credibility with the world. There is certainly no lack of evidence as grounds for such accusations.

Winckelmann complained bitterly about the philosophers of his time and their extensive influence.[27] But surely one can avoid influences simply by withdrawing into one's own specialty. It strikes us as curious that Winckelmann did not enroll in the Leipzig Academy where, under the guidance of Professor Christ,[28] he would have found it easier to pursue his major field without paying heed to any philosophers.

But in the light of events in modern times, an observation confirmed by experience is appropriate here, namely that no scholar has been able to reject or oppose or scorn with impunity the great philosophical movement initiated by Kant. The only exception is perhaps the true scholar of antiquity, who because of the peculiar quality of his specialty seems specially privileged.

By occupying himself exclusively with the best the world has produced and by comparing humbler, even inferior things to those excellent achievements alone, his erudition reaches such a high level, his judgment becomes so authoritative, his taste develops such consistency, that within his own area of competence he appears admirably, even astonishingly well trained.

Winckelmann was fortunate to become one of these scholars; of course, life and art had aided him immeasurably on his way.

Poetry

Although Winckelmann did not neglect the poets when he read ancient writers, upon closer examination of his studies and his life we detect no real inclination for poetry. On the contrary, we may say that here and there an actual dislike is noticeable. His fondness for traditional Lutheran hymns and his desire to have an authentic collection of them, even in Rome, suggest a good solid German but hardly a genuine lover of poetry.

The ancient poetic works seem to have interested him at first as documents of old languages and literature, later as source material for his study of the plastic arts. It is all the more surprising and gratifying then to see him emerge as a poet himself, and one with unmistakable talent, in his descriptions of statues and in almost all his later writings. He saw with his eyes, and grasped with his mind, works of art that defy description, and yet he felt the irresistable urge to reveal their essence in words. The utter perfection of a work, the idea which gave birth to its artistic form, the feeling its presence aroused in him—all this he wanted to convey to listener and reader. And in surveying his store of capabilities he saw himself compelled to reach for the most powerful and most effective available. He had to be a poet, whether he was aware of it, whether he wanted to, or not.

Insight Gained

Although Winckelmann was eager to gain the respect of the world, longed for literary fame, sought to make his works attractive and lend them dignity through a certain solemnity of style, he was by no means blind to their shortcomings. Indeed, he noticed them immediately, as was to be expected of anyone bent on improvement and impatient to involve himself in ever new aspects of a subject. The more didactic and dogmatic he had been in an essay, the more he had insisted on this or that elucidation of a monument, the surer he had been of a particular interpretation or meaning of a passage, then the more obvious an error seemed to him, if such was indicated by new data, and the more eager he was to correct it in some way.

If the manuscript was still in his hands, he rewrote it; if it had been sent to the printer, he sent him emendations and addenda. He made no attempt to conceal all these second thoughts from his friends, for his character was rooted in truthfulness, rectitude, directness and sincerity.

Later Works

The *Monumenti Inediti*[29] proved to be a productive project, as Winckelmann came to realize, not all at once but in the course of working on it.

It is quite evident that he was initially motivated by his desire to introduce new subjects and explain them clearly, and to expand the horizons of archeology. In addition, he was interested in testing the method he had already established in his *History of Art* on works which he presented to the reader here. But since he had already gone beyond his *History*, he finally came to the wise decision to make the first part of the *Monumenti* a corrected, edited and condensed version of the *History*, in which he would even refute some of his former views.

Conscious of earlier errors, about which non-Romans had been in no position to offer critical comment, he wrote in Italian so that the work could be judged in Rome. No only did he proceed with great caution, he also consulted experts among his friends with whom he examined the text carefully, making prudent use of their insight and judgment, and so produced a work that will be a legacy for all time. He not only wrote it, he edited it and attended to all the details of publication, including that of cost. An impecunious private citizen accomplished what would have stood a well-established publisher or a number of academicians in good stead.

The Pope

Since we have said so much about Rome, how can we omit mention of the Pope, who was of great help to Winckelmann, at least indirectly?

Winckelmann's stay in Rome coincided with the papacy of Benedict XIV, a cheerful, easygoing man who preferred to let others rule rather than rule himself. It is possible, therefore, that the various positions which Winckelmann held were obtained more through the good offices of his friends in high position than because of the Pope's awareness of his merits.

But on one occasion Winckelmann had an important audience with the head of the Church: he was granted the special distinction of being allowed to read the Pope passages from his *Monumenti Inediti*. And so from this quarter too, Winckelmann gained the highest honor that can accrue to a writer.

Character

Achievement, much more than character, appears to be what is most significant about many people, especially scholars. In Winckelmann, however, the opposite was true. Everything he produced is noteworthy and estimable mainly because his character inevitably revealed itself in the process. In the sections entitled Spirit of Antiquity, Pagan Spirit, Beauty and Friendship, we offered a few general, preliminary remarks on this topic. A closer consideration seems appropriate now as we near the end of our essay.

Winckelmann was a person who was thoroughly honest with himself and others. His innate love of truth increased as he became more self-reliant and independent, until finally he came to see the polite indulgence of error, so common in life and literature, as a crime.

Such an individual could no doubt feel at ease with himself. Yet here too we find that characteristic trait of the ancients: always being occupied with oneself without actually observing oneself. Winckelmann thought only *of* himself, not *about* himself. He was absorbed by the things he intended to do, he was interested in his whole being, the entire scope of his being, and was also confident that his friends shared these interests. We find, therefore, that everything is discussed in his letters, from the highest moral concerns to the most common physical needs. He even admitted he would rather talk about personal trifles than important matters. For all that, he remained a riddle to himself, and was sometimes amazed at his own development, especially when he compared what he had been and what he had become. But then, we may look upon all human beings as elaborate puzzles, able themselves to assemble their picture only in part, whereas outsiders can easily complete it.

Nor do we find in Winckelmann any clearly enunciated principles. In moral and aesthetic matters he was guided by his intuition and his education. He envisioned a sort of natural religion in which God, however, is only the source of beauty and has no other relation to humanity. In matters of duty and gratitude Winckelmann behaved very properly.

While his attention to personal needs was not excessive, and not always consistent, he worked very hard to provide for his old age. The means he employed in the pursuit of his goals were irreproachable, and he showed himself to be honest, upright, even stubborn, yet at the same time prudent and persevering. He never worked according to plan, but on impulse and with passion. The intensity of his joy at every discovery led inevitably to errors, which, given his lively pace of work, he eliminated as quickly as he detected them. Here we have another indication of the antique cast of his character: certainty about the point of departure and uncertainty about the goal, as well as loss of completeness and perfection in the attempt to obtain breadth.

Society

Although Winckelmann was initially not quite at ease in society—ill-prepared as he was by his early years—a sense of dignity soon made up for lack of breeding and manners, and he quickly learned to adapt to circumstances. It is evident everywhere in his letters that he enjoyed the company of elegant, rich and distinguished people and delighted in their esteem. And for easy access to society, he could not have been better off than in Rome.

He himself remarked that people of high standing in Rome, especially the clergy, no matter how ceremonious they might appear in public, were in private informal and comfortable with their companions. However, Winckelmann did not realize that behind this informality lay the oriental relationship of master and servant. Southern peoples would suffer boredom without end if they had to maintain permanently formal relations with members of their circle, as is customary in the north. Travelers have observed that slaves behave much more casually toward their Turkish masters than northern courtiers toward their princes, and, in our own country, subordinates toward their superiors. But upon closer examination we realize that these expressions of respect were actually introduced for the benefit of subordinates, who, by showing respect, always remind their superior of what he owes them.

The southerner, on the other hand, likes to have times when he can be at ease, and that is beneficial to those around him. Winckelmann describes such scenes with great relish. They made it easier for him to bear his dependence, and they encouraged his sense of freedom which was wary of fetters that might threaten it.

Visitors

Winckelmann was very happy in his dealings with the local inhabitants, but he experienced considerable pain at the hands of visitors from abroad. To be sure, nothing is worse than the ordinary tourist in Rome. In any other place, the traveler can go his own way; however those who fail to do as the Romans do are a horror to the true Roman.

The English are ridiculed because they take along their teapots everywhere and even tote them up Mount Etna. But don't all nations take their own teapots along on travels to brew the herbs they brought from home?

Such provincial sightseers—narrow-minded, unobservant, always in a hurry, arrogant—Winckelmann cursed more than once and swore never again to act as their guide, only to relent on the next occasion. He joked about his having to employ schoolmarmish methods to inform and persuade them. Yet he also benefitted considerably from serving as a guide to persons of position and reputation. We mention only the Prince of Dessau, the Hereditary Princes of Mecklenburg-Strelitz and Brunswick, and Baron Riedesel, who in his appreciation of art and antiquity proved completely worthy of our friend.

Achievement

We notice in Winckelmann a relentless striving for esteem and respect, yet he wanted recognition based on accomplishment. He always insisted on substance in subject matter, in expression and in treatment, which explains his strong antipathy for the emphasis of the French on appearances.

Having found opportunity in Rome to associate with visitors of various nationalities, he cultivated these connections with skill and energy. The honors he was awarded by academies and learned societies pleased him, indeed he actively sought them out.

His reputation was enhanced most by a work, written with quiet care, that stands as testimony to his great achievement. I refer to his *History of Ancient Art,* which was immediately translated into French and made its author famous far and wide.

What such a work accomplishes is perhaps best recognized when it first appears. We feel its effect, we enthusiastically embrace what is new and are amazed at how much we benefit from it. Subsequent, less enthusiastic generations, on the other hand, pick critically at the works of their masters and teachers and make demands it would never have occurred to them to make had not those predecessors, of whom ever more is now demanded, achieved so much themselves.

Winckelmann became known to the educated nations of Europe at a moment when he enjoyed sufficient confidence in Rome to be honored with the not unimportant post of Prefect of Antiquities.

Restiveness

Despite that intense happiness which he himself frequently mentioned, he was always plagued by a restlessness which, because it was fundamental in his nature, manifested itself in various ways.

In earlier years he had eked out an existence. Later he lived from the generosity of the court and the favor of many a benefactor, always restricting himself to the most basic needs in order not to become dependent, or more dependent than he already was. Yet he made strenuous efforts to earn his livelihood and provide for his future, a goal which finally his splendid edition of the *Monumenti* seemed most likely to help him attain.

But the precariousness of his situation had accustomed him to looking here and there for ways of supporting himself, now accepting a minor position in the house of a cardinal, in the Vatican or elsewhere, now grandly resigning if a better prospect was in the offing, all the while looking for other employment and remaining open to various offers.

Furthermore, anyone living in Rome is constantly tempted to travel to other parts of the world. One feels at the center of the ancient world and that the countries of interest to the scholar of antiquity are nearby. Greece, Sicily, Dalmatia, the Peloponnesus, Ionia and Egypt are all there as it were for the taking if one lives in Rome, and arouse from time to time in anyone an immense desire to visit them, if like Winckelmann he is born with an urge for visual experience. One's wanderlust is intensified by the many travelers stopping over in Rome to prepare for a journey to those lands, sometimes with a purpose in mind, sometimes not. And upon their return, they never weary of telling and writing about the wonders they have experienced in faraway places.

It was natural then for Winckelmann to want to visit all these places, either on his own or in the company of a well-to-do traveler sufficiently able to appreciate an informed and gifted companion.

Another cause of this inner restlessness and discontent does honor to his heart: his irresistible desire to be with distant friends. Here we seem to find the focal point of the longing in a man who otherwise was content with his immediate surroundings. He saw his friends before his mind's eyes, he conversed with them in letters, he longed for their embrace and wished to relive the days spent in their company.

His longing for those friends in the North intensified when peace was restored.[30] He felt pride at the thought of being presented to the great king who had honored him earlier with an invitation to serve him,[31] and he was eager for a reunion with the Prince of Dessau, a serene man of noble character whom Winckelmann considered God's emissary on earth. He wanted to pay his respects to the Duke of Brunswick whose great qualities he valued, to personally offer his thanks to the Minister von Münchhausen, a patron of the sciences, and to admire his immortal creation[32] in Göttingen. He also anticipated with pleasure a lively and intimate reunion with his Swiss friends.[33] Such were the allurements that filled his heart and imagination. He had long occupied and entertained himself with such dreams when, at last, he unfortunately yielded to his desires and set out on the journey which was to end in his death.

But he was already so completely devoted to Italian life that any other life seemed unbearable. When he had first traveled to Rome, the rocky, mountainous terrain of Tyrol had interested and even delighted him. Now, on the way back he felt as if he were being dragged to his fatherland through a Cimmerian gate.[34] He became so beset with anxiety that he found the idea of continuing his trip impossible.

Last Journey

When Winckelmann departed this earth, he had reached the highest level of happiness he could have wished for. His fatherland awaited him, his friends eagerly anticipated his arrival; the expressions of love and friendship which he needed so much and the bestowal of public honors he valued so highly—all that was about to be lavished on him. In this sense we may perhaps consider him fortunate to have gone on to Elysium from the pinnacle of human existence, to have been taken from us after only momentary shock and brief pain. He did not have to experience the decrepitude of age and the waning of his mental powers, did not have to actually witness the dispersal of art treasures which he had predicted, although in a different sense. He lived like a man and departed a complete human being. Now he has the advantage of being remembered by posterity as one eternally enterprising and vigorous. For a human being wanders among the shades in the form in which he left this world, just as Achilles remains for us the eternally striving youth. Yet we too derive benefit from Winckelmann's untimely departure. From his grave comes a reminder of his strength which fortifies us and arouses the urgent need to continue forever with love and dedication what he has begun.

The Collector and His Circle[1] (1799)

First Letter (From the collector to the editor of an art journal.)

Many thanks for your letter and the enclosed manuscripts which arrived so soon after you left. The two days you spent with us were most enjoyable, yet much too short, and I felt keenly the void caused by your departure. But your letter lifted my spirits, and I felt almost as happy as when you were here. The ideas expressed in your manuscript reminded me of our conversations, and I was as delighted then as I had been before to see that we agree in so many respects in our views on art.

This discovery is doubly welcome, since I have the opportunity to test your opinions as well as my own every day. All I need do is examine any part of my collection and apply our theoretical and practical maxims. Sometimes everything goes smoothly, sometimes I encounter difficulties, and sometimes I can't agree with you or even with myself. Nevertheless, it is true to say that much has been gained if one can agree on major points, if our views of art, which to be sure constantly fluctuate like the scales of a balance, are attached to a solid pivot and—to stay with my simile—the balance and scales are not tossed about at random.

The sample essays for the journal you intend to publish have strengthened my hopes and my support and interest, and I would be glad to contribute in any way I can. Theory has never been my forte, but I would certainly be happy to share with you my experiences, which you may use as you see fit. To prove the sincerity of my intentions I will begin immediately and do what you requested: I am going to write down a detailed history of my collection. Many people have been surprised at the remarkable pieces it contains, even though they were well aware of its reputation and came prepared. That happened to you too. You expressed amazement about the unusual treasures in the various sections, and you would have been even more amazed if time and personal preference had permitted you to take note of everything I own.

My grandfather needs but little commentary. He laid the foundation for the whole collection, and that is was a good one was proved to me by the attention you paid to every one of his acquisitions. Your interest in this particular pillar of our strange family edifice was marked by such love and affection that I did not mind your neglect of some other sections. I was content to concentrate with you on those works which are precious to me, too, because of their value, their age and their origin. To be sure, an art lover's character and preferences are important in determining how his love of art and his love of collecting—two inclinations often found together—will develop, but in my opinion he is just as much influenced by the age into which he is born, by the conditions under which he lives, by contemporary artists and art dealers, by the foreign countries he has visited first and by nations to which he has some personal relationship. Yes, he is influenced by thousands of such chance circumstances. How many things may converge to make him steadfast or fickle, liberal or in some respects limited, farsighted or narrow!

I thank my good fortune that my grandfather lived in the best of times and the best of situations for acquiring those items which a private collector would find almost impossible to afford today. I still have bills and correspondence pertaining to these purchases which show how incredibly prices have risen since my grandfather's time. In all countries, interest in art is now more widespread, which accounts for this tremendous increase.

Yes, the good man's collection has been for me personally, for the other works of art in my gallery, for my relationship to art and my views of it, what the Dresden collection is for the German nation: for the young, an inexhaustible repository of genuine knowledge; for the mature, a source of emotional strength and sound principles; and it is salutary for all viewers, even the most casual, because excellence affects not only the initiated. Your remark that every one of the works I inherited from my dear grandfather could rival those royal treasures of Dresden did not fill me with pride—just with satisfaction; for secretly I had thought so myself.

And now I am approaching the end of my letter without having carried out my intention. I have been rambling instead of telling my story. An old man in a good mood is prone to do both. I have barely enough space left to tell you that my nieces and I send our regards, and especially that Julie has been enquiring frequently and quite impatiently about the long-postponed trip to Dresden. Of course she hopes that on the way she will see her new friends again whom she so ardently admires. And, I may add, not one of her old friends could send heartier greetings than

Yours faithfully

Second Letter (From the collector and his niece, Julie.)

You did me two good turns in one by extending such a warm welcome to the young man who presented himself with a letter from me. You provided him with a pleasant day in your company, and he then gave me a lively oral report on your welfare, activities and plans.

Our lively conversation right after his return was the reason why I did not immediately notice how much the young man had changed during his absence. When he left for the university, he was a promising youth, well-trained in Greek and Latin, well-acquainted with Greek and Roman literature, conversant in ancient and modern history, adequately prepared in mathematics and other subjects required to become a good teacher. And now, to our distress, he has come back a philosopher! He has devoted himself primarily, nay, exclusively to philosophy, and since the members of our little circle, including myself, do not seem particularly talented in matters philosophical, we do not really know what to talk about with him. He is not interested in things we understand, and we do not understand the things he is interested in. He speaks a new language, and we are too old to learn it.

What a strange subject philosophy is, especially modern philosophy! Delving into the self, spying on your mind at work, wrapping yourself completely in yourself to better understand what the world is all about—I really wonder whether that is the right way! The hypochondriac, does he perceive things more clearly because he always digs into his inner self and thus digs his own grave? I'm sure this new philosophy is some type of hypochondria, an interest gone awry that has been given a highfalutin name! Please forgive an old man, a simple country doctor.

But be that as it may! Politics has not ruined my good humor, and neither shall philosophy. Therefore, I must hurry and take refuge in the temple of art and get to the story I promised you, lest this letter contain nothing of what I set out to write.

Only after my grandfather's death did my father reveal that he had a preference for only one type of art. He enjoyed the exact imitation of real things, a style which at that time had been developed to near perfection with water colors. At first, he was content to just purchase such paintings; later he commissioned artists to produce highly realistic pictures of birds, flowers, butterflies and seashells. There was nothing of note in kitchen, garden or field that was not immediately committed to paper with a paintbrush. Thus he recorded quite a few unusual specimens of various creatures which, I am told, are of the greatest interest to naturalists.

Gradually, he progressed to portraits. He loved his wife and his children and he valued his friends—that was the beginning of my portrait collection.

You probably remember the numerous small portraits in oil on copper. In earlier times, great masters produced similar works, perhaps for their own amusement, perhaps as a service to friends. This custom was not only laudable, but eventually led to the development of a distinct genre in which some painters specialized.

The small format has its advantages. A life-size portrait, even if only a bust or three-quarter length, takes up too much space for what it is. Every sensitive, well-to-do man feels obligated to have himself and his family painted at different stages of life. Done well on a small scale by a skillful artist, the typical portrait would take up little space and could even be joined by pictures of good friends of the family without making it difficult for descendants to find a place for them. A large portrait on the other hand—and this is particularly true today—usually departs this world along with its owner upon his death. And fashions change so rapidly that even a well-painted grandmother may not harmonize with her granddaughter's wallpaper, furniture and knickknacks.

As we know, the artist is dependent on the art lover of his time, just as the art lover is dependent on the contemporary artist. The good master hired by my father was probably the only one left who knew how to paint those miniature portraits. After his death, he was succeeded by an artist who painted life-size pictures.

For a long time, my father had wanted to engage someone who painted in this way because he wished to see himself and his family portrayed in their natural size. Just as any bird or insect to be painted was measured exactly—because in addition to other realistic features it had to be the exact size as the model—in the same way my father wanted his mirror image transferred to the canvas. Finally his wish was fulfilled by a skillful man who enjoyed our hospitality for a while. My father was handsome, my mother was a shapely woman, and my sister outshone all her peers in beauty and charm. The artist began his work, and of course one portrait was not enough. Especially my sister, as you have seen, was painted in more than one costume. A large family portrait was also planned, but it did not progress past a preliminary sketch because no agreement could be reached on style or pose.

On the whole, my father was not satisfied. The artist had been a student of the French school. Though his works were harmonious, imaginative, and appeared realistic to the casual observer, upon careful comparison with the models it became obvious that they left much to be desired. And some of them were totally spoiled because the painter, wanting to please my father, had followed his advice.

Unexpectedly, my father's wish was fulfilled in all respects. Our artist had a son, a gifted young man who had been apprenticed to a German uncle as a child and designated his heir. One day the young man visited his father, and my father discovered in him a talent that satisfied him completely. Immediately the young man was asked to paint my sister, and he did so with incredible precision. The result was not very artistic, but it was natural and true-to-life. There she stood, as if she were about to go into the garden, her brown hair partly covering her forehead, her big braids tied up with ribbons, carrying her sun hat filled with beautiful carnations (my father's favorite flowers!), holding a peach in her hand from a tree which had borne fruit for the first time that year.

Fortunately, all these items blended naturally without being trite. My father was delighted, and the old painter only too glad to surrender his position to his son. With his works, a new era for our family began, and my father considered it the happiest time of his life. We were all portrayed with our personal possessions and in our everyday environment. I need not go on about those pictures. I am sure you have not forgotten Julie's mocking zeal as she gradually assembled for you all the props from the paintings she could find to convince you of the complete realism of the imitations. There was Grandfather's snuffbox, his big silver pocket watch, his cane with the topaz knob, Grandmother's sewing basket and her earrings. Julie still had an ivory toy which she is holding in a portrait of herself as a child. She posed next to the picture, imitating it. The toy had not changed, the girl had—I still remember our jokes about that!

Within the course of a year, paintings had been made of all furnishings and utensils, in addition to the whole family. The young artist probably did not always find his job wholly fascinating, and he regained his enthusiasm only by casting occasional glances at my sister, an elixir which was the more vitalizing since he thought he could detect a sympathetic response in her eyes. To make a long story short: the two young people decided to spend the rest of their lives together. My mother looked favorably upon this decision and my father was pleased at the prospect of having this talented young man, who had become practically indispensable to him, as a permanent member of the family.

It was agreed that the young man should first take a trip through Germany and obtain his uncle's and his father's blessings before becoming one of us.

This mission was soon accomplished, and although he had not been away for long, he returned with a tidy sum of money earned at the various courts he had visited. The happy couple was married, and our family experienced a period of contentment which lasted until both had died.

My brother-in-law was a very handsome, easygoing man. His talent was sufficient for my father, his love sufficient for my sister, and his kindness made him liked by me and the rest of the family. During the summer, he went on trips and returned well remunerated. The winters were devoted to his family, and he usually painted his wife and daughters twice a year.

Because everything he painted, even the slightest detail, was so deceptively realistic, my father hit upon a peculiar idea for a painting. The picture no longer exists, otherwise I would have shown it to you when you were here. I will have to describe it and tell you how it perished.

In the last room upstairs where the best portraits are displayed, you may have noticed a connecting door; actually, it leads nowhere. In former times, when this door was opened, something more surprising than pleasing was revealed: my father, arm in arm with my mother, stepping forth, so to speak. The effect was startling because of the picture's realism, produced partially by the setting and partially by art. The portrait showed my father dressed formally, as if he were returning from a dinner or a soirée. It had been painted in this location and for this location, very painstakingly, the figures in perfect perspective when viewed from a certain vantage point, and the clothing superbly realistic.

To make sure that the light from the side would be just right, a window had been reset, and everything was arranged in such a way that the illusion would be perfect.

Unfortunately, this work of art, which so closely resembled the real thing, was destined to share the fate of real things. The canvas had been set into the door frame, and as a result was vulnerable to the dampness of the wall. The effect was even more damaging because the closed door prevented proper ventilation. Thus, after a harsh winter during which the room had not been opened, we found the picture of Father and Mother completely ruined, which saddened us all the more because they had died shortly before.

But I am getting ahead of myself, for I still have to tell you about the last happy period of my father's life.

After this picture had been completed, it seemed that it was the ultimate satisfaction of its kind in his life, that nothing could surpass it. And yet, there was still one more in store. An artist visited us and proposed making gypsum casts of the family members which he would then form in wax and tint in natural colors. As a sample he showed us the wax bust of his young assistant. It proved his talent, and my father decided to have the job done. It was successful. The artist painstakingly and realistically made a likeness of head and hands. A wig and a damask dressing gown were sacrificed for the phantom, and in this attire the wax replica of my dear old father sits today behind a curtain. I did not have the courage to show it to you.

After my parents' death, the family did not remain together for long. My sister died while still young and beautiful, and her husband painted her in her coffin. Melancholy prevented him from painting his daughters because, as they grew older, they seemed to divide their mother's beauty between them as it were, and he was too saddened by memories. He took good care of the small objects which had belonged to his wife and often painted them as still-lifes with perfect realism. These he then presented to the dearest of the friends he had acquired during his trips.

It seemed that through his grief he developed a feeling for the timeless and symbolic significance of things, whereas before he had painted objects as mere objects. Now his small, subdued paintings exhibited meaning and eloquence. In one picture, a hymn book bound in red velvet with gold clasps told of his wife's piety, another showed a pretty embroidered purse with strings and tassels from which she used to distribute alms. And there was the goblet from which she had drunk at her last communion before she died (her husband had obtained it from the church in exchange for a better one). Another picture showed a loaf of bread and the knife she had used to slice bread for the children.

Then there was a seed box for the spring planting, a calendar in which she had recorded expenses and other such items, and a crystal cup with her engraved initials, which was a childhood present from her grandfather, a fragile vessel that nonetheless outlasted its owner.

My brother-in-law continued to go on trips, and in general did not change his accustomed way of life. But because he was capable of focussing only on everyday life and because everyday life always reminded him of his bitter loss, his spirits remained low. From time to time, an incomprehensible longing seemed to overcome him, and the last still-life he painted consisted of objects that belonged to him, which, strangely chosen and assembled, hinted at transitoriness and separation, at permanence and reunion.

Several times we found him brooding before this picture, which was not at all characteristic of him, in a very emotional state. . . . Please forgive me if I stop here for today, for I have to regain my composure. This sad memory suddenly overcame me, and I must break its spell.

But I do not want to end this letter on such a melancholy note. I'll hand my pen to Julie, who will tell you. . . .

My uncle has just handed me his pen with instructions to tell you with a pretty turn of phrase that he remains 'humbly yours.' He still sticks to the formalities of those good old times when it was considered one's duty to take one's leave at the end of a letter with a graceful bow. We are no longer taught to do that, and such a formal curtsy does not seem natural or affectionate enough. A simple 'good-bye' and an imagined handshake, that's the best we can do.

Well then, how should I carry out my uncle's command, as befits an obedient niece? Isn't there any graceful flourish I can think of? And will you find it graceful enough if I assure you that the nieces are just as 'humbly yours' as their uncle? He has forbidden me to read the last page of his letter, so I don't know whether he wrote something good or bad about me. Perhaps I am vain in assuming that he has written about me at all. Anyway, he allowed me to read the beginning of his letter, and I think he slandered our good philosopher! I don't think it is kind or proper of my uncle to criticize so severly a young man who loves and admires him so sincerely, only because he is so steadfast in his pursuit of the educational goals he considers appropriate for himself. I know you will agree with me that women sometimes see things more clearly than men because we are not so one-sided and are more willing to be fair to everyone. Therefore let me assure you that the young man is certainly not uncommunicative and unsocial. He talks to me too, and even though I do not understand his philosophy at all, I do understand the philosopher—at least I think I do.

But perhaps I should thank *you* for the favorable opinion I have of him because the collection of engravings and the kind words you sent me through him have ensured him a warm reception.

I don't quite know how to express my gratitude for your generous present. I have the distinct feeling that it was meant to tease me. Did you want to make fun of 'your obedient servant' by sending her these elfin fantasy-creatures, these strange fairies and spectral beings created by my friend Füssli?[2] Poor Julie can't help it that strange and imaginative things fascinate her, that she is fond of pictures with fantastic subjects, and that she enjoys these weaving, fleeting dreams fixed on paper!

Enough of that! You made me very happy, although I do realize that I have taken on a burden by accepting you as my second uncle. As if my first weren't trouble enough! He has the same bad habit of wanting to enlighten children about the things they enjoy!

My sister, on the other hand, handles these things much better: she simply pays no attention. And since in our family everyone is obligated to like something that has to do with art, she has chosen to like things which are charming and pleasant to have around.

Her fiancé (now they are engaged—when you were here, things were still up in the air) sent her the loveliest colored engravings from England, and she likes them very much. You should see those tall beauties dressed in white with pink ribbons and pale blue veils! And those interesting mothers with their well-fed babies, and those handsome fathers! Once they are all under glass and in mahogany frames that are adorned with those little metal rods that came with them, they will surely turn up their noses at my Titania and her fairy entourage worrying about enchanted Bottom!

Now I am giving you the impression that I'm finding fault with my own sister! Well, the best method to defend oneself is to be a little intolerant of others. And now I have finally filled these pages after all, without realizing it, and I have come so close to the bottom of the last one that I have only enough space left to write March 10th and the signature of your loyal friend who bids you an affectionate good-bye.

Julie

Third Letter (The collector to the editor.)

In her postscript to my last letter, Julie spoke in defense of our philosopher. Unfortunately, her uncle cannot as yet do the same. The young man not only insists on a particular way of thinking which I do not find at all convincing, he is also preoccupied with topics which I do not consider—or have ever considered—important. I seem unable to reach him through my art collection, which normally helps me establish some kind of relationship with almost anyone, and he has even lost the historical and antiquarian interest in it which he formerly seemed to have. His main pursuit is ethics, a topic about which I know very little, except what my heart tells me. Some of his scholarly zeal is also directed toward natural law, for which I see no need because our courts are fair and our police force quite effective. His ultimate goal is constitutional law, a subject which my uncle ruined for me when I was still quite young. Consequently, the conversations to which I had been looking forward have not materialized. I do respect him as a decent person and I like him because he is a good fellow, and I would want to assist him because he is a relative. But that does not change the fact that we have nothing to say to each other. My engravings leave him silent, my paintings leave him cold.

Yet as I vent my displeasure on someone as I am doing now, like a typical uncle in a German comedy, past experiences come forward to remind me that exaggerating the traits which may separate us is not a good way to establish a relationship.

For this reason it is probably more prudent to wait and see how matters develop. Meanwhile I do not wish to neglect my obligations towards you, and so I continue my report about those who laid the groundwork for my collection.

My father's brother, after an honorable career as an officer, was consulted from time to time on various matters of government and finally on quite important cases. He was acquainted with almost all the princes of the period, who often presented him with gifts adorned with their miniature portraits in enamel, so that he developed a fondness for and an appreciation of such works of art. He gradually acquired the portraits of living as well as deceased rulers when the golden snuffboxes and diamond frames were sold back to the goldsmiths and jewellers. Finally my uncle owned a veritable 'Who's Who' of his century in portraits.

Because he traveled much and always wanted to have his treasured collection close to him, he took it with him, since it did not take up much space. Whenever he showed it, he was without fail given a portrait of some person, living or deceased, which had been lying forgotten in a jewelry box. For a collection like his has a way of attracting isolated pieces, and its sheer size tends to overcome and destroy the love an owner may feel for a particular item.

From portraits (some full-sized, for instance princesses pictured allegorically as huntresses and nymphs) he extended his collection to other miniature paintings, always putting more emphasis on technical excellence than on higher artistic quality, which can indeed be attained in this genre. You have seen the best pieces in this part of my collection, to which I have made only an occasional addition.

And now at last I must talk about myself, the present happy owner (although often enough the harried custodian!) of this well-known and highly praised collection.

From an early age, my preference was diametrically opposed to that of my uncle and even of my father. I cannot say for sure whether I inherited my grandfather's more serious leaning, or whether I deliberately rejected what my father and my uncle liked because I felt that urge to oppose my elders which is so common in young people. In any case, my father would only accept the most exact imitation, the most painstaking execution which made a work of art almost identical with an object in nature. My uncle would only find a small painting acceptable which was, one may say, a composite of an infinite number of minute dots. He always kept a magnifying glass handy, since he believed he could augment the miraculous nature of such a work by enlarging it. I, on the other hand, could only find pleasure in a sketch which at the same time suggested clearly and vividly a final work that might result from it.

The excellent pieces of this type in my grandfather's collection should have taught me that a sketch can be done with just as much precision as with expression; but they merely fanned my enthusiasm and provided no guidance. Boldly casual patterns, exuberant use of ink, strong strokes—that was what excited me. I even knew how to interpret sketches that were merely hieroglyphs of a figure, bare outlines, and I loved them wildly. Such works were the beginning of the small collection which I started in my youth and continued when I was older.

So I was and remained in constant opposition to my father, my brother-in-law and my uncle. This situation persisted and intensified because neither they nor I could find a way to compromise.

Although, as I said before, I tended to prize only the expressive sketch, this does not mean that I did not include many finished works in my collection. Without actually realizing it, I learned to appreciate the successful transformation of an expressive draft to an expressive final work. I learned to value precision, although I always considered it absolutely essential that the most precise stroke should also express feeling.

The original etchings of various Italian masters, which are still part of my collection, contributed to the deepening of my understanding. Thus I was making progress, and I was soon spurred on by a new ambition.

Order and completeness were two qualities I wanted my little collection to exhibit. I studied the history of art, I classified my pictures according to schools, masters and periods, I set up a catalogue, and I must say it is to my credit that I made an effort to obtain at least one of the works of any artist about whom I had become even the least bit knowledgeable. I did not want simply to repeat the good things I had heard about him but to have the actual evidence before me.

This was the state of my collection, of my knowledge and interests when the time came for me to enter the university. My liking for science (medicine, to be exact), the absence of all works of art, the presence of new things and the start of a new life—all that made me neglect my love of art. The only opportunity I had to train my eyes was afforded by the best of the illustrations in my anatomy, physiology and natural history texts.

Just before the end of my student years, I had the opportunity to go to Dresden. This visit provided me with a new awareness which was to have a decisive effect on my whole life. I was transported, almost delirious when I walked through the hallowed halls of that gallery! How many things I had only seen in my mind's eye I now saw in reality! How many gaps in my knowledge of art history were filled! I began to realize how many steps there were in that magnificent pyramid of art! I remembered the family collection with the greatest pleasure and congratulated myself that someday it was to be mine. Since I could not be an artist, I would have been in despair had I not been destined, even before I was born, to be an art lover and collector.

What effect other collections had on me, what else I did to increase my knowledge, and how my love of art accompanied all my activities like a guardian angel—I will not go into all that. Suffice it to say that I devoted all my other faculties to my chosen profession, that my practice demanded almost all my attention, and that this occupation, as removed from art as it may be, only intensified my love for art and my passion for collecting.

The rest you can easily guess, since you know me and my collection.

When my father died and I inherited this treasure, I had sufficient expertise to fill any gaps I found. I did so not only as a collector who fills gaps because they are there, but also to some extent as a connoisseur, who must recognize which deserve to be filled. And I still believe my path to be the right one because my likes and dislikes have been seconded by knowledgeable men of my acquaintance. I have never been to Italy, yet I have tried my best not to remain provincial in my taste. You be the judge of whether I have succeeded. I do not deny that in some respects I could have and should have refined my taste more. But who would want to live with completely refined taste!

But enough about myself, for now and evermore. May all my egotism find an outlet in my collection! Let 'Give and Take' be our watchword, which no one will bid you with more enthusiasm and greater affection and trust than

Your obedient servant

Fourth Letter (The collector to the editor.)

Once again you have given me convincing proof of your friendship not only by sending me the first finished sections of the *Propylaea* so promptly, but also by communicating to me some things in your letter which, because of the considerable detail, made your intentions clearer and the overall effect more telling. It was a most kind response to the watchword at the end of my last letter, and I thank you for your favorable reaction to the short history of my collection.

The printed material and your written commentary reminded me and my loved ones of those pleasant hours you granted us when, in spite of the unfriendly season, you went considerably out of your way to see a private collection. You found satisfaction in some of its parts, and you did not hesitate to offer your sincere friendship to its owner. I find in these pages the same principles you expressed then, the main ideas which occupied you at that time. I see that you have not deviated from your course, that you have made progress; and may I hope that you will be interested in how I have been faring here? Your essays encourage me to continue my report, and your letter asks me to do so. You know the history of my collection, and that gives me courage too, for I wish to put several requests and confessions before you.

When we contemplate a work of art, it is commendable and proper that we always keep in mind a lofty, unattainable ideal; that we always apply the highest standard possible when judging the artist's achievement; that we always seek out the truly perfect; that we always refer the art lover as well as the artist back to the fountainhead of art and always try to raise his perspective too; that in history as well as theory, in critical evaluation as well as in practice we always aim at the ultimate. Such efforts cannot fail to be fruitful.

Does not the minter try in every way possible to purify precious metals? Does he not use the specific weight of pure gold and silver as a fixed standard so that he may recognize possible alloys? Whether we add copper in any amount, increase the weight, lower the value, give certain names to coins and silverware, it does not matter. From small change of the poorest quality to counterfeit coins, all will be recognized for what they are. Touchstone and crucible are incorruptible judges of the real value!

I certainly do not want to criticize you for your seriousness and high standards. Yet, in reference to my metaphor, I would like to call your attention to some intermediate categories which neither artist nor art lover can afford to ignore in everyday life.

But I cannot proceed directly in my discussion of such wishes and proposals because I have something on my mind—actually, a request.

I must make a confession, lest I feel unworthy of your friendship. I am sure it will not offend you, or even displease you—so I'll risk it! Any step forward is a risk, and only by taking risks do we make progress. Here it is then, so that you won't think that what I have to say is more important than it really is.

Even though the owner of a collection is more than willing to show it to other people, he gradually becomes a little spiteful—no matter how patient and goodhearted he may be—if he has to show it too often. He hears total strangers casually express their feelings and thoughts about objects with which he is intimately familiar. We do not often find occasion to inflict our political views on strangers, nor would it be wise to do so. But works of art are provocative, and people talk about them without inhibitions. No one has doubts about his feelings, and that is as it should be. No one has doubts about his judgment, and that is not quite as it should be.

As long as I have owned my collection I have met only one man who did me the honor of believing me capable of judging its worth. He said: "I don't have much time. Show me the best, the most remarkable and the rarest item in each section." I thanked him, saying he was the first to make such a request. I trust he did not regret his confidence in me; at least he seemed quite satisfied when he left. I do not mean to imply that he was an outstanding connoisseur or art lover; perhaps his request was even proof of a certain indifference. Perhaps a man who loves a part of something is more interesting than one who only appreciates the whole. In any event, he is worth mentioning because he was the first and last person to escape my secret spite.

I must confess that even you aroused feelings of petty malice in me, which, I hasten to add, did not affect my respect and love. Not only did I send the girls away—you must forgive me, I couldn't help smiling when you kept looking furtively at the door that had closed behind them while we were examining the antique bronze pieces. But the door remained shut. The girls had disappeared for good without having finished their wine and biscuits. I had sent them away because I wanted my antiques to be the object of your undivided attention. Please forgive me and remember that I compensated you the next morning in the summerhouse when I introduced you not only to the painted members of the family but to the live ones as well, and gave you, in addition to the beautiful view of the area, the pleasure of a lovely conversation. It just occurs to me that I started a sentence with 'not only' and did not complete it grammatically. Perhaps I should start anew.

When you entered my gallery, you did me the particular honor of seeming to assume that I shared your views and valued most highly the same works you value. I admit that in general our judgments did coincide. But occasionally I detected a strong preference, perhaps even a prejudice. I let it pass. You, for your part, pointed out the value of some seemingly insignificant works which I had overlooked among the many items of my collection.

After your departure we talked about you at length. We compared you with others who had called upon us, and that led to a general comparison of previous visitors. We found great differences in their tastes and attitudes, but we discovered a recurrence of certain preferences in various people. Using the guestbook to refresh our memories, we began to group them according to their tastes. Subsequently, what had been a mere pastime became something more serious, and we observed our new guests more closely and put them into categories with the others.

I said 'we' because, as usual, I availed myself of the girls' help. Julie proved to be especially eager and was immediately successful in classifying people. Women know instinctively men's likes and dislikes. Caroline for her part was not kindly disposed toward visitors who did not praise the beautiful and rare pieces of English mezzotint which adorn her quiet room. You belong to that group, but this lack of appreciation has not damaged you seriously in the sweet child's eyes.

Art lovers of our sort (quite naturally we will discuss them first) are actually quite common, if one makes allowances for varying degrees of prejudice, of spontaneity and circumspection, of flexibility and strictness. Hence, I have high hopes for your *Propylaea,*[3] not merely because I assume that people like us exist, but because I actually know such people.

Although I cannot reproach you for your seriousness in matters of art or for your strictness towards artists and art lovers, I still must say something on behalf of art and its friends, since all kinds of people will read your publication, even if only those who have seen my collection. On the one hand, I would request that you exhibit a degree of tolerance toward all types of art, and that you not reject the most limited artists and art lovers as long as they pursue their preferred ways without presumption. On the other hand, you have my full support if you oppose those who, with limited concepts and with incurable bias, want to make a preferred and limited part of art into the whole. For this purpose, let us set up a new system of classification for art collections, not according to bronzes and marbles, ivory or silver, but one in which the artist, the connoisseur, and especially the art lover are themselves categorized.

At this point I can only give you a very general outline. The result can be easily summarized; my letter is getting too long, anyway. My introduction is detailed, and you will have to help me formulate the conclusion.

As usually happens, our little academy did not think of examining itself until much later, and we soon discovered in our family a representative for almost every category.

There is a group of artists and art lovers whom we have called the Imitators. Their only interest and their greatest pleasure is imitation raised to a high degree of perfection. My father and my brother-in-law belong to this group; the former as art lover and the latter as artist are extreme examples of this tendency. For such people, imitation must constantly strive to make the copy as nearly identical with the original as possible.

Since this requires great accuracy and care, they are closely related to another class whom we have called the Dotters. Their primary interest is not so much imitation as workmanship. Their favorite objects are those that require the most dots and lines. I am sure this class will remind you of my uncle. The artist in this group seeks to fill space infinitely, so to speak, and tries to convince us visually that matter can be divided ad infinitum. A talented artist like this earns our esteem if he does a miniature portrait of a beloved one in such a way that what our heart treasures about that person becomes a physical presence for our eyes to see, like a jewel set among jewels.

Natural history also owes much to this category of artists.

As we were talking about this class I realized that I belonged to a very different group, if only because of my earlier predilection. All those who want to express too much with few strokes—just as the Dotters may often express too little with many strokes and dots—we called Sketchers. We were not referring to those masters who make a rough draft, a sketch, of the work to be executed so as to get a critical overview of what they are doing. The term "Sketcher" properly refers to those who never develop their talent beyond sketches and hence never reach the goal of art, the final execution, just as the Dotter is often not aware of the essential starting point of art, which is inventiveness, or imagination.

The Sketcher, on the other hand, often has too much imagination. He loves poetic, even fantastic subjects, and his expression is always a little excessive.

He rarely commits the error of being too tentative or understated. On the contrary, this quality often goes along with good execution.

When we came to the class where the tentative, the pleasing, the graceful predominate, Caroline immediately declared herself an adherent and protested solemnly against giving it a facetious label. Julie, on the other hand, does not care whether she and her friends, those poetic and imaginative sketchers and painters, are judged with severity or lenience.

After discussing the tentative styles we naturally came to speak of woodcuts and engravings of the early masters, whose works, in spite of a harsh, severe and rigid style, still delight us because of their rough-hewn, solid quality.

We thought of many other types which, however, could perhaps be grouped among the previous ones, such as Caricaturists who only emphasize the characteristically repugnant, the physically and morally repulsive; Improvisers who sketch out anything on the spur of the moment with great dexterity and speed; Scholar-Artists whose works are incomprehensible without commentary; Scholar-Art-Lovers who cannot leave the simplest, most obvious work without commentary, and others whom I will discuss at another time. Today I want to conclude with the hope that the end of my letter may give you reason for making fun of my presumptuousness and therefore may atone for its beginning where I dared to smile at a few endearing weaknesses of my friends. You may repay me in kind if you don't find my boldness too objectionable; chide me, point out my own foibles. This way, you will increase my gratitude, but not diminish the devotion of your

Eternally faithful

Fifth Letter (The collector to the editor.)

Your cheerful response assures me that my letter found you in the best of spirits and that it did nothing to diminish that blessed state. Your reply was also a pleasant gift at a pleasant moment.

If it is true that good fortune usually comes alone, not in three's like misfortune, then I have just experienced the exception to that rule. Your letter could not have arrived at a more propitious time, and your comments about my curious classifications could not have borne fruit more swiftly than at that very moment—they were like seeds falling on fertile soil. Let me tell you what happened yesterday so that you will know what new star has risen and what fortunate configuration occurred when it converged with the constellation of your letter.

Yesterday we received a visit from a stranger[4] whose name was familiar to me and who has the reputation of being a connoisseur. I was pleased to see him, provided him with a general introduction to my collection, let him choose the items he wished to see and showed them to him. I soon noticed how knowledgeable he was about art and especially art history. He recognized the masters as well as their school, and in dubious cases he would give excellent reasons for his doubts. It was a pleasure to converse with him.

Perhaps I would have expressed my own opinion more freely if, from the first, my resolve to sound out my guest thoroughly had not restrained me. Many of his judgments were in agreement with mine, and some made me admire his discerning and practiced eye. The first thing that struck me was his pronounced antipathy toward all mannerists. That troubled me, since some of my favorite pictures belong to this category, and I was all the more eager to learn the reasons for his dislike.

My guest had arrived late, and when the fading light prevented us from looking at any more pictures, I asked him to join us for supper. We had invited our philosopher too, because we have become a little more friendly lately. I will tell you briefly why.

It is a good thing that heaven, anticipating the peculiarities of men, has provided a means to bring them together as often as it causes dissension among them. Our philosopher had not seen Julie since childhood and was taken with her charm. Intuition led him to entertain uncle as well as niece, and now our conversations usually focus on human interests and passions.

Before we all gathered for supper, I took the opportunity to defend my mannerists against the visitor. I spoke of their beautiful artistic temperament, their fine technique and their gracefulness. However, anticipating objections, I added: "I only say this to explain why I tolerate them. Because if we look for sublime beauty in their works—which is the highest principle and the highest purpose of art—that of course is quite a different matter."

I did not quite like his smile because it seemed to express complacency and a sort of pity for me. He replied: "So you also adhere to the traditional view that beauty is the ultimate goal of art?"

"I know of no higher one," I said.

"Can you tell me what beauty is?" he exclaimed.

"Perhaps not," I said, "but I can show you beauty. Let us take a quick look, and by candlelight if need be, at a beautiful plaster cast of Apollo and a beautiful marble bust of Bacchus which I own, and let us see if we cannot agree that they are beautiful!"

"Before we embark upon this investigation," he said, "it might be advisable to consider the word beauty and its origin more closely. The German word for beauty, *Schönheit,* comes from *Schein,* appearance. Beauty is simply appearance and cannot be considered the ultimate goal of art. Only what is undeniably characteristic deserves to be called beautiful. Without character there is no beauty."

I was somewhat taken aback by his words and replied, "If we grant for the sake of argument that what is beautiful must be characteristic, we can only conclude that the characteristic is at best the basis of beauty. But we cannot conclude that they are identical. Character is to beauty what the skeleton is to the living human being. No one will deny that the bone structure is the basis of all highly developed forms of life. It is the foundation, it determines form, but it is not form itself. Even less does it produce the final manifestation which, as essence and outer shell of an organic whole, we call beauty."

"I can't be bothered with similes," our guest replied, "and your own words indicate that beauty is something incomprehensible, or the result of something incomprehensible. What we cannot understand does not exist. What we cannot make clear with words is nonsense!"

I: "Can you really express clearly in words the effect a colorful object has on your eyes?"

HE: "Again, that is an example I cannot be bothered with. Character, at any rate, can be proved. You never find beauty without character, because otherwise it would be vacuous and insignificant. Everything beautiful that the ancients created is purely characteristic, and only from this special quality does beauty originate."

Our philosopher had arrived and started chatting with my nieces. When he heard our animated discussion he joined us; and my guest, as if spurred on by the presence of a new listener, continued:

"It is a pity that good minds, respectable people, should popularize such false principles which have merely the appearance of truth. No one repeats them more glibly than those who do not know or do not understand the subject. Thus Lessing[5] foisted on us the principle that the ancients created only beauty, Winckelmann lulled us to sleep with his 'quiet grandeur, simplicity and calm' instead of telling us that the art of antiquity appears in every conceivable form. But these gentlemen only concentrate on Jupiter and Juno, the Genii and the Graces, and they do not talk about the ugly bodies and heads of barbarians, the disheveled hair and dirty beards, the scrawny physiques, wrinkled skin, protruding veins and sagging breasts of old age."

"For heaven's sake," I exclaimed, "did any great period in the history of ancient art actually produce important works with such loathsome subject matter? Are you sure they are not minor or occasional works, products of an art form that had to submit to the fashion of the time, an art in decline?"

HE: "I'll give you a list of them so that you can examine them and judge for yourself. But I am sure you won't deny that the *Laocoon*, the *Niobe* and the *Farnese Bull*[6] are major works. Just look at the *Laocoon* and behold nature in tumult and despair: the final choking agony, desperate straining, convulsive twitching, the effect of corrosive poison, violent reaction, failing circulation, suffocation, paralytic death."

The philosopher seemed to look at me in amazement, and I said: "I shudder, I am horrified at the mere description. Indeed, if what you say about the *Laocoon* is true, where is the grace that one claims to see in it, as in every true work of art? But I don't want to get involved in that. You will have to settle it with the editors of the *Propylaea*, who profess the very opposite of what you say."

"I foresee no trouble there," my guest replied. "All of antiquity supports my point of view. For example, is there anything more horrifying than the raging terror and violent death in the portrayals in the *Niobe* group?"

I was taken aback by his assertions because just a short time before I had been looking at the prints in Fabrioni,[7] which I immediately fetched and opened: "I cannot find a trace of the raging terror of death. What I do see in the statues is utmost subordination of the tragic situation to the lofty concepts of dignity, nobility, beauty and restrained bearing. Everywhere I see the artistic purpose to make body and lines appear graceful and pleasing. The character only appears in general lines, which permeate the works like a spiritual skeleton as it were!"

HE: "Let's look at the bas-reliefs at the end of the book."

We turned to them.

I: "Frankly speaking, I do not see anything at all that is horrifying here either. Where are raging terror and death? All I see are figures so artistically mingled and so superbly and diversely arranged that they give me the most pleasant feelings, even while they remind me of their tragic fates. Everything characteristic is presented with restraint, all violence is neutralized. Hence I would say that what is characteristic is the basis on which simplicity and dignity rest. The highest goal of art is beauty, and its ultimate effect is aesthetic pleasure.

"The element of grace which, to be sure, cannot be tied directly to the characteristic, is especially striking in this sarcophagus. Are not Niobe's dead daughters and sons used as adornments? This is the supreme sybaritism of art! Art no longer uses flowers and fruits as ornaments, it uses human corpses, the greatest sorrow that can befall a father or a mother, the sudden death of their children. Yes, and the lovely spirit standing by the tomb with his lowered torch,[8] he stood at the working artist's side and inspired his earthly talent with heavenly grace."

My guest looked at me, smiling, and shrugged. "Alas," he said when I had finished, "alas, I see that we cannot come to an agreement. What a pity that a man of your knowledge and your intelligence cannot see that those are merely empty words; that notions such as beauty and ideal must seem like dreams to a sensible person, dreams which he of course does not want to see transformed into reality, indeed finds repugnant."

During the last part of our conversation, our philosopher became a little restive, although in the beginning he had seemed to listen with indifference and calm. He shifted his chair, seemed about to say something a few times, and finally, when there was a pause, began to speak.

But he will write and tell you himself what he said. He came back early this morning because his participation in yesterday's conversation suddenly broke the barriers, and the first signs of a blossoming friendship are beginning to appear.

I want to put this letter in the morning mail. I have kept a few patients waiting because of it, but I hope Apollo, the patron of both doctors and artists, will forgive me.

Some strange things may happen this afternoon: Mr. Characteristic will be back, and half a dozen strangers are planning to visit. The weather is beautiful, and people are traveling again.

Julie, the philosopher and I have formed an alliance against that group, and we shall not miss a single one of their quirks!

But hear first the end of yesterday's debate and accept best regards from your hurried, but ever faithful

Friend and servant

Sixth Letter (Continuation by the philosopher.)

Our dear friend has allowed me to sit at his desk, and I thank him for his trust and for giving me the opportunity to correspond with you. He calls me a philosopher; he would call me a student if he knew how much I still desire to educate and inform myself. But unfortunately, one appears arrogant to others even if one thinks oneself only halfway toward one's goal.

Last night I interjected myself rather forcefully into a discussion on the visual arts without having much first-hand information on the subject, what knowledge I possess having come from literature.[9] But I am sure you will forgive me when you see from my report that I spoke only in generalities, and that I based my right to speak on some familiarity with ancient poetry.

I must say, I felt outraged by the way my opponent was treating my friend. I am still young and perhaps become outraged at the wrong time, which is why I deserve the title "philosopher" even less. But the man's remarks were an attack on me, too. For if the connoisseur and the art lover must not abandon beauty, then the student of philosophy cannot allow ideals to be relegated to the realm of fantasies.

Now let me tell you the gist of the conversation, at least as I remember it.

I: "Might I be permitted to say a word?"

GUEST (rather snidely): "Go right ahead. But please, no fantasies."

I: "I do know something about ancient literature, but I am not well informed about the visual arts."

GUEST: "I'm sorry to hear that. In which case we'll probably have a hard time coming to an understanding."

I: "But all the arts are so closely related that there should be no misunderstanding among adherents of even the most distant branches."

UNCLE: "Proceed."

I: "The writers of ancient tragedy treated their subject matter in just the way the sculptors did, unless these prints of Niobe's family are quite different from the original."

GUEST: "They are close enough. They give an incomplete, but not a false impression of the original."

I: "Good. Then we can use them as a working basis for our discussion."

UNCLE: "What was it you wanted to say about the methods of the ancient tragedians?"

I: "Very often, especially in the early period, they chose unbearable subjects and intolerable events."

GUEST: "Are you saying that the old myths were unbearable?"

I: "Indeed they were, almost like your description of the *Laocoon* group."

GUEST: "You found it unbearable?"

I: "Pardon me, not your description, but what you described."

GUEST: "In other words, the work itself?"

I: "Not at all! Rather what you see in it: the plot, the story, the skeleton, what you call the characteristic. Because if *Laocoon* were really the way you described it, it would deserve to be smashed to pieces, and the sooner, the better."

GUEST: "You are using strong language."

I: "I'm only following your example."

UNCLE: "Well then, what about the ancient tragedies?"

GUEST: "Those unbearable subjects."

I: "Right! But let's also talk about the treatment of these subjects, which made everything bearable, tolerable, beautiful and graceful."

GUEST: "Well, I suppose that was achieved by means of 'simplicity and quiet grandeur'?"

I: "So it seems."

GUEST: "And by means of the moderating principle of beauty?"

I: "No doubt."

GUEST: "You mean to say that the ancient tragedies were not terrifying?"

I: "Scarcely, as far as I can tell—if we listen to the poets themselves. Of course, if we only pay attention to the subject matter of poetry, if we speak of a work of art as if we had personally experienced the events it depicts, then we could even call Sophoclean tragedies disgusting and repulsive."

GUEST: "I'm not qualified to judge poetry."

I: "Nor am I qualified to judge the visual arts."

GUEST: "It will probably be better if each of us stays in his own field."

I: "But still, there is one general point where the effects of all art—poetic as well as visual—converge and from which all the laws of art derive."

GUEST: "And what would that point be?"

I: "The human soul."

GUEST: "Ah yes! You and your new breed of philosophers[10] always want to play according to your own rules. Of course, it is easier to shape the world in accordance with an idea than to subordinate ideas to things as they are."

I: "This is not a dispute on metaphysics."

GUEST: "I should hope not!"

I: "For argument's sake I will grant that we can conceive of nature as existing without man. But art, by necessity, depends on man, for art exists only through and for man."

GUEST: "I don't see where you are heading."

I: "By making that which is characteristic into the goal of art, you yourself appoint man's logical understanding as the judge of what is characteristic."

GUEST: "Of course! What I can't grasp with my logical understanding doesn't exist for me."

I: "But man is not merely a thinking creature, he also has feelings. He is a whole, an amalgam of diverse yet closely connected forces. And the work of art must address itself to the whole and must reflect this rich unity, this harmonious diversity in man."

GUEST: "Don't lead me into such labyrinths. Who could ever get us out again?"

I: "In that case it would be best to terminate our discussion and go back to our original positions."

GUEST: "For my part, I feel I am on solid ground."

I: "Perhaps some simple means might be found, if not to share, then at least to understand the other's position."

GUEST: "You tell me how."

I: "For the moment, consider how the creative process began."

GUEST: "Very well."

I: "Let's accompany the work of art on its way to perfection."

GUEST: "I'll only go along if we follow the road of practical experience. I refuse to tread the steep paths of speculation."

I: "May I start from the beginning?"

GUEST: "Please do."

I: "Say a man has a liking for some object or other. Or some living creature."

GUEST: "Like that nice little dog over there."

JULIE: "Come here, Bello! It's no small honor for you to serve as an example in such a learned discussion."

I: "The dog is certainly pretty enough. Now, if the man in question had an imitative urge, he would try to portray this dog in some way. But even if his imitation turned out well, we would not have gained much because at best we would have two Bellos instead of one."

GUEST: "I'm withholding comment until I see what you are getting at."

I: "Assume that this man, whom we may already call an artist because of his talent, is still not satisfied. He finds his interest too narrow, too limited. He looks for other dogs, other types, other breeds, and in the end visualizes not a particular dog, but rather the concept of 'dog.' And finally he is able to represent this concept by means of his art."

GUEST: "Bravo! A man after my own heart! I'm sure his work of art would turn out to be characteristic!"

I: "No doubt."

GUEST: "And I would be content with that. I would ask for nothing else."

I: "But the rest of us must continue."

GUEST: "I'll stop right here."

UNCLE: "I'll go along to see where we are heading."

I: "Our hypothetical artist's approach may have produced at best a certain standard for depiction, exemplary and scientific, but not satisfying to the soul."

GUEST: "How could one possibly fulfill all the odd demands of that precious soul?"

I: "Its demands are not odd, it only insists on its legitimate rights. An old myth tells us that Elohim once resolved: Let us fashion man after our own image. Hence man is justified in saying: Let us fashion gods after our own image."

GUEST: "I think we are now venturing into a very dark region."

I: "There is only one light to show us the way."

GUEST: "And that is?"

I: "Reason."

GUEST: "It's difficult to say if reason is a guiding light or a will-o'-the-wisp."

I: "We don't have to call it reason. But let's try to determine what demands our mind makes on a work of art. It should not only gratify a limited interest, not only satisfy our intellectual curiosity, not only order and consolidate our knowledge. Something higher within us must be awakened. We want to venerate and be worthy of veneration ourselves."

GUEST: "Now you're losing me!"

UNCLE: "But I think I understand to some extent. How well, I will try to make clear with an example. Assume the artist has cast a bronze eagle which is a perfect generic representation. Now if he were to put it on Jupiter's sceptre, do you think it would be totally suitable there?"

GUEST: "Well, that would depend."

UNCLE: "I say not. The artist would have to add something."

GUEST: "What?"

UNCLE: "That is hard to put in words."

GUEST: "I thought so!"

I: "Yet I think I can come close to it."

GUEST: "Well, go ahead."

I: "He would have to give to the eagle what he gave to Jupiter in order to make him a god."

GUEST: "And what might that be?"

I: "The divine quality, which of course we would not recognize if man could not feel it and produce it himself."

GUEST: "I'll stay where I am and let you people lose yourselves in the clouds. I can see that you are trying to describe the high style of Greek art. But I only admire this style because it is characteristic."

I: "For us, it is something more. It satisfies an important demand, but one that is not yet the most important."

GUEST: "It would seem that you're very difficult to satisfy."

I: "One is justified in demanding much if there is much to be attained. Let me be brief. The human mind is in an exalted state when it venerates, when it worships, when it elevates an object and in turn is elevated by it. However, the mind cannot stay long in this state. The generic representation left it cold, the ideal elevated it beyond itself. But now the mind longs to return to itself. It would like to savour again its earlier liking for the individual object, without, however, returning to the limitations of this position and without giving up that which is significant and elevating. What would happen to the mind in this dilemma if beauty did not step in and solve the problem! Only beauty can give life and warmth to what is presented with scientific exactitude. By muting what is significant and elevated, and suffusing it with extraordinary charm, beauty brings the individual object back to us. A beautiful work of art has come full circle: It is again something individual that we can take to our hearts and make part of us."

GUEST: "Have you finished?"

I: "For now. The little circle is complete, and we are back where we started. I have tried to explain the soul's demands and how they are met. I have nothing more to add." (Uncle was summoned to an emergency case and left.)

GUEST: "During arguments you philosophers have a way of hiding behind peculiar words as if behind a shield."

I: "I can assure you that I did not speak as a philosopher. It was all a matter of experience."

GUEST: "What no one else can grasp, you call experience!"

I: "Each experience needs the appropriate organ."

GUEST: "Some special organ I suppose?"

I: "No, not a special one, but it must have a specific quality."

GUEST: "And what might that be?"

I: "It must be able to produce."

GUEST: "Produce what?"

I: "Experience. There is no experience which is not produced, brought forth, created."

GUEST: "Well, that's the limit!"

I: "That applies especially to artists."[11]

GUEST: "You don't say! Then the portrait painter would be in an enviable position! Think of all the people who would flock to him if he could produce portraits without having to inconvenience his customers with so many sittings!"

I: "Your example does not worry me at all. On the contrary, I am convinced a portrait can only be good if it has been created by the painter in the true sense of the word."

GUEST (jumping up): "That's going too far! I wish you were just pulling my leg and this were only a joke. How pleased I would be if that were the answer to the problem. How glad I would be to extend my hand in reconciliation to a decent man like you."

I: "I'm sorry, but I'm absolutely serious. This is my firm conviction, and I must stand by it."

GUEST: "Well, in that case I guess we should shake hands only to say good-bye, especially since our host has been called away and we have lost the mediator in our heated dispute. Good-bye, mademoiselle. Good-bye, sir. I shall enquire tomorrow when it would be convenient to pay my respects again."

He stormed out of the room, and Julie had barely time to give the maid a signal to hurry after him to light his way. I stayed behind with Julie. Caroline had left some time ago; I think it was just after my opponent had declared that pure beauty without character was insipid.

"You went too far, my friend," said Julie after a short pause. "Although I don't quite think he was right, I certainly cannot give you my unqualified support either. I'm sure you were just teasing him when you said at the end that a portrait painter literally had to create the picture!"

"Dear Julie," I replied, "I really wish I could explain to you what I mean. Perhaps I will succeed some day. But I would think that you whose mind is so active and wide-ranging, you who not only understand the artist but even anticipate him in certain ways, you who can visualize so vividly things you have never seen—you should be least surprised when we speak of creating, of bringing forth."

JULIE: "I think you are trying to win me over to your side. It won't be difficult because I like listening to you."

I: "Let us think well of man and not let it bother us if what we say about him sounds a bit bizarre. Does not everyone concede that a poet is born, not made? We all attribute creative power to genius and do not think for a second that we are saying anything paradoxical. There is no denying that works of the imagination are creative. Surely, the unresponsive, the insensitive will never recognize what is good, noble, beautiful—either in themselves or others. But where would the ability to do so come from if not from within us? Ask your own heart! The heart does not just act intuitively, it also knows how to act, isn't that true? Does not the capacity to do good rejoice in a good deed? Who feels strongly without having the desire to express what he feels? And what do we express but what we create! And not just create so that it exists, once and for all, but so that it lives and grows and is reborn and creates again? And this is precisely the divine power of love, which man never stops celebrating in song, saying that it brings forth the magnificent qualities of the beloved subject each moment anew, that it forms them in the minutest detail, embraces them as a whole, does not rest by day or night, delights in its own work, is amazed at its own restless activity, finds the familiar ever new because it is reborn each moment in the sweetest of all activities. Yes, the image of the beloved cannot grow old because every moment is the moment of its birth.

"Today I committed a grievous sin. I acted contrary to my principles when I spoke about a subject I had not studied thoroughly. And right now I am on the verge of an even more reprehensible action. Silence befits a man who feels his imperfections. Silence also behoves a lover who has no hope of happiness. Let me depart, Julie, lest I become doubly worthy of reproach."

I was in quite a state and seized her hand. She held my hand, kindly. I am sure, kindly. Pray heaven that I was not mistaken, that I am not mistaken!

But let me continue with my report. Julie's uncle came back. He was kind enough to praise what I had criticized in myself and was satisfied that my ideas on the visual arts agreed with his. He promised me that he would soon help me get the practical experience which I might still need. Julie promised jokingly she would give me lessons too, if I became more talkative and more sociable—I know very well that she can do with me as she will!

The maid came back and expressed pleasure with our guest's generosity because he had given her a handsome tip for lighting his way. She was even more impressed with his good manners: he had thanked her most kindly and had even called her 'my pretty child.'

I was in no mood to spare him and exclaimed: "Ah yes! If you deny the ideal you can easily mistake the common for the beautiful."

Julie reminded me jokingly that justice and fairness were also ideals we should strive for.

It had gotten late. Julie's uncle asked a favor of me, which turned out to be a favor for myself. He gave me a copy of his letter to you in which he had tried to define the various types of artists and art lovers. He also gave me your reply, asking me to study both, to think about them, and to be present when the expected gallery visitors arrived; perhaps I could help add more categories. I spent the rest of the night with this assignment and came up with an impromptu scheme, not very thorough, but at least amusing. It has special value for me personally because Julie found it highly entertaining when she read it this morning.

I have to end now. I have just realized that my letter can be mailed together with my friend's which is still here on the desk. On quickly re-reading what I have written, I notice that I could have said many things differently and should have been more precise in my formulations. If I were to follow my impulse, I would burn rather than mail these pages. But if we only communicated what is perfect, there wouldn't be much to communicate! And blessed be our guest for having made me so angry and agitated, which in turn led to this correspondence with you and to the prospect of a new and pleasant relationship.

Seventh Letter (Julie to the editor.)

Another letter from Julie! Again you see the handwriting which you once analyzed graphologically and said revealed an objective, discerning mind that comprehends and communicates with ease.

Well, today I'll surely need those qualities if I'm to carry out a task which was literally forced on me. I feel neither qualified nor able to do it, but it's the gentlemen's wish, and so be it!

I am supposed to report to you what happened yesterday and describe the people who visited our gallery. And then, I am to explain that delightful scheme which in future will pigeonhole and label all artists and art lovers who focus on one particular aspect and are unable to embrace the whole. I don't mind the first part of my assignment, since it is basically a factual report. The second part I don't think I'll get to today, and tomorrow I'll try to find a way to get out of it.

But since I'm sure you would like to know why this particular task was assigned to me, let me tell you briefly what happened last night before we went to bed.

We had been sitting together—my uncle, our young friend (who doesn't want to be called "philosopher" anymore), Caroline and I—discussing the events of the day and grouping ourselves and our friends into various categories. And when we were about to say good night, Uncle began: "Today we have thought so often of our absent friends and wished they were here. Well then, who is going to give them a quick summary of the day's events and the progress we have made in assessing ourselves and others? We mustn't fail to inform them so that they can respond and thus keep our little project moving along."

To that I replied: "It seems to me that the matter would be handled best if Uncle summarized the day's events and our friend could be persuaded to compose a short essay on the new theory and its application."

"Since you mention the word 'theory'," replied our friend, "I can't help recoiling with horror and must politely decline, despite my wish to please you in everything. I don't know what it is these days that causes me to make one mistake after another. First I broke my silence and babbled about the visual arts—about which I know nothing—and here I am about to let myself be persuaded to write up some kind of theory on a subject I do not really grasp. Allow me the sweet pleasure of having committed these blunders out of affection for my dearest friends. But spare me the shame of exposing my imperfections to strangers whose good opinions I value."

To this my uncle quickly replied: "As far as I am concerned, it is simply out of the question for me to sit down and write a letter this week. I have to spend all my time on local and out-of-town patients; I must make house calls, write case histories, visit some patients in the country. You young people will have to fight it out among yourselves. But I would suggest that Julie do the job, simply starting with the report on today's events and ending with the definition of the theory. She has a good memory, and I could tell by her jokes that she is sometimes quicker than we in logical conclusions. All she needs is good will, and that she usually has."

That's what they said about me, so that's what I have to put down. I resisted as well as I could, but in the end I had to give in. I have to admit I was ultimately persuaded by a few encouraging words from the young man, who seems to have gained a strange hold over me.

Now my thoughts are directed toward you, and my pen hastens to meet you, as it were. As I write I feel as though I were gradually reducing the distance that separates us. . . Now I have arrived, and I hope my report and I will be kindly received.

We had hardly finished lunch yesterday when two visitors were announced, a tutor and his young charge.

Set for mischief and eager to meet our first prey, we all hurried to the gallery. The young man was handsome and quiet; his tutor was well-mannered enough, but not exactly refined. After the usual preliminaries the tutor began to look around among the paintings and asked permission to take notes on the most outstanding. My uncle was kind enough to point out the best in each section, and the visitor jotted down the artists' names and the titles, always asking what each painting had cost and what its present cash value was. Of course an answer could not always be provided.

The young man was more pensive than attentive and seemed to linger longest before lonely landscapes, rocky terrain and waterfalls.

Then the guest from the previous day arrived, whom I will call Mr. Characteristic from now on. He was in a very good mood, joked with Uncle and our friend about their argument of the day before and assured them he would convert them yet. My uncle immediately started to chat with him and led him to an interesting painting. Our friend seemed moody and cross, and I scolded him. He confessed that his opponent's relaxed manner had annoyed him momentarily, and he promised to cheer up.

We were watching my uncle chatting amiably with his guest when a lady entered with two travel companions. Caroline and I, dressed in our finest in anticipation of this visit, hastened over to welcome her. She was polite and sociable, and we were not put off by a certain sternness in her because it suited her age and social position. She was a head shorter than my sister and I, yet she seemed to look down on us and relish the superiority of her mind and experience.

We asked her what she would like to see. She assured us that she preferred to walk through galleries by herself and to let her feelings guide her. We let her be guided by her feelings and kept a respectful distance.

When I heard her express her disapproval of some Dutch paintings and their mundane subject matter to one of her companions, I thought I could perhaps be of some help. I placed a little box containing a beautiful reclining Venus on the easel. There is disagreement on who painted it, but everyone agrees that she is superb. I opened the doors and asked her to view it in the proper light. But what a hostile reception I got! She had hardly glanced at the picture when she lowered her eyes and immediately turned to me with some indignation. "I would not have expected," she exclaimed, "a modest young girl to show me such a picture." "What do you mean?" I asked. "You do not know?" she replied.

I pulled myself together and said with feigned innocence: "No, milady, I do not see anything wrong in showing you this picture. On the contrary, I wanted to express my respect for you by letting you see this treasure of our collection right away. Normally, we show it at the end."

LADY: "Are you saying that this nudity does not offend you?"

JULIE: "Why should I be offended by the greatest beauty the eye can behold? And besides, I am familiar with the picture; I have seen it since I was a child."

LADY: "I must disapprove of tutors who did not conceal such objects from you."

JULIE: "Pardon me, but why should they have done that? And how could they have done that? I had instruction in natural history. They showed me the birds with their feathers, animals with their fur, even fish with their scales, and you say they should have concealed from me the human form, to which everything points and leads so forcefully? Would that have been possible? I am sure if they had covered all human beings with cloaks, my mind would not have rested until it had invented the human figure. And am I not a woman myself? How can you conceal a human being from another human being? And besides, isn't it a good lesson in modesty to show us women—we who always think ourselves so pretty—what true beauty is?"

LADY: "Humility comes from within, mademoiselle, and true modesty needs no external stimulus. It seems to me a womanly virtue to be able to control one's curiosity and to restrain one's inquisitiveness, at least so as to avoid subjects that may prove dangerous in so many respects."

JULIE: "There may be people, milady, who can be taught to accept such negative virtues. As far as my education is concerned, my dear uncle will have to bear the blame. When I was old enough to think about myself, he often said to me: Make it a habit to contemplate nature freely; it will always stimulate serious thinking, and may the beauty of art hallow the sensations which result."

The lady turned to her silent companion and said something in English. Apparently she was not quite happy about my freedom and turned away. Since she was not far from an Annunciation, I accompanied her there. She looked at it attentively and finally expressed her admiration for the angel's wings and how realistic they were.

After lingering over this picture for quite some time, she finally hurried to an Ecce Homo[12] which she contemplated with rapture. Since I do not find the effect of that suffering countenance at all salutary, I wanted Caroline to take my place. I beckoned to her, and she left the young baron with whom she was standing by the window and who was just putting a piece of paper into his pocket.

Asked what they had been talking about, she replied: "He read me some poems addressed to his sweetheart, songs written to her during his long travels. The verses are quite nice; have him show them to you."

I had no occasion to speak to him however, since he had just gone over to the lady and introduced himself as a distant relative. Naturally her ladyship turned her back on her Lord Jesus in order to greet his lordship, her cousin. Art seemed forgotten for a while, and a lively conversation ensued on family and other matters.

Meanwhile, our young philosopher friend had joined one of the lady's companions and discovered he was an artist. He asked him questions about one painting after another, hoping to learn something, as he assured me later. Yet his hope was not realized, since the artist, who seemed quite knowledgeable, concentrated on pointing out specific flaws. The design was wrong in this picture, the perspective in that one; this one lacked harmony, in that one the application of colors was inadequate; in another the brush strokes were poor; this shoulder did not sit correctly on the body; this halo was too white, that fire too red; in this one a figure did not stand on the right plane. These and other remarks interfered with the enjoyment of the pictures.

I could tell that my friend did not find that particularly edifying, and to rescue him, I called the tutor over and said: "You have noted the value of the best pictures. Here's an expert who can point out their flaws. I'm sure it would be interesting to keep a record of them too." I had no sooner extricated my friend than we got into an almost worse predicament. The lady's second companion, a scholar who had been walking around by himself examining the pictures through a lorgnette, started a conversation with us and complained that so few pictures exhibited proper concern for costume. He said he found the anachronisms particularly unbearable. How could anyone tolerate Saint Joseph reading a bound book, Adam digging with a shovel, and the saints Jerome, Francis and Catherine all together with the Holy Infant in the same picture! He had found too many such flaws to feel comfortable in our gallery.

Out of politeness as host, my uncle had of course talked to the lady as well as the other visitors from time to time. However, he seemed to get along best with Mr. Characteristic, who recalled having met the lady at some other private gallery. The guests began to walk back and forth and talk about things other than art, paying only cursory attention to the exhibits in the other rooms, so that finally, surrounded by works of art, they were miles away from art itself.

In the end, it was our old servant who became the focus of attention. He could be called deputy custodian of our gallery because he takes people around when my uncle cannot be present or if it is obvious that the visitors are only curiosity seekers. He has thought up some funny stories that he always tells when he gets to certain pictures. He quotes exaggerated prices of some paintings to cause astonishment, takes visitors to the room with the puzzle pictures, shows them a few unusual relics, and provides special entertainment with some mechanical curios.

This time he had taken charge of the lady's servants and some other people of this type, and he was more successful in entertaining them than we were with our group. Finally he had a piece performed for his audience by a mechanical drummer that my uncle had long before banished to a storage room! Our refined group also gathered around, and they all found this insipid spectacle delightful. And so night came before they had seen even a third of the collection. The visitors could not possibly stay another day! They hurried back to the inn, and we spent the evening by ourselves.

And now we could speak our minds! We traded stories and reviewed our visitors' spiteful comments. Our guests may not always have been kind in their judgment of our pictures, but I must confess that we were not very kind in our judgment of the viewers either.

Caroline was especially peeved because she had not succeeded in diverting the young gentleman's attention from his distant sweetheart to herself. I told her that in my opinion there was nothing more excruciating for a girl than having to listen to a love poem addressed to another woman. Yet she insisted that she had found it to be a beautiful and edifying experience, that her lover was absent too, and that she hoped his conduct in the presence of other girls was as exemplary as the young stranger's.

Then as we ate a cold supper—during which we did not forget to drink to your health—our young friend was asked to present his system for categorizing artists and art lovers, which he did after some hesitation. I can't go into the matter now because I'm getting writer's cramp and am exhausted. Also, I want to see if I can't get out of this obligation. Telling you about our visitors' quirks was tolerable, but I hesitate to get more deeply involved. So, for today, I beg your indulgence if I slip away quietly.

Julie

Eighth Letter (Julie to the editor.)

Once again Julie's handwriting! However, today I am doing it willingly. One might even say I'm writing to you simply to spite the men. After my stubborn refusal yesterday to take on the last part of the job and write up the second part of our account, they decided to have a serious scholarly session tonight to discuss the matter fully and help me with my report to you. Now that the men have generously agreed to do their share, I have taken heart and feel qualified to do the job myself. There will be a pleasant surprise for them tonight, I hope! Men plan so many things, yet they would never carry them through if women did not step in at the right moment and graciously assist them in these tasks that are easy to begin but difficult to complete.

Something peculiar happened when we tried to classify the art lovers who visited us yesterday. They didn't fit anywhere, we simply couldn't find a category for them.

When we confronted our philosopher with this fact, he said: "My system may be flawed, but it is to its credit that with the exception of Mr. Characteristic none of the visitors fits into my categories. These categories comprise various kinds of one-sidedness, which must be considered shortcomings if the artist is limited by nature, and flaws if he deliberately persists in his limitation. But pretentiousness, eccentricity and incongruity are not provided for in my system. My six categories designate the qualities which, all combined, would describe the true artist as well as the true connoisseur. Unfortunately, as I know from my scant experience and as our observations confirm, they all too often occur singly."

Now down to business!

First Category: *Imitators*

Imitation can be considered the basis of the visual arts. Whether imitation was the origin, is another question. If the artist starts out as an imitator, he may yet rise to the highest level. If he stays with imitation we may call him a Copyist, thus attaching a somewhat disparaging connotation to the term. If a person with this bent feels the desire to progress only within his limited area of interest, he will see the need for utmost realism; the artist will strive to achieve it, and the art lover will want to experience it. If they fail to find the transition to true art, they will go completely astray. The artist will end up painting statues; the art lover will have himself immortalized in a damask dressing gown, as our dear grandfather did.

A predilection for silhouettes is related to imitation. A collection of them may be interesting if kept in a portfolio. But let's not decorate walls with these sad, half-real specters!

The Imitator only reproduces the subject, without adding anything to it or telling us anything beyond the obvious. He draws us into a single, very limited world; we marvel at his being able to do this, and it provides us with some pleasure. But the work cannot really satisfy us because it lacks the beautiful radiance of artistic truth. If this radiance is present, even just a trace, the work has great charm, as we can see from many German, Dutch and French portraits and still lifes.

(N.B. Don't be misled and imagine that I thought all this up by myself just because you see my handwriting! At first, I wanted to underline what I copied verbatim from the notes I have. But that would have required too much underlining. Besides, I'm sure you will notice when I am simply quoting; you may even find your own words from your letter.)

Second Category: *Imaginers*

Our friends had a lot of fun with this group. Somehow the category seemed to cause them to go a little overboard! Although I was sitting right there and confessed that I belonged to this group and asked them to be just and polite, I could not prevent them from coming up with quite a number of terms, by no means all of which were laudatory. They called them for example Poeticizers, for instead of recognizing the poetic side of the visual arts and taking that as a guide, they compete with poets by chasing after effects which are the domain of poetry, while failing to understand and exploit the strengths of their own art. They called them Illusionizers because they strive for illusionary effects and try to cater to the imagination without worrying about substance. They called them Phantomists because they were attracted by empty phantoms; Phantasmists because dreamlike distortions and incoherence are always in evidence; Nebulists because they depend on clouds to provide their airy visions with an appropriate context.

They finally even resorted to alliteration and word play to ridicule my Imaginers, calling them the Heads-in-the-Clouds-Crowd! They insisted that they were without substance, belonged neither here nor there and lacked both artistic truth and the beauty of reality.

If a false naturalism was attributed to the Imitators, the Imaginers were reproved for falsifying nature, and similar shortcomings. Of course I realized that the men wanted to tease me, but I still did them the favor of losing my temper.

I asked them if genius did not manifest itself primarily through inventiveness? If they could deny this gift in the Poeticizers? If we should not be grateful when the mind was delighted by fantasy? If this quality which they were maligning with so many peculiar labels was not the basis of the highest art? If it was not the potential road to it? If there was anything more powerful to counteract the tedium of the prosaic than this capacity to create new worlds? If it was not a rare talent? Even if it had gone astray, should we not talk about it with reverence?

The gentlemen soon surrendered. They reminded me that they were only speaking of one-sidedness; that this very quality, precisely because it could be so beneficial to the whole of art, was so much more damaging when it claimed to be self-contained, autonomous and independent. The Imitator, they said, never harms art because with his efforts he brings it to a level where the true artist can and must assume responsibility. The Imaginer, on the other hand, does infinite harm because he pushes art beyond its limits, where only the greatest genius can reclaim it from vagueness and boundlessness and lead it back toward its true essence and its own proscribed domain.

There was some more argument back and forth, and finally they asked me if I didn't have to admit that satirical caricature (an aberration that was most damaging to art, taste and morals) had developed in this manner and was continuing to do so?

Of course I could not defend caricature, although I cannot deny that this ugly stuff sometimes amuses me, and that gloating, this original and favorite sin of all of Adam's children, is a rather savory dish!

But back to my report!

Third Category: *Characterizers*

You are already familiar with this group, since you have received enough information about the argument the other day with a remarkable representative of the category.

This group can certainly count on my approval. For if my beloved Imaginers supposedly play with character traits, then something characteristic must be present in the first place. If I am to enjoy the significant, then I can certainly accept treating the significant seriously. If these Character people pave the way for my Poeticizers and save them from becoming Phantasmists or even members of the Heads-in-the-Clouds-Crowd—more power to them!

Since his last conversation with Mr. Characteristic, my uncle seems to like him better, and he defended this group. He suggested that in a certain sense they could be called Rigorists. He claimed that their method of abstracting, of reducing matters to basic principles was always instructive and productive, and that compared to the shallowness of some other types of artists and art lovers, the Characterizers were especially valuable.

But our stubborn young philosopher balked again, and said that their one-sidedness, precisely because they seemed to be right, was doing more harm by limiting art than the expansiveness of the Imaginers. He assured us he would not renounce his feud with them.

It is a strange thing about philosophers; they seem so flexible in certain matters and so unbending in others. If I could only figure them out!

Looking through his notes, I see that he has attached all sorts of outlandish labels to the Characterizers. He calls them Skeletonizers, Angularists and Pedants, and he says in one place that a purely logical perspective, a purely intellectual approach in art is neither sufficient nor helpful. I am not going to wrack my brain figuring out what he means!

Furthermore, he claims that the Characterizers lack the fine, light touch without which art is unimaginable. I think I can agree with him there.

Fourth Category: *Undulators*

This name was given to those who stand in contrast to the last group. Their fondness for the soft and pleasant that is without character and significance provides at most a trite charm. We also called them Serpentiners,[13] thinking of the time when people considered the Serpentine Line the model and symbol of beauty and believed this represented a step forward. The preference for serpentine lines and softness in the artist as well as in the art lover is due to a certain frailty, indolence and, if you will, an unhealthy sensitivity. Works of art in this category impress those who want to see only a little more than nothing in a picture, whose most pleasant feelings are aroused when they see a colorful soap bubble floating through the air. Since works of this type can hardly have substance or real content, their value usually depends on technique and a certain superficial charm. They have neither significance nor impact, and that is why they are generally welcome, like a shallow but pleasant charmer at a party. After all, small talk is meant to be only a little more than nothing.

As soon as the artist or art lover devotes himself exclusively to this approach, art disappears like the sound of a vibrating string or like water in the sand.

His art becomes ever flatter and weaker. Colors in paintings fade, lines in engravings become indistinct, and so, in the end, to the delight of the delicate art lover, everything gradually turns to haze.

We did not dwell long on this category because my sister, as you know, is very serious about this matter and immediately gets annoyed if anyone disturbs her misty realm. Otherwise I would have tried to force the term Nebulists on this class and thus liberated my Imaginers. I hope, dear sirs, you will take that into consideration in the course of your revision.

Fifth Category: *Miniaturists*

The members of this class got off rather lightly. No one felt he had good reason for criticism. There were many things in their favor, not much to hold against them.

Their products, at least from a practical point of view, are really quite convenient. With the greatest of care, the artist fills a small space with tiny dots, and the art lover can store the result of many years' labor in a small box. If their work is good, the artists deserve the name Miniaturists. If they lack all artistic spirit, have no feeling for the whole and are incapable of lending their work unity, then the derogatory nickname Dotter is more fitting.

The Miniaturists still remain in the realm of true art. They are, however, similar to the Imitators in that they remind the true artist that the particular quality the Miniaturists possess is just one among the others he must have if he is to achieve perfection in his work.

I have just remembered that my uncle wrote you in some detail about this category. So let's not disturb those gentle souls any further and wish them expressiveness, significance and unity in their work!

Sixth Category: *Sketchers*

Since my uncle had already confessed to membership in this group, we were inclined not to be too harsh on them. However, he himself pointed out that the Sketchers could promote just as dangerous a one-sidedness in art as the champions in the other categories. Art should not merely speak to the mind by way of our visual sense, it should also satisfy the visual sense itself. Then the mind can join in and give its approval. But the Sketcher speaks directly to the mind and thus dazzles and delights the inexperienced. An interesting idea, presented vaguely and, as it were, symbolically, passes through the eyes without providing visual pleasure, stimulates the mind, wit and imagination, and the art lover, taken by surprise, sees what is not there. There can be no talk of design, proportion, form, character, expression, composition, harmony and execution, for all these qualities only seem to be present. Mind speaks to mind, and the means by which this should happen is rendered useless.

Fine sketches by great masters, those fascinating hieroglyphs, most often account for this predilection. But they gradually lead the true art lover to the threshold of true art, and once he has had a glimpse of what lies ahead, he will not go back. The aspiring artist has more to fear than the art lover if he continues to linger in the area of designing and sketching, for even though he gains admittance to the domain of true art most rapidly through this portal, he is most likely to run the risk of tarrying endlessly at the threshold.

Those are essentially my uncle's words.

But I have forgotten the names of the artists who, despite their promising talent, did not pass the threshold and so were never able to fulfill the hopes which were placed in them.

In my uncle's collection there is a special portfolio with drawings by artists who never progressed beyond the sketching stage. He said that an interesting study could be conducted by comparing their sketches to those of great masters, who were able to complete their works.

After we had considered each of our six categories individually for some time, we tried to combine various characteristics from different categories, as they are often combined in individual artists—something I have touched on in the course of my report. The Imitator sometimes joined the Miniaturist, sometimes the Characterizer. The Sketcher might make common cause with the Imaginer, Skeletonizer or Undulator, and the last felt quite comfortable in the company of the Phantomist.

Any combination brought about a higher work of art than did absolute one-sidedness, a quality which is actually quite rare, as we realized when we tried to find examples.

In this way we had soon proven our original hypothesis. Only a combination of all six categories produces the perfect artist, and the true connoisseur must embrace all six categories.

The first half of our six groups is too serious, rigid and constrained; the other half is too playful, easygoing and casual. True art can result only from a close union of seriousness and play.[14] If we line up truly opposite categories, we get the following:

Imitator—Imaginer
Characterizer—Undulator
Miniaturist—Sketcher

Each pair then represents one of the three requirements for a great work of art, as the following general diagram shows:

Seriousness	*Seriousness and Play*	*Play*
alone	combined	alone
one-sidedness	development towards diversity	one-sidedness
manner	style	manner
Imitators	Artistic Truth	Phantomists
Characterizers	Beauty	Undulators
Miniaturists	Perfection	Sketchers

So there you have a complete overview! I am finished with my assignment. I will take my leave of you as quickly as possible this time, since I am convinced my report is only the beginning and that discussions both pro and con must start at the very place where I leave off. The other matter of concern to me—a confession which really has nothing to do with art—I will deal with shortly in a separate letter. I'll need a new quill for that, since this one is so worn I have to use the back to sign a name which I hope you will look upon with as much favor as ever,

Julie

PART TWO
Essays on Literature

I
LITERARY CRITICISM

Shakespeare: A Tribute[1] (1771)

It seems to me that the noblest of our sentiments is the hope of continuing to exist even after destiny has apparently returned us to a state of non-existence. This life, gentlemen, is too short. Proof of this is the fact that man, whether prince or pauper, sage or simpleton, will tire of everything but living, and the fact that no one attains the goal he has so ardently sought. Even if things go well for a time along the way, finally, often within reach of one's objective, one stumbles into a trap set by God knows who—and counts for nothing.

Count for nothing? I, who mean everything to myself! Everything I know, I know only through myself! Thus exclaim those who have self-awareness, striding briskly along life's path in preparation for the unending path beyond. Of course, each advances at his own speed. While the one sallies forth at a lively pace, the other dons seven-league boots and overtakes him, and two steps bring him as far as a day's journey the first. Be this as it may, this persevering wanderer remains our friend and companion while we observe and admire the other's gigantic strides, following his trail and comparing his stride with our own.

Let's set out on our journey, gentlemen! Examining a single footprint of that kind excites and inspires us more than gawking at a royal parade of thousands.

Today we honor the memory of the greatest wanderer, and in so doing we honor ourselves. For we carry within us the seeds of the achievements we value in others.

Do not expect me to write much or in an orderly way. Peace of mind is no festive robe. And as yet, I have not thought much about Shakespeare. Vague notions and feelings are the most I have been capable of. The first page I read made me a slave to Shakespeare for life. And when I had finished reading the first drama, I stood there like a man blind from birth whom a magic hand has all at once given light. I realized and felt intensely that my life was infinitely expanded. Everything seemed new to me, unfamiliar, and the unaccustomed light hurt my eyes. Gradually I learned to see, and, thanks to my awakened spirit, I still feel intensely what I have gained.

I never doubted for a moment that I would renounce the traditional theater. The unity of place seemed to me an oppressive prison, the unities of action and time burdensome fetters on our imagination. I struggled free—and knew for the first time that I had hands and feet. And now when I saw what harm the keepers of the rules had done me in their dungeon, and how many free spirits were still cowering there—my heart would have burst had I not declared war on them, had I not tried daily to destroy their prison towers.

The Greek theater, which the French took as their model, was so constituted internally and externally that it would have been easier for a marquis to imitate Alcibiades[2] than for Corneille to follow Sophocles.

First in the service of religion, then solemnly political, the tragedy presented to the people with the simplicity of perfection great individual deeds of their forefathers. It aroused feelings of wholeness and greatness in the soul, for it was itself whole and great.

And in what souls!

Greek souls! I cannot find words to describe what that means, but I can feel it, and for brevity's sake I refer to Homer and Sophocles and Theocritus, who taught me to feel what it means.

Now I hasten to add: "Little Frenchman, why are you wearing Greek armor? It is much too big and heavy for you."

That is why all French tragedies are parodies of themselves.

How regulated everything is! They resemble each other like shoes and are not without their boring spots, typically in the fourth act—but sad to say, you gentlemen know that from your own experience, and I say no more.

I don't know who first had the idea of putting historical-political spectacles on the stage; that is a good question for anyone interested in writing a scholarly treatise. Whether or not the honor of being the originator falls to Shakespeare, it was he who raised this type of drama to a level that we must still take to be the highest, totally beyond the imagination of most. And so there is little chance that anyone will match, much less surpass him.

Shakespeare, my friend, if you were still among us, I would want to be nowhere but in your company. How happy I would be playing the supporting role of Pylades to your Orestes, rather than that of the most venerated high priest in the temple of Delphi.

I will stop now, gentlemen, and continue writing tomorrow, for I have struck an emotional chord which you may not find edifying.

Shakespeare's theater is a colorful gallery[3] where the history of the world passes before our eyes on the invisible thread of time. The structure of his plays, in the accepted sense of the word, is no structure at all. Yet each revolves around an invisible point which no philosopher has discovered or defined and where the characteristic quality of our being, our presumed free will, collides with the inevitable course of the whole. Our corrupted taste, however, so beclouds our vision that we almost require a new Creation to escape the Darkness.

No Frenchmen, or Germans infected by their tastes, not even Wieland,[4] have come off very honorably in this regard, or in others either. Voltaire, who has always specialized in lese majesty, has proved himself here as well to be a veritable Thersites.[5] If I were Ulysses, he would cringe under the blows of my scepter.

Most of these gentlemen take particular offense at Shakespeare's characters.

But I cry: Nature! Nature! Nothing is so like Nature as Shakespeare's figures.

Now they're coming at me from all sides!

If they would only give me room so that I can breathe and speak!

Shakespeare competes with Prometheus, imitating him by forming human beings feature by feature, but on a colossal scale—that is why we don't recognize them as our brothers. Then he brings them to life by breathing his spirit into them. He speaks through them all, and we recognize the kinship.

And how can our century dare judge Nature? How should we know Nature, we who from childhood have felt in ourselves and seen in others nothing but restraint and artificiality? I often feel shamed by Shakespeare, for it sometimes happens that at first glance I think, "I would have done that differently." Later I recognize that I am a poor wretch, that Nature proclaims her wisdom through Shakespeare, and that my characters are mere soap bubbles whafted about by fanciful whims.

Now let me finish—though I haven't even started yet.

What noble philosophers have said about the world applies to Shakespeare too: What we call evil is only the other side of good; evil is necessary for good to exist and is part of the whole, just as the tropics must be torrid and Lapland frigid for there to be a temperate zone. He guides us through the entire world, yet we pampered novices cry out at the sight of a grasshopper: "Master, it's going to eat us alive!"[6]

To work, gentlemen! Take your trumpets and drive forth those noble souls from the Elysium of so-called good taste, where, drowsy in monotonous twilight, they live, yet do not live; have passions in their hearts but no marrow in their bones, and, because they are not tired enough to rest and yet too lazy to act, they stroll aimlessly among the myrtles and laurels, idling and yawning away their shadowy lives.

Shakespeare Once Again[1] (1815)

So much has been said about Shakespeare that it would seem nothing more could be added. And yet it is characteristic of ideas that they stimulate new ideas. On this occasion, I intend to discuss Shakespeare from more than one point of view: first as a poet in general, then in comparison to ancient and contemporary writers, and finally as a playwright. I shall attempt to establish what effect the imitation of his style has actually had on us, and what effect it is able to produce. I shall express my agreement with existing opinions by reiterating them; my disagreements I shall state briefly and in a positive spirit, without engaging in polemics. Let me proceed to the first of these items.

I. Shakespeare as a Poet

The highest goal man can achieve is the awareness of his own attitudes and ideas—knowledge of himself which provides him with the means to gain intimate knowledge of the minds of others. There are people who have an innate talent for this and who, through experience, develop and refine it for practical purposes, deriving from it an ability to profit mainly from worldly matters. The poet too is born with this talent, except that he does not develop it for practical and mundane purposes, but rather for a higher, spiritual, universal one. By calling Shakespeare one of the greatest poets, we imply that there were few who perceived the world as he did, few who, by expressing their visions, allowed the reader to share so fully in their awareness of the world. Shakespeare makes the world completely transparent for us. All of a sudden, we find ourselves the confidants of virtue and vice, greatness, pettiness, nobility, and depravation—and all this, and even more, by the simplest of means. If we try to determine what those means are, it seems at first as if Shakespeare were appealing to our visual perception. But that is a delusion. Shakespeare does not write for the eye. Let me attempt to explain what I mean.

The eye may be called the most perceptive of our senses, and hence the most effective means of communication. But the inner sense is even more perceptive, and it is to this sense that the word speaks most directly. After all, it is the word that comes to our aid when the object which our eyes perceive is strange and incomprehensible. Shakespeare addresses our inner sense, which immediately activates our creative imagination and brings about a total effect which is inexplicable to us. And that is the cause of the delusion I referred to, the impression that everything is happening right before our eyes. But if we examine Shakespeare's works carefully, we find that they contain much more action conveyed by the word than physical action. He makes things happen which are easily imagined, indeed are better imagined than seen.

Hamlet's ghost, Macbeth's witches, many a gruesome scene become meaningful only through the power of the imagination, and this is true of many minor scenes as well. When reading we readily accept such things as a matter of course, whereas during a stage performance we may find them disturbing, even repugnant.

Shakespeare achieves his effects through the living word, and the living word is best conveyed by reading aloud because then the listener is not distracted by either a skillful or an awkward stage presentation. There is no higher or purer pleasure than listening with closed eyes to a naturally expressive voice reciting, not declaiming, a Shakespeare play.[2] We follow the simple thread of the plot and the unfolding events. To be sure, the description of certain characters causes us to form mental images of them, but actually, we are supposed to discover what is happening in the characters' minds through a sequence of words and speeches. All participants seem to have agreed among themselves not to leave us in the dark about anything. Heroes and foot soldiers, gentlemen and slaves, kings and messengers, all conspire to achieve this end. We may even say that minor figures are often more active in this regard than leading ones. Everything that fills the air, unspoken, during a historical event, everything that is lurking in the human heart in moments of great distress—it is all expressed in words. What the mind anxiously represses and conceals is revealed frankly and without inhibition. We experience the truth of life, and we do not know how.

Shakespeare resembles the world spirit in that he permeates the world as it does, and nothing remains hidden from either. But whereas it is the task of the world spirit to keep secrets before, and even after, the event, it is the poet's calling to reveal secrets and to take us into his confidence, if not before, then certainly during the event. The depraved man in power, the well-meaning dullard, the passionately involved man, the detached observer—they all wear their hearts on their sleeves, often improbably so. Everyone is eloquent and loquacious, and come what may, the secret must out, even if the stones have to speak! The inanimate world too is eager to hold forth, and all things participate: natural phenomena of heaven, earth and sea, and thunder and lightning. Wild beasts lift their voices, often seemingly as imagery, yet always as part of the revelation.

Even the civilized world must surrender its treasures. Art and science, craft and trade, they all bear gifts. Shakespeare's works are one great bustling fair, and he owes the richness of his wares to his native land.

England is ever present in Shakespeare's works, this land, surrounded by the sea, shrouded in mist and clouds, active in all corners of the earth. The poet lived during a great and important era, and he portrayed its culture, strengths and even weaknesses in a positive spirit. Indeed, he could not have such an effect on us had he not been a true child of his time. No one has more disdain for externals than he; his interest is directed toward man's inner self, and here all human beings are alike. Shakespeare's portrayal of Romans has been called superb. I disagree. His Romans are all Englishmen through and through—but they are human beings, thoroughly human, and may just as well wear the Roman toga as any other costume. Once we have accepted that, we look upon Shakespeare's anachronisms as admirable, for it is precisely his disregard for externals which makes his works so true to life.

I trust these few words will suffice, although they by no means do complete justice to Shakespeare's accomplishments. His friends and admirers will have much more to add. Let me conclude this part with the following observation: It would prove difficult to find another poet whose every work is based on a different idea which pervades the whole drama.

Coriolanus, for example, is permeated by anger at the refusal of the masses to recognize the superiority of able men. In *Julius Caesar,* everything hinges on the idea that able men refuse to accept a leader because they wrongly assume they can rule as a group. *Anthony and Cleopatra* says with a thousand tongues that pleasure and action are incompatible. We could continue in this vein and find ever more reasons for admiring Shakespeare.

II. Shakespeare in Comparison to Ancient and Contemporary Writers

What inspires Shakespeare's great mind is the real world. To be sure, he intersperses magical elements throughout his works at appropriate moments, and we do find soothsaying and madness, dreams, premonitions, omens, fairies and gnomes, ghosts, demons and sorcerers. But by no means do these chimera play a major role in his works. Rather, it is the reality of Shakespeare's own world and its vitality which form the broad basis of his writings—hence our impression of their genuineness and concreteness. This has led to the conclusion that Shakespeare is not so much a modern poet, a romantic,[3] as a representative of the 'naive' school because his values are rooted in the here and now, and because he hardly ever approaches the realm of romantic yearning, and if he does, only very gingerly.

Nevertheless, upon closer scrutiny we realize that Shakespeare is very much a modern writer, far removed from the ancients. The tremendous gulf separating him from them has nothing to do with literary form—which is really not to the point here—but rather with the essence of his writings, their innermost spirit.

Before I proceed, I wish to emphasize that it is not my intention to present the terminology I use as exhaustive or definitive, nor do I intend to add a new antithesis to those already known to us. The antithesis I am going to discuss is already contained in the existing ones, as we shall see. These antitheses are:

ancient	modern
naive	sentimental
pagan	Christian
heroic	romantic
real	ideal
necessity	freedom
moral obligation *(Sollen)*	desire *(Wollen)*

The greatest and most common torment man may encounter springs from the conflict between moral obligation and desire, but also between moral obligation and its fulfillment, and between desire and its fulfillment. The last two are the cause of so much inner confusion throughout man's life. The superficial confusion that results from casual errors and can be resolved easily and without serious consequences is the source of comic situations. Serious dilemmas, unresolvable or unresolved, produce our tragic moments.

The predominant conflict in ancient literature is the one between moral obligation and its fulfillment, in modern literature between desire and fulfillment. For the moment, let us incorporate them in the other antitheses to see what results. I submit that in both ancient and modern times, sometimes one category, sometimes the other is predominant. However, since no absolute separation can be made between moral obligation and desire in man, it is only logical that both must always exist side by side, although one may be predominant and the other subordinate. Moral obligation is imposed on man: it is a hard master; desire man creates for himself: his will is his heaven. A persistent moral obligation is bothersome, and not being able to fulfill it is frightful; a persistent desire is pleasant, and with a good measure of will power one may even get over the lack of fulfillment. Let us look at card games as a type of literature, since we find these two elements there too. The rules of the game in combination with chance represent obligation, which for the ancients was represented by fate. Desire in combination with the player's skill counteracts obligation. In this respect, I am tempted to call the game of whist ancient. The rules of the game put limitations on chance, even on desire. With a given number of partners and opponents and the cards that have been dealt me I must control a number of unavoidable chance happenings. In other card games, such as ombre, it is just the opposite. There are no limits on my desire and daring because I can revoke my hand, assign different values to my cards, discard some or all of them, count on luck, and even turn the worst hand into a winning one. This type of game closely resembles modern thinking and modern literature.

Ancient tragedy is based on an inescapable moral obligation which can only intensify and gain momentum if it clashes with an opposing desire. Essentially, this is where the frightfulness of the oracles resides, a domain where *Oedipus* reigns supreme. In *Antigone,* however, obligation in the form of duty seems less harsh. Indeed, there are many variants of obligation, but it is always despotic, no matter whether it is embodied by reason, as in moral code or civil law, or by nature, as in the laws of birth, growth and decay, of life and death. We recoil from all these laws, without realizing that they serve the welfare of the whole. Desire, on the other hand, is free, is perceived as free and favors the individual. Therefore desire is insidious, and it took possession of man as soon as he encountered it. Desire is the god of modern times. Having become his worshippers, we are afraid of the opposing force, and that is the reason why our art and our way of thinking will always remain distinct from those of the ancients. Through moral obligation tragedy becomes great and powerful, through desire weak and insignificant. Desire gave rise not to tragedy but to so-called drama, in which desire takes the place of awesome moral obligation. But precisely because desire comes to the aid of our weakness, we feel grateful when in the end, after painful expectation, we receive some pitiful consolation.

If after these preliminary observations we return to Shakespeare, it is with the hope that the reader himself will be conducting his own comparisons and applying my theories. Shakespeare is indeed unique in that he fuses ancient and modern with such exuberance. In his plays, obligation and desire clearly try to counterbalance each other. Both are powerful contestants, yet Shakespeare always sees to it that desire remains at a disadvantage.

Perhaps no other poet has portrayed more magnificently the underlying connection between desire and moral obligation in individuals. As a character with a role in life, the individual is under an obligation, that is, he is constrained, destined for a specific function. Yet as a human being, he has desires; he is unconstrained, and his desires have no specific target. Already at this point, an inner conflict arises, and Shakespeare gives it special emphasis. But then an external conflict is added, a conflict which is often aggravated by the fact that, for various reasons, an unrealizable desire is raised to the level of a compelling obligation. I refer the reader to my earlier discussion of *Hamlet*[4] where I demonstrated this theory. The principle applies broadly in Shakespeare, however. Many of his characters get into predicaments which they are not equipped to handle. Hamlet does so because of the ghost, Macbeth because of the witches, Hecate[5] and the superwitch, his wife, and Brutus because of his friends. Even in *Coriolanus* we find a similar pattern. In short, we may say that the motif of desire that overpowers the individual is characteristically modern. But since Shakespeare permits this desire to originate from without rather than from within, it becomes a type of obligation close to the ancients' concept. All protagonists in ancient literature desire only what is humanly possible, and that is the reason for the beautiful balance between desire, obligation, and fulfillment. However, their sense of obligation tends to strike us as too extreme and unconvincing, and as a result, despite our admiration, we are not deeply affected. A necessity that excludes freedom to some extent, or altogether, no longer appeals to our modern sensibilities. Shakespeare, on the other hand, closely approximates the modern view. To our amazement and joy, he fuses the ancient and the modern by changing necessity to moral necessity. If we want to learn anything from Shakespeare, this should be the subject of study. I do not wish to chide or condemn our modern romantic literature, but I do maintain that it is extolled, unjustifiedly, as the exclusive model to follow and is praised beyond its merits, which obscures and distorts its strong, robust and admirable features. Instead, we should endeavor to reconcile that great and seemingly irreconcilable antithesis of modern and ancient, especially since a great and peerless master—whom we hold in such high regard and often praise without really knowing why—has already wrought the miracle. Of course, Shakespeare enjoyed the advantage of living in a creative age and in a vigorous Protestant country where the madness of bigotry was silent for a while and where, therefore, a true believer in Nature like Shakespeare was free to develop his pure inner self religiously without paying tribute to any organized religion.

The above remarks were written during the summer of 1813, and I ask the reader not to carp and criticize, but rather bear in mind that they represent only one individual's attempt to point out the different ways various poets have tried to reconcile and resolve that immense antithesis which has assumed so many guises. To say more would be superfluous, especially if we consider that since the time this was written, so much has been said about the subject, and so many excellent explanations have been proffered. I refer particularly to Blümner's[6] commendable treatise, 'On the Concept of Fate in the Tragedies of Aeschylus,' and its excellent review in the supplement of the *Jenaische Literaturzeitung*. I shall now proceed to my third point, which deals directly with German theater and with Schiller's resolution to make it thrive in the future.[7]

III. Shakespeare as Playwright

To the lover of the arts, the enjoyment of any work means savoring it as a whole. That is to say, he submits to its total impact and is imbued by the sense of unity the artist has given it. The critic, on the other hand, must analyse and dissect it because his purpose is to evaluate and judge, to teach and inform. I tried to do justice to this requirement when I discussed Shakespeare first as a poet in general, and then in comparison with ancient and modern writers. Now I wish to proceed to my third and last point, Shakespeare as a playwright.

To be sure, Shakespeare's fame and accomplishments are part of the history of literature. But we are doing an injustice to all playwrights before and after him if we record his achievements exclusively in the history of the theater.

A universally recognized genius may use his talents in a problematical way; not everything the master does is masterful. While Shakespeare's name is an essential part of the history of literature, he is only a peripheral part of the history of the theater. Yet, since he absolutely deserves our admiration as a writer for the theater, we must examine the conditions under which he had to write, but without extolling those conditions as virtues or models.

There are closely related literary forms which in practice are often combined, such as epic, dialog, drama, and stage play. The epic requires oral delivery by one individual to an audience; dialog requires conversation in a closed circle to which an audience is allowed to listen; drama requires conversation supported by action, even if the action is only created by our imagination; a stage play requires all three together, and insofar as it also involves our visual sense, it can be effective as long as it presents a locale and characters to which we can relate.

In this sense, Shakespeare's works are predominantly drama. His method of revealing what happens in mind and soul captivates the reader. Stage requirements are unimportant to Shakespeare, so he does not pay much attention to them, nor do we as we read. We skip along from locale to locale, our imagination fills in all the episodes he omits, and we are even grateful to him for stimulating our minds in such a rewarding way. By presenting everything in the form of a stage play, Shakespeare facilitates the task of our imagination, for we are more familiar with the "stage that represents the world" than with the world itself. No matter how fantastic the things we read and hear, we still think that they would be effective in the theater, which might explain why so many bad plays have been adapted from popular novels.

However, strictly speaking, nothing is truly suitable to the theater which is not also perceived as symbolic: an important action which anticipates an even more important one. That Shakespeare knew how to achieve this supreme effect is evident in the scene where the heir to the throne takes the crown from the side of his sleeping, dying father, puts it on his own head and struts off.[8] But such symbolic episodes are few, are isolated jewels in the midst of quantities of material which is not suitable for presentation on the stage. As a matter of fact, the stage almost always presents an obstacle to Shakespeare's creativity. His great talent is that of an epitomizer, one who extracts the essence, and since the poet is the very epitomizer of nature, we must acknowledge Shakespeare's great accomplishment in this regard as well. At the same time however—and this reflects well on him—we must reject the notion that the stage is a vehicle worthy of his genius. Yet it is precisely the limitations of the stage which force him to discipline his poetic talent. In adjusting to these constraints, he does not choose specific material for a specific work as some writers do, but rather, he decides on one idea as the central point, and then makes the world and the universe relate to it. His method of condensing events of ancient and modern history enables him to use material from any chronicle, sometimes even following his source verbatim. He does not proceed as conscientiously with tales, as is evident in *Hamlet*. *Romeo and Juliet* is closer to the original, yet he all but destroys its tragic quality by introducing two comic characters, Mercutio and the Nurse, roles which were probably played by two popular actors, the Nurse most likely by a man. Upon close examination of the play's structure, we notice that these two characters and all that relates to them only appear in farcial interludes, which we find objectionable on the stage, since we are accustomed to a logical, consistent way of thinking.[9]

Shakespeare is most impressive when he revises and adapts existing plays. This can be clearly shown in *King John* and *King Lear* by comparing them with the older versions.[10] But even in these instances, Shakespeare is again more poet than playwright.

In conclusion, let me proceed to the solution of the riddle. The imperfections of the English stage in Shakespeare's time have been well established by scholars. There was no demand at all to strive for realism as we know it, which became possible gradually through improvements in machinery and in the art of perspective and costuming. It would be very difficult for us to return to that early, rudimentary stage, for we could not possibly sit in front of a bare scaffolding with simple props which only suggest reality, with a green curtain symbolizing the king's chamber, and a trumpeter who keeps trumpeting at regular intervals, and the like. What present-day audience would tolerate that? Staged under such conditions, Shakespeare's plays were fascinating fairytales, told by a limited number of persons who wore costumes for better effect and characterization and who moved about, entered and exited when necessary. It was left to the spectator to imagine the countryside and the royal court on the barren stage.

Schröder[11] gained the distinction of having introduced Shakespeare's plays to the German stage solely by becoming the epitomizer of Shakespeare the epitomizer! Schröder used only what is effective on the stage and discarded everything else, even some essential things if he thought they would not produce the proper effect on his countrymen or would seem to contradict the spirit of his time. For example, it is true that by excising the first scenes of *King Lear* he destroyed the essence of the play. But he was justified in doing so, for in the first scene, King Lear seems so absurd that in the subsequent parts of the play we cannot altogether condemn his daughters' actions. We feel sorry for the old man, but we do not feel profound pity for him. And that was Schröder's intent: to arouse our pity for Lear and our abhorrence for the daughters who are indeed unnatural but by no means totally culpable.

In the source Shakespeare adapted, this scene produces the most delightful effects later in the play. Lear flees to France, while daughter and son-in-law, succumbing to some romantic whim, set out on a pilgrimage to the seashore and meet the old man, who does not recognize them. Here everything turns sweet, while Shakespeare's penchant for the tragic turns it bitter. A comparison of the two plays is always a source of pleasure for the critical reader.

For many years the misguided notion has been gaining ground in Germany that if Shakespeare's plays are performed on the German stage, not a single word must be omitted even though that may make actors and audience choke. Attempts to put this notion into practice, prompted by an excellent and accurate translation, have resulted in failure everywhere. The serious and repeated efforts in the theater in Weimar are a case in point. If we want to see a truly Shakespearean play, we must return to Schröder's approach. Yet the senseless demand persists: when we perform Shakespeare, we must not omit the slightest detail! Should the proponents of this opinion prevail, Shakespeare will within a few years disappear from the German stage altogether. However, that would not be as deplorable as it may sound because the reader, in private or in the company of others, would delight in him in an even purer way.

An attempt has been made to adapt *Romeo and Juliet* for the theater in Weimar in accordance with the points discussed at length above. I shall describe the guiding principles of that venture at some future occasion. It will then perhaps become clear why the adaptation was unsuccessful, despite the fact that the staging is by no means difficult, although it must be handled with artistry and care. Similar projects are now in progress, but since persistent endeavors do not always produce immediate results, their impact may not be felt until some time in the future.

Laurence Sterne[1] (1827)

Given the rapid pace of general education today, we tend to forget those to whom we are indebted for providing us our initial stimulation and first influences. We believe that what exists and happens must exist and happen in just that way. But we stray onto the wrong path precisely because we lose sight of those who have shown us the right path. With that in mind, I would like to call attention to a man who helped initiate, and became the spokesman for, an era in the second half of the past century which produced more profound understanding of human nature, noble tolerance and gentle love.

This man, to whom I owe so much,[2] often comes to mind. I also think of him when there is talk of errors and truths—concepts which fluctuate constantly among mankind. We may add a third, less absolute term, namely idiosyncracies, for there are certain aspects of human behavior which are best characterized by this word. Idiosyncracies seem erroneous to the outsider, true to those who possess them, and on closer examination of great psychological importance. They are the qualities which constitute the individual. What is general becomes specific through these traits and, even at their most eccentric, there is still a shimmer of human intelligence, reason and good-will in them, which attracts and fascinates us.

Yorick-Sterne, that most sensitive observer of human nature, has coined a charming term for the idiosyncracies of human actions, calling them 'ruling passions.' And it is true, they are what drive the individual in a certain direction, push him along a single track and keep him ever alive and active, without need for reflection, conviction, purpose or will power. It is obvious how closely related this process is to habit, for habit, after all, provides a path of indolence along which our idiosyncracies can freely saunter.

On Byron's *Manfred*[1] (1820)

The tragedy *Manfred* by Byron impressed me as a wonderful, deeply moving work. This strangely brilliant poet has assimilated my *Faust*,[2] and in his melancholy way has drawn the strangest nourishment from it. He has used motifs which suited his purpose in his own way, with the result that none is the same anymore, and this is precisely the reason why I cannot praise him enough. The transformation is so complete that one could give highly interesting lectures on that subject alone and on the similarities and dissimilarities between his work and its model, though I cannot deny that the gloomy intensity of a boundless, profound despair gradually becomes somewhat wearisome. However, any dissatisfaction we may experience is always coupled with admiration and respect.

In this tragedy we find the quintessence of the attitudes and passions of a most remarkable talent born to suffer. Byron's way of life and his style of poetry hardly permit fair and impartial judgment. He has often enough confessed what tormented him and has portrayed it repeatedly, so that scarcely anyone sympathizes with his unbearable pain on which he harps incessantly.

Specifically, there are two women whose ghosts haunt him relentlessly, and in *Manfred* they also play an important role, one under the name of Astarte, the other without form and presence, a mere voice.

Of the terrible experience Byron had in his liaison with the first woman, the following is told: As a dashing, highly attractive young man, he won the affections of a Florentine lady; the husband found out and murdered her. But that same night, someone killed the murderer himself in the street, yet no suspect was found. Lord Byron departed from Florence, and such ghosts have been trailing after him ever since.

This incredible-sounding event is made to seem completely real to us through the countless allusions to it in his poems. Cruelly exacerbating his inner torment, for example, he sees his own life reflected in the fate of the king of Sparta. The story is as follows: Pausanias, a Lacedaemonian general, first gains glory for his important victory at Plataea, but because of his arrogance, stubbornness and crude behavior, he later loses favor with the Greeks, and because of his alleged secret dealings with the enemy, the trust of his countrymen. He becomes guilty of a heinous act which haunts him till his ignominious death. For while commanding the fleet of the Greek allies in the Black Sea, he had fallen desperately in love with a beautiful Byzantine girl. Her parents, after much resistance, finally had given their consent, and the girl was to be taken to the general at night. In her modesty she asks the servants to extinguish the light, and groping her way in the darkened room, she knocks over a lamp. Pausanias wakes up, and suspecting the presence of assassins, seizes his sword and slays his beloved. He is never able to forget the horrifying scene, and its memory pursues him so relentlessly that all appeals to gods and exorcists prove in vain.

What pain a poet's heart must endure if he chooses such a story from ancient times, makes it his own and burdens his dramatic alter ego with it. The following monologue, overflowing with discontent and despondency, now becomes comprehensible in the light of these remarks. We recommend it as a useful exercise in declamation. Here we have an intensified Hamlet. Skill is required, especially in setting off the interpolated material while maintaining the flow and sense of the whole. It will also be obvious that a certain impetuous, even eccentric expression is required to convey the poet's intent.[3]

We are the fools of time and terror: days
Steal on us and steal from us; yet we live
Loathing our life, and dreading still to die.
In all the days of this detested yoke—
This vital weight upon the struggling heart,
Which sinks with sorrow, or beats quick with pain,

Or joy that ends in agony or faintness—
In all the days of past and future, for
In life there is no present, we can number
How few—how less than few—wherein the soul
Forbears to pant for death, and yet draws back
As from a stream in winter, though the chill
Be but a moment's. I have no resource
Still in my science.......................................
..........and the Spartan Monarch drew
From the Byzantine maid's unsleeping spirit
An answer and his destiny—he slew,
That which he loved, unknowing what he slew,
And died unpardon'd.................................
If I had never lived, that which I love
Had still been living; had I never loved,
That which I love would still be beautiful—
Happy and giving happiness. What is she?
What is she now?—a sufferer for my sins—
A thing I dare not think upon—or nothing.

On Byron's *Cain*[1] (1824)

Having heard extraordinary things about this work for almost a year, I finally read it myself, and was filled with astonishment and admiration, an effect which all good, beautiful and great achievements have on truly receptive minds. I took pleasure in discussing it with friends, and resolved at the same time to say something about it publicly. However, the more deeply we penetrate the product of a mind like Byron's, the more we feel how difficult it is to describe it to ourselves, let alone to others. Perhaps I would have remained silent about this work, as I do about so many others of excellence, had not an external stimulus made me reconsider.

A Frenchman, Fabre d'Olivet, has translated *Cain* into unrhymed verse, and believes to have refuted its assumptions in a series of philosophical and critical notes. I have not, to be sure, laid eyes on this work, but the *Moniteur*[2] of October 30, 1823 sided with the poet, and in expressing views on certain passages that are completely in harmony with my own, rekindled my interest, as usually happens when we finally hear a sympathetic voice among the many that are indifferent and confused. For then we feel encouraged to express our approval. First, let us listen to the advocate himself:

"This scene, which builds to the climax of Eve's curse of Cain, is in our opinion evidence of the vigor and profundity of Byron's ideas. It reveals Cain as a son worthy of such a mother.

"Here the translator asks where the poet found his model for Eve. Lord Byron could answer: in human nature and through observation of human nature, as Corneille found his Cleopatra and the ancients their Medea, and in history which presents us with so many characters dominated by boundless passions.

"A keen observer of the human heart knows to what extent its varied emotions may go astray—especially in women, who seem equally unrestrained in good and evil. With this in mind, we certainly cannot accuse Byron of having sinned against truth or having willfully gone beyond what is plausible, even though he is dealing here with the newly created world and the first human family. He portrays a corrupted human being, while Milton describes with striking vividness a human being in a state of beauty and original purity.

"At the moment when the terrible curse passes Eve's lips—the episode for which Byron is criticized—she is no longer a paragon of perfection and innocence. The Tempter's venemous beguiling words have had their effect on her and have forever debased those magnificent qualities of mind and soul which the creator of life had destined for far nobler ends. At this point, pure, sweet contentment with herself has already changed to vanity, and the curiosity aroused by the enemy of mankind, which led to her fateful disobedience, has thwarted the creator's intentions and marred the crowning achievement of his creation.

"Eve's preference for Abel, and the frenzied maledictions she hurls at his murderer Cain are quite consistent with the person she has become. The weak but guiltless Abel, a reincarnation of the fallen Adam, must be dearer to his mother because he makes the humiliating memory of her transgression less painful for her. Cain, on the other hand, having inherited more of Eve's pride and having retained the strength that Adam has lost, suddenly stirs up all her memories and all her feelings of self. Mortally wounded in the object of her maternal preference, she lashes out in her pain at the murderer, although he is her own son. It is befitting for a genius as powerful as Lord Byron to depict this scene with such awesome veracity. He had to deal with it in this particular way, or not at all."

We can adopt this view without reservation and apply it, not just to this scene, but to the work as a whole. If Lord Byron wanted to write a *Cain,* he had to deal with the subject in this particular way, or not at all.

Since the work is now generally available in the original and in translation, we need not publicize or recommend it here. Nonetheless, we do feel impelled to make a few observations.

Lord Byron is a poet whose fervent mind penetrates with unequalled acuity into things past and present, and anticipates future events that may result from them. He has conquered new territories for his boundless talent, yet what he will accomplish in them is impossible to predict. However, we can define his approach to a certain extent.

Byron adheres strictly to biblical tradition. His first human couple gives up its original purity and state of innocence for a guilt of mysterious origin, and the resulting punishment is passed on to all descendants. This overwhelming burden is placed on the shoulders of Cain, the representative of discontent mankind that has been plunged into deep misery for no fault of its own. The first son, oppressed by such weighty knowledge, is especially troubled by the idea of death, of which he has as yet no clear concept. Although he may wish his present distress to end, he is repelled by the notion of exchanging it for a totally unfamiliar condition. From this we see that the first, uneasy son of man was already burdened with the full weight of a theology that attempts to explain and reconcile, and yet is always at odds with itself—the same theology that still preoccupies us today.

These disturbing thoughts so familiar to human beings rage within Cain's soul and cannot be banished by the devout meekness of his father and brother, or the loving, sympathetic assistance of his sister-bride. To intensify his inner turmoil beyond endurance, Satan approaches him, a powerfully seductive spirit, who first causes Cain moral uncertainty, but then takes him on a miraculous journey through time and space. He shows him the past as extraordinary and great, the present as small and insignificant, and the future as ominous and desolate.

Cain returns to his family where he finds everything as he left it. He himself is more perturbed, though morally no worse than before, and he finds Abel's insistence that he participate in an offering unbearable. We will say no more than that the scene in which Abel is killed is extremely well motivated and, as a result, what follows is equally impressive. There lies Abel! This is Death, of which so much has been said and of which mankind knows just as little as before!

But we should not forget that the coming of a saviour is suggested throughout the play. Thus in this regard, as in all others, the poet has indeed reflected our religious concepts and doctrines.

We have nothing to add to the French critic's eloquent words of praise for the scene with the parents in which Eve finally curses the speechless Cain, We need only express our admiration and awe regarding the end of the poem.

Let us quote an imaginative friend who shares our high esteem for Byron. She expressed the view that everything that can be said about religion and morality in this world is contained in the last three words of the play.[3]

Dante[1] (1826)

While recognizing the great qualities of mind and spirit in Dante, we shall nevertheless be aided in our appreciation of his works if we bear in mind that during his lifetime (he was a contemporary of Giotto) visual art re-emerged in all its natural vigor.[2] Dante too came under the sway of the markedly allegorical spirit evident in art. He grasped objects so clearly with his visual imagination that he could reproduce them in sharp outline. As a result, we behold even the most abstruse and the strangest things as if they were drawn from nature. Furthermore, the terza rima[3] rarely if ever causes him difficulty; rather, it helps him in one way or other to obtain his artistic objective and sharply delineate his characters. The German translator for the most part has followed him in this, has visualized the poem to be translated, and sought to do in his own language and his own rhymes whatever was necessary to convey the sense of the original. Any criticism I may have pertains to the poem itself.

The whole design of Dante's Hell has at the same time micro- and macroscopic dimensions, and confuses us. We are to imagine circles within circles extending from the top to the deepest abyss. But that immediately suggests an amphitheater which, no matter how immense, always presents itself to our imagination as something artistically confining, since from above we see clearly into the arena, but also the arena itself. If we look at Orcagna's frescos of Hell, we seem to be seeing in reverse a portrayal of Cebes' stages of the human soul.[4] Dante's concept has a more rhetorical than poetic effect: the imagination is aroused, but it is not satisfied.

While we cannot praise the whole, the strange richness of the individual locales surprises, amazes and confuses us, and finally, against our will, we are filled with admiration. Dante paints his scenery with the utmost exactitude and precision, and thus obscures our perspective as we proceed on our journey; yet we must praise his imaginativeness in the depiction of the physical properties of Hell and the description of the characters themselves, their punishments and torments. As an example we choose the 12th Canto.[5]

The place we reached to clamber down the cliff
  was alpine and, for what was there as well,
  such as all eyes would turn from with relief.
As is the landslip this side Trent, which fell
  on the Adige[6] in flank, through lack of prop
  it may be, or through earthquake (who can tell?);
for from the mountain-crest which let them drop,
  down to the plain the shattered rocks so lie
  as to afford some passage from the top;

So down by that discharge of stones we hied,
and oft, by reason of the unwonted load,
under my feet the scree would slip and slide.
I went bemused; and he: 'Perchance some food
for thought this ruin gives thee, where on guard
is set that bestial wrath I've just subdued.
Know, therefore, that the other time I fared
down here to lower hell, this precipice
not tumbled yet, still stood with face unscarr'd.

But of a truth, discern I not amiss,
shortly ere His descent, who the great spoil
of the utmost circle carried off from Dis,[7]
the gulf to its depth, through all its loathsome coil,
so trembled that the universe, methought,
felt love, which more than once in vast turmoil,
as some deem, hath the world to chaos brought:
and at that moment, both elsewhere and here,
on this old cliff the ruin thou seest was wrought.

First I should mention the following. Although in the original-language edition I own, published in Venice in 1739, the passage *e per quel* to *schiva* [lines 2 and 3 above] is interpreted as referring to the Minotaur,[8] I can only see it as a reference to the locale. The area was mountainous, alpine *(alpestro);* but that description was not vivid enough for the poet. What else there was *(per quel ch'iv' er' anco)* [line 2 above] was so terrible that it confused the eye and the mind. In order to clarify the spectacle for himself as a poet and for his readers, Dante mentions, not so much metaphorically but as a concrete example, a landslide that presumably had blocked the road from Trento to Verona in his day. Great slabs and boulders of jagged primeval rock were no doubt still newly piled up there. There they lay, not weather-beaten, nor overgrown and concealed by vegetation, but in such a way that the large individual pieces, resting precariously upon one another, could easily be made to teeter by the weight of a man. That is what happens here as Dante descends.

But the poet wants to present far more than a natural phenomenon. He uses Christ's descent into Hell as a convincing poetic means to bring about this and other landslides in the *Inferno*.

The wanderers now approach the river of blood, whose crescent course is bordered by a level beach, where as ferocious guards thousands of centaurs race about. Virgil has come close to Chiron[9] on the level ground, but Dante is still laboriously making his way among the rocks. We are made to look back at Dante when the centaur Chiron says to his companions:

'Have ye noticed how
the one behind there moves what he doth touch?
Thus are not wont a dead man's feet to do.'

Need we ask our imagination whether this immense mountain- and rock-slide seems completely real?

In the other cantos, in different settings, we can show just such emphasis and elaboration through the repeated use of similar situations. Parallel passages of this kind best demonstrate the very essence of Dante the poet.

The difference between the living Dante and the departed spirits becomes obvious at other times too, such as when the inhabitants of Purgatory are frightened because he casts a shadow, by which they recognize that he is alive.

On Calderon's *Daughter of the Air*[1] (1822)

De nugis hominum seria veritas
Uno volvitur assere.(Jacob Balde)[2]

The truth underlying the follies of man
Can be seen on a single stage.

And indeed, if one were looking for a story of human folly written in the elevated style of the stage, then this drama would no doubt be an excellent choice.

To be sure, we often get so carried away by the fine qualities in a work of art that we consider and proclaim any new examples of excellence we encounter to be the best of all. Yet this never proves harmful, because in order to substantiate our opinion we study the work lovingly and with even greater care in seeking to clarify its merits. That is why I do not hesitate to confess that in reading the *Daughter of the Air* I more than ever admired Calderon's talent and respected his lofty spirit and the clarity of his thinking. To be sure, it should be noted that the subject matter is superior to that of his other plays, since the plot involves strictly human motives, and nothing demonic is added except where necessary to develop and motivate the extraordinary, the excessive, in human nature. Only the beginning and the end are miraculous, everything else follows a natural course.

Whatever else can be said about this play applies to all of Calderon's works. There is no true realism; on the contrary, his plays are quite theatrical, even stagey. There is absolutely no trace of what we may call poetic illusion, especially the kind that appeals to our emotions. The structure is readily grasped, the scenes follow logically in a kind of choreography that is artistically satisfying, and reminiscent of techniques employed by our modern comic operas. The main inner motivation is always the same: a conflict of duties, of passions, of obligations which is produced by contrasting characters and circumstances.

The main action follows its majestic and poetic course. The minor scenes, which move along in graceful minuet-like patterns, are rhetorical, dialectical and sophistic. All human types are represented, including the fool, whose ordinary common sense immediately acts to destroy, if not indeed to prevent, any poetic illusion that lays claim to our sympathy and affection.

Upon closer reflection we must admit that in this kind of drama, human conditions, feelings and events cannot be presented on stage in their original natural state. They must first be modified, fashioned and refined, and are so presented here. Calderon stands at the threshold to an overly refined culture; he presents a quintessence.[3]

Shakespeare, on the other hand, offers us a full, ripe cluster from the vine. Whether we eat the grapes one by one, crush them, press them, drink them as juice or sip them as wine—we are refreshed whatever we do. In Calderon, however, nothing is left to the discretion of the audience. We are offered highly distilled spirits, seasoned with many spices and sweetened, and we must either accept the drink as it is, a zesty, delicious stimulant, or refuse it.

But the reason we so admire the *Daughter of the Air* has already been mentioned: it benefits from its excellent subject matter. Unfortunately, in a number of Calderon's other plays we find the highminded, enlightened poet forced to be a slave to solemn fanaticism and to embue irrationality with artistic purpose. This arouses unpleasant feelings of ambiguity towards the poet himself, since the material is offensive, while the treatment is delightful. *Devotion to the Cross* and *Dawn in Copacabana* are cases in point.

We take this opportunity to confess publicly what we have often said privately: It should be considered the greatest advantage to Shakespeare that he was born and raised a Protestant.[4] He always seems human and thoroughly familiar with what it means to be human. He stands above irrationality and superstition, and uses them merely as devices. He compels supernatural beings to serve his dramatic purposes, summoning tragic ghosts and comical imps to help him attain his goal. In the end, everything is resolved without the poet's every encountering the dilemma of having to deify an absurdity—the saddest predicament for any man conscious of his intelligence.

We return to the *Daughter of the Air* and add the following. If we are easily able to transport ourselves to such a remote culture, without knowing the locality, without understanding the language; if we feel at ease with a foreign literature without previous historical study; if we can imagine the style of life in a certain era and the mentality of a people through a single example—to whom are we indebted? Of course to the translator, who has spent a lifetime tirelessly using his talents for our benefit. We wish to convey our warmest gratitude on this occasion to Dr. Gries, who has presented us with a gift of incalculable value, a translation which makes us forget the original because its clarity attracts us immediately, its grace captivates us, and the perfect harmony of all its parts convinces us that it could and should not have been any different.[5]

Such outstanding qualities may only be truly appreciated by older people, who are free to enjoy excellence for its own sake. Young people, on the other hand, struggling, competing and trying to get ahead, do not always acknowledge an achievement by others which they have set as a goal for themselves.

Honor to our translator, who focused all his faculties on one goal and kept to a single course so that we may derive enjoyment in a thousand different ways!

A German Gil Blas[1] (1821)

The manuscript submitted to us is the diary of a man who since childhood has been cast here and there by fate. If we give it the above title, we must immediately make it clear that whereas the French *Gil Blas* is a work of art, our German Gil Blas is a work of nature, and for this reason they appear worlds apart. However, in regard to content they do permit comparison, because in the German work too the protagonist is basically a decent human being, and yet indolent as befits a subordinate who has had to obey orders since childhood. He who depends on others is no more scrupulous than they expect him to be. Thus our hero is broadminded to the point of intrigue and pandering. But since he cannot completely deny the law-abiding burgher in himself, he worsens his lot whenever he attempts to act in conformance with his sense of morality and duty. Because all this comes about quite naturally as an outgrowth of circumstances and not as a result of artful irony designed to tease us, we are attracted by the simple, calm presentation of events, which are always of human interest, though not of particular importance. In regard to his time, however, our hero's unfolding life story is noteworthy in that, driven by circumstances as well as his own restlessness, he is witness to many recent historical events.[2]

It is not surprising that the author wishes to see his work published, since he is justified in attaching some importance to his efforts and would no doubt, like any writer, welcome a reasonable honorarium. But the story should not be edited for publication, for it could not be turned into a sophisticated work of art. It is precisely the epic flow of days and years with their immense variety of recurring events that characterizes our hero's life. And since we are used to so many accounts of everyday happenings in newspapers, we should here not mind accompanying a poor wretch on his way through life.

Only a few passages, where veracity exceeds the limits of propriety, would have to be excised. Otherwise it could be printed as it is, for basically it is quite well written. Similar books in lending libraries and reading rooms are very much in demand, and this work should also prove profitable. It could be called the Bible of servants and journeymen, and among the lower classes there is probably no one who will not find some aspects of his own life portrayed here. The middle class will note pleasantly informative descriptions of its family customs. Especially the charity of women toward such privileged young vagabonds is presented most commendably and is characterized differently in different areas. In northern Germany and in Holland, the roving journeymen benefit greatly from women's memories of seafaring husbands and sons, and similar goodwill is encountered farther south in Germany. Yet it is a Frenchwoman who finally provides the most amusing example. Our young adventurer is returning as the servant of an emigre from the unfortunate Champagne region. Impoverished masters dismiss their servants, who in turn are forced to steal in order to escape starvation. Our hero is caught in the act of stealing a chicken on a French farm, and with much shouting and screaming is dragged into the house. The farmer's wife in unperturbed and says only: "Let him go. He's just a poor German servant who was curious what a French chicken tastes like."

Even the upper classes will find this book rewarding, especially if it occurs to them to ask how it would be if their servants were to write such confessions. And we must admit that reading this rather long tale prompted us to reflect seriously. For we thought we perceived in this work a moral order that knows ways to occupy, test, feed and sustain a basically good, capable, active, even restless man, and finally knows ways to calm his spirit through training and to compensate him for his sufferings with a haven where he can lead a modest existence.

Faust[1] (1828)

In looking at the French translation of my *Faust* in a deluxe edition, I am reminded of that period in my life when the work was conceived, planned and finally, in a peculiar frame of mind, written down.[2] The favor it has met with here and abroad and which now finds expression in such an exquisitely produced volume, may well be due to the curious character of the work, in that it represents a permanent record of the development of a mind, tormented by everything which tortures all human beings, stirred by the same things that trouble us all, engulfed by what we all abhor, and delighting in the things we all desire. The author has long since put these states of mind behind him, and the world too has, as it were, very different battles to wage. However, human nature in its capacity for joy and sorrow is generally unchanging, and the last born will still find reasons to enquire what those before him enjoyed and suffered in order to learn how to contend with what is in store for him as well.

My poem, not surprisingly, given its nature, was conceived in a gloomy state of mind. And while there is diversity, there is also something foreboding in its world. Yet in French, a language that illuminates everything and lends itself to reflection, the work seems much brighter and more deliberately constructed. And as I look at it in this folio edition, with superb paper, print, design and binding, I almost feel the impression fading which the poem used to make on me when I occasionally picked it up to reassure myself of its existence and qualities.

It is particularly remarkable that a visual artist became so intimately acquainted with my work that he was able to capture the original gloomy mood and trace the restlessly striving hero with just as restless a pen.

Mr. Delacroix is a painter of undeniable talent, who however proves troublesome to the Paris art world—as the young often do to us of the older generation—since one can neither deny his achievements nor applaud a certain lack of restraint in his style. He seems to have felt at home with my work and to have treated it as his own invention—this strange creation that vascillates between heaven and earth, between the possible and the impossible, the most coarse and the most delicate, or whatever other extremes the imagination may conjure up. Thus, his illustrations counteract the splendor of the deluxe edition, the mind is led from clear print into a gloomy world, and the primitive feeling of a legendary tale is again evoked. This is all we venture to say. We trust that anyone who reads and views this impressive edition will have similar feelings and share our satisfaction.

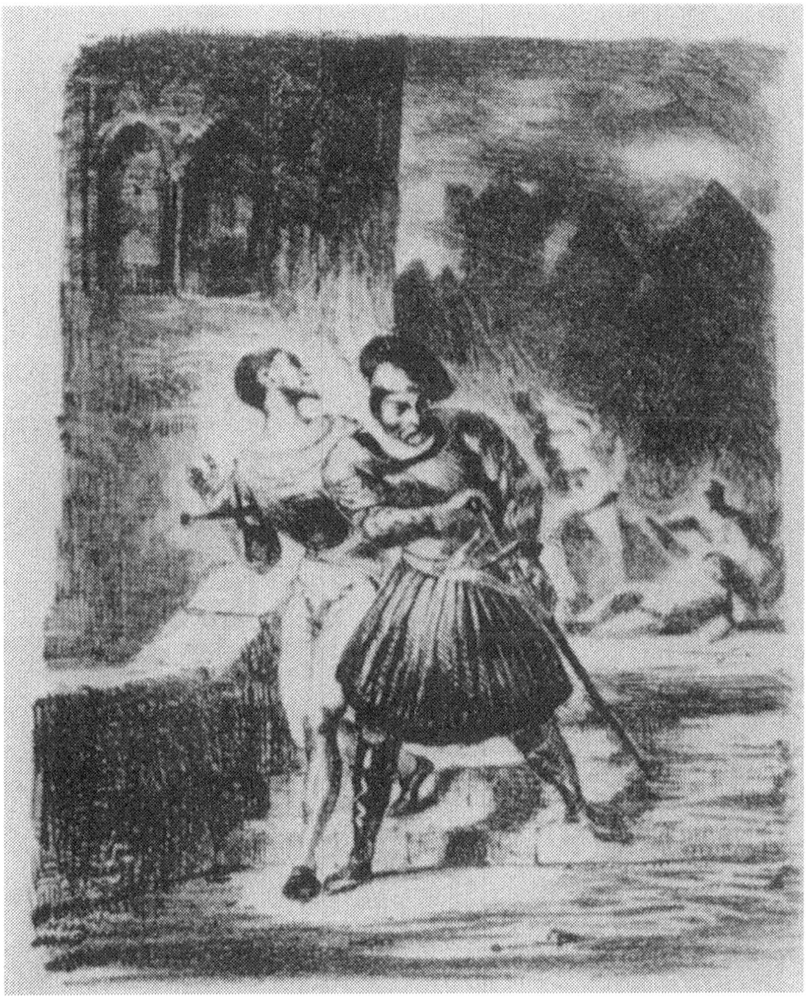

Goethe's *Faust*. A lithograph by Delacroix. (Courtesy of the Picture Collection, the Branch Libraries, New York Public Library.)

II
LITERARY THEORY

Response to a Literary Rabble-Rouser[1] (1795)

In this years's March issue of the *Berlinisches Archiv der Zeit und ihres Geschmacks,* an article appeared on German prose and rhetoric, which the editors—as they themselves confess—were reluctant to publish. We for our part do not criticize their decision to accept this immature effort; if it is a journal's responsibility to preserve material that is representative of an era, it must also include the era's improprieties.[2] To be sure, adopting an authoritative tone and certain mannerisms thought to be characteristic of a well-informed mind is anything but unusual among our critics; but individual lapses into more primitive behavior must also be noted, as they do occur. However, we, the editors of the journal *Die Horen,* would like to state for the record what has been frequently and perhaps more eloquently expressed by others: Besides those who make unreasonable and exaggerated demands on our writers, there are also reasonable and grateful minds who quietly support these men who reap such meager rewards for their efforts.

The author of the *Archiv* article deplores the scarcity of first-rate classical prose works in Germany; then he passes with one giant step over almost a dozen of our best authors. He does not even refer to them by name,[3] subjects them to lukewarm praise and sharp criticism and characterizes them in a manner which makes it almost impossible to identify them from his caricatures.

We are convinced that no German author thinks of himself as a writer of classics. We are likewise convinced that the requirements every German author sets for himself are stricter than those muddled and presumptuous demands of a crude troublemaker who attacks a respected group of writers, who certainly do not expect unqualified praise for their every effort but who are entitled to respect.

It is certainly not our intention to comment on the poorly conceived and poorly written text. We are confident that after reading the pages in question, our readers will react with indignation and repudiate the rude arrogance with which the author tries to invade the territory of his betters with the intent to usurp their places; they will agree with our calling this piece a blatant case of literary rabble-rousing. Only a few remarks shall be made in reply to this insolence.

People who consider it indispensable that their spoken or written words express specific concepts rarely use terms such as "classical work" or "classical writer." When and under what circumstances, in any nation, does one become a writer of classics? There are a number of preconditions: If the writer finds in the history of his nation great events which together with their consequences form a harmonious and significant whole; if his countrymen exhibit nobility in their attitudes, depth in their feelings, and strength and consistence in their actions; if he himself is permeated with the spirit of his nation and if he, because of an intuitive understanding of this spirit, feels capable of identifying with the past as well as with the present; if his native country has attained a high cultural level, thus facilitating his own educational process; if he has collected sufficient material and is aware of the perfect and not so perfect attempts of his predecessors; and if enough favorable external and internal circumstances coincide to make his apprenticeship less arduous so that in his mature years he is in a position to conceive a great work, organize it, and produce finally a coherent and unified whole.

These are the preconditions which are absolutely essential for a writer, especially a prose writer, to become "classical." If an unbiased and fair critic were to compare them with the conditions under which the best German writers of our century have in fact labored, their successes would fill him with awed admiration and their failures with sincere regret.

An outstanding piece of writing, just like an outstanding speech, is only a product of the author's life. Neither the writer nor the practical man of affairs can be held responsible for the circumstances and conditions into which he is born and under which he must work. Everyone, even the greatest genius, suffers from his century in some respects, just as he profits from it in others. And only a mature nature can produce an excellent national writer.

We cannot criticize the German nation because it is politically splintered despite its representing a geographic unit. We do not wish for the political turmoil that would pave the way for classical works in Germany.

The most unfair criticism is the one based on a distorted perspective. We should look objectively at past and present conditions and at the individual circumstances which formed our German writers; then it will be easy to find the criteria by which to judge them. There is no real cultural center in Germany where writers can gather and find a common guideline to aid their development and individual fields of interest. Born in various parts of the country, educated in very different ways, they are usually isolated and exposed to the impact of quite varied circumstances; they are inspired by their predilection for this or that model in German or foreign literature; without guidance, they have to work by trial and error to test their abilities. Only gradually, after a long process of soul-searching, do they become sure of what they *should* do, and then, only experimentation tells them what they *can* do. Again and again, the budding writer is bewildered by the demands of a mass public without taste that devours the good and the bad with equal relish. Then again, he receives encouragement from contact with the educated, who unfortunately are scattered all over the country, and he gains reassurance from the knowledge that there are contemporaries who labor and struggle as he does. Finally, the German writer reaches the stage in life where he has to support himself and his family and is forced to work in a field that is alien to his calling. Greatly discouraged and saddened, he must often perform work for which he has no respect, in order to produce the means that would allow him to pursue what his mind has been trained to do, the only thing he considers worthwhile. What respected German writer[4] would not recognize himself in this portrait? Which of them would not admit with some regret that in the beginning of his career he often enough pined for an opportunity to place the unique gifts of his individual genius at the service of a common national culture which unfortunately did not exist? To be sure, the education of the higher classes through foreign customs and literature was quite beneficial, but it also prevented the Germans from developing sooner as Germans.

Consider now the achievements of German poets and prose writers of note! With what scrupulousness, with what devotion they have followed the path prescribed by their clear and well-defined convictions! It is no exaggeration to suggest that any capable, diligent literary scholar could develop a complete theory of style by comparing all editions of our Wieland[5] and merely noting, stage by stage, his successive corrections. Wieland is indefatigable in his pursuit of excellence, and we may take great pride in him, notwithstanding the grumblings of Smelfungi.[6] If every conscientious librarian sees to it that a collection such as this is assembled while it is still possible, the coming century will make use of it with gratitude.

In a future issue of our journal, we hope to present a study of the development of our best writers as revealed in their works.[7] Perhaps the writers will want to contribute information. They may be assured that we are not interested in intimate personal confessions. We would leave it to their discretion to tell us which factors have contributed most to their development and which have presented the greatest obstacles. Their personal participation would be invaluable; it would add new dimensions to what can be gleaned from their works.

Such a study would prove quite helpful because there is one fact which inept critics disregard almost completely. Nowadays, a talented young man has the good fortune to be able to develop his talent earlier and find a lucid style appropriate to his subject. To whom does he owe that but to his predecessors, who in the last half of this century persevered in their own development in the face of all sorts of obstacles, each in his own way? As a result, a kind of school was founded, and the young man who enters in now enjoys a much larger and better defined circle than the writer of earlier times, who only after groping his way in the faint light of dawn was able to expand the circle, and that only gradually and as it were by chance. The would-be critic who wants to help us find the way with his feeble torch arrives too late—daybreak is here, and we will not close the shutters again.

It is not proper to vent one's bad humor in good society. Only a case of very bad humor can make a man deny the existence of excellent writers in Germany at a time when almost everyone writes well. It does not require much effort to find a pleasing novel, a well-told tale, or a lucid essay on this or that subject. Our critical publications, journals, compendia—they prove again and again that a uniformly good style *does* exist. The Germans are gaining more and more expertise and a clearer perspective. A worthy philosophy,[8] in spite of the resistance of doubting minds, helps them to become more aware of their intellectual potential and make use of it. The numerous examples of style, the previous labors and endeavors of so many accomplished writers enable the beginner at an earlier stage to present in an appropriate style and with lucidity and grace what he has received from the outside world and developed further within himself. Thus any kindly disposed and fair-minded German will see the writers of his nation at an encouraging stage of development. He is furthermore bound to be convinced that the public will not be misled by an ill-tempered, small-minded critic, who should be excluded from literary society, as should everyone whose destructive efforts only make active members irritated, supporters less interested, and onlookers distrustful and indifferent.

On Epic and Dramatic Poetry[1] (1827)

Both epic and dramatic writers are subject to general poetic laws, especially the laws of unity and development. In addition, both treat similar topics and can employ various structural devices. The fundamental difference between them is that the epic writer narrates an event as having happened in the past, while the dramatist represents an event as happening in the present. In order to define specifically the laws which they have to follow, it might help to say that the epic writer is by nature a rhapsodist and the dramatic writer an actor. The rhapsodist is surrounded by a quiet group of attentive listeners, whereas the actor's audience is impatient both to watch and hear. If we keep this analogy in mind, it will not be difficult to determine what is most suitable to each genre, which subjects and literary devices each writer prefers. I say 'prefers' because, as I suggested above, neither one has an absolute claim on anything.

Epic poetry and tragedy should both be concerned with human issues, and the subject matter should be significant and elevated. Ideally, the characters should be living during a cultural period when spontaneous actions are still possible, when human beings do not act from moral, political or social motives, but from purely personal ones. In this respect, the Greek myths from the heroic era were especially suitable material.

The epic poem presents primarily individual action, the tragedy individual suffering. The epic poem depicts man's physical interaction with the world: battles, journeys, or any kind of enterprise which requires broad, descriptive treatment. Tragedy portrays man interacting with himself, with the result that the action of a genuine tragedy can be quite limited in scope.[2]

Structural elements can be classified into five groups:

1. Progressive elements which promote the progress of the action and are used predominantly in drama.
2. Retrogressive elements which divert action away from its goal and are used almost exclusively in epic poetry.
3. Retarding elements which delay or prolong the action and are used effectively in both epic and dramatic writing.
4. Retrospective elements which incorporate previous events into the action.
5. Prospective elements which anticipate events that are to happen after the action; both retrospective and prospective elements are used by epic as well as dramatic writers to flesh out their work.

The worlds to be presented are the same for both.

1. The physical world:
   a) The immediate world of the characters: the dramatist normally restricts himself to one locale, whereas the epic poet ranges more freely over a larger area.
   b) The more distant world, in which I include all of nature: the epic poet, who appeals primarily to our imagination, makes this world more accessible through imagery, which the dramatist uses more sparingly.
2. The world of the mind:
   It is used by both and is best represented without embellishment in its normal and abnormal aspects.
3. The world of phantasies, premonitions, apparitions, chance, and fate:
   This world can be used by both; however, it must be represented concretely. This causes special problems for modern writers because,

try as they may, they cannot easily find substitutes for the ancients' miraculous creatures, gods, soothsayers and oracles.

Regarding the manner of treatment as a whole, we see the rhapsodist as a wise man who recites events which lie completely in the past and surveys them with serene detachment. His presentation aims at reassuring his audience so that they will listen to him willingly and patiently. He makes all parts of his recitation equally interesting, since he is not able immediately to counteract overly vivid impresssions. He takes his audience back and forth in time, as he sees fit. His audience follows him wherever he leads them because he is only appealing to the imagination, which creates its own images, and to a certain degree it makes little difference to our imagination what kind of images are created. The rhapsodist himself should not appear as a higher being in his poem. It would be best for him to recite behind a curtain so that his audience will not associate any particular personality with what they hear and will imagine that they are listening only to the muses themselves.

With the actor it is just the opposite. He represents a specific individual and wants us to concentrate exclusively on him and his immediate surroundings. His goal is to make us empathize with his mental anguish and his physical suffering, share his difficulties and forget ourselves. Like the rhapsodist, he must give his presentation a certain balance. However, he can afford to produce far more vivid impressions because, due to his physical presence, even a rather strong impression can be neutralized by a weaker one. It is an absolute necessity that the audience be constantly engaged and not be allowed to assume a position of detached contemplation. The actor wants them to be passionately involved and their imagination completely inactive; so he must not appeal to it, and even what is being narrated has to be made visual.

Didactic Poetry[1] (1827)

It is inappropriate to group didactic poetry together with lyric poetry, epic and drama. Anyone who remembers that the last three differ only in form, whereas didactic poetry gets its name from its contents, will realize that it cannot be included in the same category.

All poetry should be instructive, but unobtrusively so. It should draw our attention to something worth learning; but it should be left to us to draw the lesson from it, just as we learn from life.

Didactic poetry is clearly a hybrid between poetry and rhetoric. Sometimes it comes close to one, sometimes to the other. It can also vary in poetic value, yet it is always, like descriptive and satirical poetry, a secondary or sub-category which any valid theory of esthetics should rank between poetry and rhetoric. That by no means diminishes its intrinsic value because, in addition to being instructive, it is an art form that is embellished by pleasing rhythmic effects and ornaments of the imagination and can be presented gently or vigorously. From the rhymed chronicles to the mnemonic verses of the older pedagogues up to the very best works in this category—they all have their value, but they must be judged as works of an individual genre and according to the appropriate criteria.

If we look at didactic poetry closely and objectively, we realize immediately that it is valuable as a means of reaching a wide audience. Even the most talented poet should not consider it beneath his dignity to deal in this way with a significant subject. The English have produced some excellent examples of didactic poetry. Such poems first ingratiate themselves half jestingly, half seriously with the audience and then provide explanatory remarks so that the intended message can be understood. Teachers of esthetics, ethics and history are presented with a splendid opportunity to eliminate some confusion here; they can help their students see the merit of the best of such works, not according to the usefulness of their contents, but to their value as poetry.

Actually, didactic works should be eliminated completely from courses in esthetics, but they could be treated in special courses or perhaps in public lectures for those who have studied poetics and rhetoric. As in any field, a good theoretical understanding would be advantageous for practical application because many people would realize how difficult it is to weave a work out of knowledge and imagination, that is, combine two opposite elements into one living organism.

The teacher would have to explain how this combination might be achieved, so that his listeners could avoid blunders if they should try their hand at it.

Among the many ways and methods of bringing about this combination, humor is the most reliable, and, if genuine humor were not so rare, it could be considered the easiest.

It is hard to imagine a stranger notion than choosing geology as the subject for a didactic poem, and indeed a quite imaginative one. And yet, a member of the Geological Society in London did just that to promote and popularize the study of a subject which is indispensable for any traveler.[2]

On Greek Tetralogies[1] (1823)

It cannot be denied that until now Greek tetralogies have been thought of as developing the same material in three stages. The first part offered exposition, background and the central theme of the entire work. In the second, frightening consequences assumed monstrous proportions.

In the third, however, despite additional developments, a reconciliation occurred in some manner or other. It was optional, and sometimes quite appropriate, to add a fourth, more cheerful part, so that the audience, simple people in need of peace of mind and domestic comfort, could go home happy.

Agamemnon, for example, is killed in the first part, Clytemnestra and Aegisthus in the second, but in the third part Orestes, the matricide, pursued by the Furies, is acquitted by the Athenian superior court of appeals, for which event a great, city-wide commemorative ceremony is instituted.[2] Here we can imagine that the poet might have done well to add a piece in a lighter vein.

Greek mythology is admittedly very rich and extensive, and the poet in search of material will easily be persuaded that from every branch of its endless family tree a number of trilogies could be developed. Yet it is still understandable that with the constant demands for more and more novelty and excitement it was not always possible to find a coherent sequence of events.

Is it not likely then that the poet soon realized that the audience was not at all interested in the sequence of events? Would he not have exploited the fact that he was dealing with a frivolous public? For he would rather abandon his convictions than struggle all alone and in vain.

On this account we also find most natural and reasonable the theory which maintains that a trilogy or even a tetralogy did not require a connected plot, nor, consequently, a development of the material as described above, but rather a development of the method of presentation on the basis of a varying content adequate to produce the desired effect.

Accordingly, the first part had to be grand and awe-inspiring, the second had to elevate and delight the senses, emotions and mind through the chorus and song, and the third had to be exciting and charming by means of obvious effects, such as splendid costumes and crowds. The last part, on the other hand, as a pleasant conclusion, could be as cheerful, lively and outrageous as it wished.

Let us find parallels for both theories in our time. The German stage offers an example of the first in Schiller's *Wallenstein*. To be sure, the dramatist did not plan to imitate the ancients, but his material was so vast that as it was being written it gradually divided itself into several parts, even against the author's intentions. In keeping with modern taste, he presented as his first part a humorous, light, satyr-like piece, *The Camp*. In the second part, *The Piccolomini,* we witness the rising action, which is still being retarded by pettiness, error, and chaotic passions, though tender sublime love strives to refine what is coarse, mollify what is savage, and unbend what is rigid.

In the third part all attempts at mediation fail. This part we must call highly tragic in the deepest sense and admit that mind and emotions could not bear anything to follow.

To find an example of the thesis that presumes the presenting of completely unrelated events in an effective sequence, we must now cross the Alps and imagine the Italians as an audience, a nation fully devoted to the present.

When in Italy, we saw a wholly serious opera in three connected acts, which proceeded in the normal way. But between the acts, two ballets were presented, as different from each other as from the opera itself. The first was heroic, the second more in a comic vein, to give the dancers an opportunity to show their skill and strength. When this second ballet was over, the third act of the opera continued as decorously as if there had been no farcial interlude. The whole presentation concluded with seriousness, solemnity and splendor. What we had witnessed was a pentalogy, in its own way perfectly satisfactory to the audience.

To mention another example. We saw three-act plays by Goldoni,[3] in somewhat more modest productions, where complete two-act comic operas were splendidly performed as interludes. Play and opera had nothing in common, either in content or form, and yet people were delighted to hear the popular ouverture of the opera immediately after the end of the first act of the play. After the opera's brilliant first-act finale, the second act of the play was just as welcome. And when the second act of the opera had in turn heightened the spectators' delight, they were still most eager to see the third act of the play, which was then always presented in a highly satisfactory manner. The actors, feeling challenged by their melodious colleagues, made a supreme effort, and since they knew that the audience was in excellent spirits, they were in fine spirits themselves and performed delightfully. At the end, thunderous applause greeted this pentalogy, the last part of which had the same effect as the fourth part of a tetralogy: it sent everyone home satisfied, cheered, yet also calmed.

On Interpreting Aristotle's *Poetics*[1] (1827)

Anyone fairly well acquainted with the theory of poetics in general and the theory of tragedy in particular will recall a passage in Aristotle's *Poetics* which has caused interpreters much difficulty and whose exact meaning is still a matter of controversy. In his definition of tragedy, Aristotle seems to stipulate that the spectator's mind be purged of pity and fear through the presentation of actions and events that evoke these emotions.

I think that I may best be able to convey my ideas and convictions regarding this passage by translating it.

"Tragedy is the imitation of a significant and complete action which has a certain length and is not narrated by a single character but presented in poetical language by separate characters, each of whom plays his own role. However, after a certain course of events which evoke pity and fear, the tragedy concludes by neutralizing those emotions."

By this translation[2] I believe to have clarified the passage which has so far been considered obscure, and I would only add the following remarks: How could Aristotle possibly have thought of the effect—indeed the delayed effect—which a tragedy might have on the spectator, when in his characteristically objective way he was in fact discussing the structure of tragedy? Impossible! He states clearly and correctly: once tragedy has gone through a series of events arousing pity and fear, it must conclude on stage, before our eyes, with the neutralization and reconciliation of such emotions.

By catharsis he means this reconciliatory conclusion, which is actually expected of all drama, indeed of all poetic works.

In tragedy this is accomplished by some type of human sacrifice, either actually performed or, through divine intervention, replaced by a surrogate, as with Abraham or Agamemnon. In any case, a reconciliation, a solution is indispensable as a conclusion if the tragedy is to be a perfect work of art. However, the surrogate solution, which is prompted by the desire for a happy denouement, brings the work closer to the intermediary form of the drama, as with the return of Alcestis.[3] In comedy, on the other hand, we usually find marriage as a means of disentangling all sorts of predicaments, which are actually a lesser form of fear and hope. Although marriage may not be the end of life, it represents a significant and serious caesura in life. No one wants to die, everyone wants to get married: this is the half facetious, half serious difference between tragedy and comedy according to Aristotle's aesthetics.

Furthermore, we note that the Greeks used the trilogy for the purpose of catharsis.[4] There is probably no more powerful example than *Oedipus at Colonus*. Because of daemonic personality traits, the somber intensity of his life, the propensity for precipitous actions, indeed, because of the very nobility of his character, this half-guilty criminal becomes the victim of ever inscrutable, inexplicably relentless forces and plunges himself and his family into deep and utterly hopeless misery. Yet in the end, after reconciliation and atonement, he is elevated to the company of the gods, becomes the benevolent guardian spirit of the land

and is deemed worthy of the honor of a special sacrificial ceremony.

This is the principle on which the great master's maxim is based: the hero of a tragedy must be portrayed as neither completely guilty nor completely innocent. In the first case, the catharsis would only follow from the plot itself. A murdered villain, for example, would seem only to have escaped punishment by law. In the second case, catharsis would be impossible: fate or human beings would have to bear the burden of too grave an injustice.

Although I do not wish to engage in polemics in discussing this or any other subject,[5] I feel compelled to point out how others have dealt with the interpretation of this passage. Aristotle had said in his *Politics* that music could be an aid to moral education because sacred melodies could soothe a mind that has been excited by orgies, and hence could have a similar effect in counterbalancing other emotions. I do not deny that an analogy exists between these two cases, but they are not identical. The type of music determines its effect, as Handel has shown in his *Alexander's Feast,*[6] and as we can verify for ourselves at any dance when a waltz follows a dignified and proper polonaise and drives young people into a frenzy.

But music cannot affect morality, nor can the other arts, and it is always wrong to expect them to do so. Only philosophy and religion can achieve this; piety and a sense of duty require inspiration, and the arts can accomplish such an awakening only by chance. But what the arts can and do achieve is the softening of crude manners, which, however, may lead to effeminacy.

Whoever is in pursuit of truly moral education of the mind knows and will concede that tragedy and tragic novels do not soothe the spirit, but rather unsettle the emotions and what we call the heart. The result is a vague, uncertain mood, cherished by young people who, therefore, are passionately fond of literature of that kind.

Let us return to our original point and repeat: Aristotle speaks of the structure of the tragedy, with the dramatist in mind who contemplates producing a tragedy that is noble and appealing, pleasing to eyes and ears, and that is a unified whole.

Once the poet has fulfilled his duty, has tied significant knots and unravelled them appropriately, the same will happen in the spectator's mind. The complications will confuse him, the solution will enlighten him, but he will not go home a better person. Rather, he would be amazed at himself—if he were unusually observant—for coming back home just as frivolous or stubborn, as aggressive or meek, as kind or unkind as he was when he left. There would seem to be little more to say regarding this point, although further discussion could always shed more light on the theme.

Plato as Party to a Christian Revelation[1] (1826)

No one would be satisfied with what he has received from the Eternal Creator if he had to admit that all his brothers have been just as well provided for. Everyone claims that a special book, a special prophet has prescribed a particular course of life especially for him, and that this path alone leads to salvation for all.

Those who embrace such an exclusive doctrine have always been amazed to find that outside their circle there are also sensible and decent people interested in developing their moral character as much as possible. They have no choice but to concede that these outsiders have also benefitted from a revelation, perhaps a special revelation.

Be that as it may, this opinion will prevail among those who desire privileges and confer them on themselves. The sight of God's wide world, the recognition of the endless, immutable workings of His universe are not to their liking. On the contrary, they consider privileges, exceptions and miracles for the sake of their precious selves, their church, their school, as perfectly natural.

Even Plato has been honored before by being made a part to a Christian revelation, and in this role he is presented to us in the translation at hand.[2]

The reader of an author such as Plato, who for all his achievements is still vulnerable to charges of sophistry and casuistry, feels the need for a clear, critical presentation of the circumstances of and the motives for his writing. Such explanatory remarks seem especially desirable for those who study Plato not for some vague edification—far lesser writers can furnish that—but rather to become acquainted with an illustrious man as an individual. For it is not what others *seem* to have been that educates us, but the recognition of what they really were and are.

How grateful we would have been to the translator, had he, in addition to explanatory notes, presented a brief introduction to the ancient writer as well as the main idea and intent of each work, as did Wieland when translating Horace.[3]

How, for example, can *Ion* be offered as a canonical work when this little dialogue is nothing but a persiflage? Probably because at the end there is mention of divine inspiration! Unfortunately, however, here as in several other places, Socrates is merely speaking ironically.

Through all philosophical writings there runs a polemical thread, even though it may be scarcely perceptible. Whoever philosophizes is at odds with the modes of thought embraced by his predecessors and contemporaries. That is why Plato's dialogues are often not only directed at something, but also against something. It would be most valuable if a translator were to elucidate the two 'somethings' and, to a greater degree than heretofore, make them easily comprehensible to the German reader.

We take the liberty of adding in this connection a few more words concerning *Ion*.

A fictitious figure—as we may characterize the Socrates who is modelled as little on the real person as he is on the character created by Aristophanes—this Platonic Socrates meets a rhapsodist, a reciter, a declaimer famed for his recitals of Homeric poems who has just won a prize and intends soon to win another. Plato depicts Ion as an extremely limited person who, to be sure, can recite Homeric verse with expression and move an audience. He is also a person who does not hesitate to talk about Homer, but probably more to paraphrase than to explain a passage, more to seize the opportunity simply to say something than to bring his audience closer to the spirit of the poet through his own interpretation. He admits openly that he falls asleep when the works of other poets are read or interpreted—what kind of a person can this be? It is obvious that all he did was acquire a skill through family tradition or practice. He was probably favored by an attractive appearance, a good voice and a receptive heart, yet he remained a natural talent, a mere performer, who had never given thought to his own art or art in general. He did nothing more than perform a restricted and mechanical routine, yet he still thought of himself as an artist, and was probably considered a great artist by all of Greece. Plato's Socrates takes on this simpleton and annihilates him. First he makes him feel his limitations, then he demonstrates his insufficient knowledge of details in Homer, and finally, since the poor devil has been reduced to a state of helplessness, he convinces him that he is the recipient of direct divine inspiration.

If that is hallowed ground, then the stage of Aristophanes is also a sacred place. Plato's Socrates has no intention of proselytizing Ion, nor is it the author's goal to preach to the reader. Ion, the famous, admired laureate for hire is meant to be shown with all his weaknesses exposed. A more fitting title would be: Ion, or The Confounded Rhapsodist, for the dialogue has nothing at all to do with poetry.

As a matter of fact, in this as in other Platonic dialogues, the incredible stupidity of some characters is emphasized to make Socrates alone appear truly wise. If Ion had only a glimmer of knowledge about poetry, he would have had a ready answer to Socrates' teasing question: Does the charioteer or the rhapsodist understand Homer better when he speaks about chariot racing? Ion's answer could have been: Of course the rhapsodist, because the charioteer only knows if Homer speaks correctly; but the judicious rhapsodist knows if he speaks appropriately, if he has fulfilled his obligation as a poet, not as a reporter of a race. In judging an epic poem, only intuitive perception and feeling are needed, not factual knowledge, although one should also have a general awareness of the world and all that pertains to it. Why must we have recourse to divine inspiration here, unless we want to mystify people? There are many instances in the arts where realism is simply disregarded because the artist finds it necessary to sacrifice all subordinate matters to higher purposes. I myself have heard more than one coachman criticize old cameos which portray horses without harness pulling a chariot. Of course the coachman was right to find this completely unrealistic, but the artist was right too not to let the beautiful shape of the horse's body be spoiled by lines. This poetic license, these hieroglyphs, which all art requires, are poorly understood by those who want all truth to be realistic, and thereby force art from its natural sphere. Ambiguous statements by famous ancient writers that may be appropriate in context should not be reprinted without clarifying commentary; otherwise they can result in misinterpretation. The same holds true for such false teachings about inspiration.

It happens again and again that someone without poetic talent succeeds in writing a perfectly praiseworthy poem. That only proves what lively interest, a proper frame of mind and strong feelings can achieve. Hatred, it is said, can enhance inspiration, as can all passion that spurs us to action. Even the recognized poet is only at certain moments capable of displaying his talent at its highest level. This peculiarity of the human mind can be understood psychologically, and without recourse to miracles and the workings of strange powers, if we have enough patience to study natural phenomena. Such knowledge is made available by science, whose accomplishments are of course easier to smugly disregard than to examine judiciously and fairly.

A peculiar thing about this Platonic dialogue is that Ion admits to his ignorance about the arts, prophecy, charioteering, medicine and fishing, but then maintains that he feels eminently qualified to be a general. This was in all likelihood a pet notion of the talented but foolish Ion, a quirk he may have picked up from his intimate association with Homeric heroes, and which was not unknown to his audience. Have we not noted this and similar quirks in men more sensible than Ion shows himself to be here? Who in our day believes he would not make a good general?

With true Aristophanic malice, Plato delays the last blow meant for our poor sinner. Ion stands there dazed, and when Socrates finally offers him the choice between the title of scoundrel or man inspired by god, Ion naturally chooses the latter and, in a state of total bewilderment, politely expresses his gratitude for having been made a fool of. Indeed, if this is hallowed land, Aristophanes' theater is sacred ground too!

Certainly, if someone were to analyze for us what men like Plato said seriously, jokingly or half-jokingly, either out of conviction or for argument's sake, he would render us an extraordinary service and contribute immeasurably to our education. For the times are past when sybils pronounced their prophecies in caves. We demand critical interpretation, and we want to be able to judge before we accept something and apply it to ourselves.

Stages of Man's Mind[1] (1817)

The primeval phase of the world, of nations, of individual human beings is the same. At first everything is enveloped by a desolate void, but the spirit already contemplates the creation of the animate and inanimate world. While the primitive masses look about with fear and amazement in search of the barest necessities, a more advanced spirit gazes at the great phenomena of the world, perceives what occurs there, and gives utterance to what exists with profound awareness as if it came into being before his very eyes. Therefore, in the earliest stage we have the contemplation and the philosophy of nature, the defining and the poetry of nature—all in one.

The world gets brighter, and the obscure elements become clearer and take on outline. Man reaches out in order to gain mastery of them in a different way. This new man surveys the world with a simple, healthy sensuousness which sees nothing but itself reflected in things past and present. He gives new shape to old names, anthropomorphizes and personifies things, and beings living and dead, and imparts his own character to all creatures. Thus primitive faith lives and thrives, and, often recklessly, rids itself of all abstruse remnants from the primeval epoch. Poetry flourishes, and only he who has innate primitive faith or can acquire it, is a poet. This epoch is characterized by a free, robust, serious, noble sensuousness, which is elevated through the power of the imagination.

But since man knows no limit in his pursuit of self-improvement and because the enlightened aspect of existence is not always to his liking, he longs to return to mystical experience and searches for a higher power behind the world of appearances. And just as poetry creates dryads and hamadryads and makes them subjects of higher gods, so theology creates a hierachy of demons that are envisioned to be ultimately dependent on one god. We may call this time the sacred epoch. Although it is essentially a product of reason, the rational spirit gradually loses its influence. Primitive faith is reclaimed, modified to suit the time, and the miraculous is proclaimed to have objective rather than poetic validity. To this the intelligent mind must object, although in its ideal state and form it worships the primitive beginnings, takes pleasure in the poetic primitive faith, and values the noble human need to accept a supreme being. However, intelligent man strives to clarify everything, to find reasonable explanations for even the most mysterious phenomena. To be sure, he does not reject primitive faith and organized religion, but he presumes that they are based on something comprehensible, praiseworthy and useful. He seeks significance, transforms the specific into the general, and from national, provincial and even individual traits he deduces characteristic features applicable to mankind in general. We cannot dispute the noble, pure and sensible aspirations of this epoch; yet it benefits the talented individual rather than entire nations.

As this attitude becomes more prevalent, it is immediately followed by the last epoch. We may call it the prosaic epoch because its aim is not to humanize the essence of previous epochs and make them understandable to everyone, but instead, it vulgarizes the old and venerable. And in doing so it utterly destroys innate feelings, primitive faith and organized religion, and even the presumption of the intellect that there is a laudable purpose behind the unfamiliar phenomena.

This epoch cannot endure long. Man in his need, stimulated by events in the world, retrogresses and abandons the guidance of the intellect. He intermingles religion, primitive faith and primeval beliefs, he clings to one tradition, then to another. He delves into the mystical, replaces poetry with the merely fantastic and elevates it to dogma. Instead of teaching prudently and exerting influence patiently, he sows herb and weed indiscriminately. There is no point of reference to guide him; everyone claims to be teacher and leader and presents his perfect folly as a perfect ideal.

And so the value of any mystical idea is destroyed, and even primitive faith is desecrated. Qualities that formerly diverged naturally in their development, now interfere with each other as hostile elements. And so, chaos has returned—not the original that was fertile and life-bearing, but a chaos of death and decay which even the Spirit of God could not use as material to create another world worthy of Him.

Basic Origins

Considered in depth, appropriately defined

Poetry	Primitive Faith	Robust	Imagination
Theology	Rising to the Ideal	Sacred	Reason
Philosophy	Intellectual Doubting	Sensible	Intellect
Prose	Dissolution into the Ordinary	Common	Sensuality

Intermingling, Hostility, Dissolution

Justus Möser: Superstition and Poetry[1] (1823)

It is a pleasure to say a few words about this excellent man who, although never a personal acquaintance of mine, greatly influenced my development through his writings and, more indirectly, through my correspondence with this daughter, in which I found her father's views of me expressed with insight and shrewdness. He was common sense personified, a worthy contemporary of Lessing, the epitome of critical thinking. The occasion for my remarks here is the news that a substantial volume of Möser's posthumous papers will be published next year as a sequel to his 'History of Osnabrück.' Even as fragments they deserve to be preserved, since the manifestations of such a mind and character, like nuggets of gold or gold dust, are as valuable as ingots and even more valuable than gold coin.

Here is only one sample of his sublime ideas, which prompt me to add a few similar thoughts and views of my own.

"On Our Ancestors' Superstitions: So much has been said about the superstitions of our ancestors and so many negative conclusions have been drawn about their intelligence that I feel compelled to say a few words, if not to vindicate, then at least excuse these good people. In my opinion, all their so-called superstitious ideas had the sole purpose of putting a mark on certain truths (which then became the 'mark of truth'), in order to remember them easily, just as their purpose in attaching a piece of wood to a key was so as not to lose it, or to find it more easily. For example, when a child put a knife on the table in such a way so that someone might hurt himself with it, they told him, if angels were to walk across the table, they would cut their feet. They said that, not because they believed it but to help the child remember. Another saying of theirs was that for every grain of salt we waste in life, we must wait one hour before the gates of heaven. This was intended as a reminder for their children or their hired help, as a warning against their negligence in small matters, which adds up in the long run. They said to a vain girl who, even at night, could not pass a mirror without stealing a glance at herself, that the devil peeks over the shoulder of one who looks at herself in the mirror at night—and other such sayings meant to teach a lesson or help one remember it. In brief, just as we use the animal world in our fables, our ancestors used the world of spirits to drive home a truth for a child."

Möser does an excellent job of contrasting religious fables and those dealing with worldly affairs. The latter develop our good sense by pointing out advantage and disadvantage; the former aim at moral education and make use of religious illustrations. In the worldly fables, Renard the Fox is the most important figure, in that he is well aware of his advantage and pursues his goal without the least regard for others. In the religious fables, angels and devils are almost the sole characters.

Origines[2] says, his contemporaries believed hot springs were tears shed by banished angels.

Superstition is the poetry of life. Both invent imaginary beings and sense the strangest connections between things that are in fact real and tangible, at times in a sympathetic, at times in an antagonistic relationship.

Poetry can always free itself from such shackles, which in any case it always puts on voluntarily.[3] Superstition, on the other hand, is comparable to magic ropes that grow ever tighter the more we struggle. Even an enlightened age is not immune to it. And if superstition appears in a dark century, the beclouded mind of man soon reaches for the impossible, seeks to influence the realm of spirits and of things distant or in the future. A wondrous, rich world emerges, yet enveloped by a murky atmosphere, and shrouds of fog obscure whole centuries and become ever more dense. Imagination broods over a confused sensuousness. Reason, like Astraea,[4] seems to have returned to her divine place of origin, and common sense despairs because it is unable to prevail.

The poet is not harmed by superstition because in lending only figurative value to its half-truths, he can in many ways put them to positive use.[5]

On Carlyle's *German Romance*[1] (1828)

To clarify the title of this work we should point out that the volume contains samples of Romantic literature, including fairly tales, selected from works of German authors who have distinguished themselves in this style. There are stories of varying length by Musäus,[2] Tieck, Hoffmann, Jean Paul Richter and Goethe, translated into flowing, graceful English. Particularly noteworthy are the introductory notes on each author. We commend them highly, as we do the author's earlier biography of Schiller, and recommend to our newspapers and journals their translation and publication, unless that has already been done unbeknown to us. The biographical material is presented with care and provides essential knowledge about each author's character and its influence on his writings. Here, as in Schiller's biography, Mr. Carlyle evidences an objective, clear and deep understanding of German literary matters. He makes the particular concerns of our nation his own, he gives every author his due, each in his own category, and thus resolves to some extent the conflicts unavoidable within the literature of any nation. For to live and to be active means forming factions and taking sides. No one is blamed for struggling to attain position and rank, which will furnish him a livelihood and provide him the influence to ensure further success.

This struggle within a nation often long obscures the literary horizons. The outsider, however, waits for the dust to settle, the haze to disappear and the fog to lift; then he can see those distant regions with their areas of light and shade distinctly, and he observes them with the serenity of one gazing at the moon on a clear night.

At this point I would like to recall a few observations which I wrote some time ago.[3] Though it may be objected that I am repeating myself, I would hope that repetition may occasionally serve some purpose.

It is evident that the best poets and writers of all nations have for some time been concentrating their efforts on universal human concerns. In every specific literary mode, whether its content is historical, mythological, mystical or fictional, we increasingly see a writer's national and individual characteristics illuminated from within by these universal concerns.

Although a similar concern prevails in everyday life, pervades even what is brutal, savage, cruel, false, selfish and deceitful on this earth, and seeks to spread benevolence everywhere, we do not have the right to hope that universal peace will result. But we do have hope that unavoidable controversies will gradually become less acrimonious, wars less cruel and victory less arrogant.

What points and works toward this goal in the literatures of nations, is what all nations have to recognize. We must get to know the particular characteristics of nations to understand them, to be able to have dealings with them. For these idiosyncracies are like language and currency: they not only facilitate dealings among nations, they make them possible.

The surest way to truly universal tolerance is to accept the particular characteristics of individuals and whole peoples, yet at the same time to adhere to the conviction that the truly valuable is characterized by its being part of all mankind. For some time now the Germans have been contributing to such mediation and mutual acceptance. He who studies German finds himself in the marketplace where all nations offer their wares. He plays the role of interpreter while enriching himself.

And that is how we should see the translator, as one who strives to be a mediator in this universal, intellectual trade, and makes it his business to promote exchange. For whatever one may say about the shortcomings of translations, they are and will remain most important and worthy undertakings in world communication.

The Koran says: "God has given each people a prophet in its own language." Thus every translator is a prophet among his people. Luther's translation of the Bible has had the greatest impact, even though critics quibble and carp to this day. And what is the purpose of that gigantic effort of the Bible Society, but to transmit the gospel to every people in its own vernacular?

Advice For Young Poets[1] (1832)

Frequently young German writers send me their poems with the request not only to judge them but also to give them my thoughts regarding creative writing as a profession. As much as I appreciate this confidence, it is impossible, on an individual basis, to reply adequately in writing; indeed, an oral reply would be difficult enough. However, since such inquiries generally focus on the same issue, I have decided to address this subject in the following remarks for future reference.

The German language has now reached such a high level of development that anyone can express himself according to his ability;[2] he can do this in prose or poetry, and in any way appropriate to the subject or feeling he wishes to convey. As a result, anyone who has reached a certain level of education through listening and reading and has attained some clarity about himself, may soon feel the urge to communicate his thoughts and opinions, his insights and feelings with a certain eloquence.

However, it might be difficult, if not impossible, for the young person to realize that by so doing little has, in fact, been accomplished. To be sure, upon closer examination of writings of this kind we realize that the author may be more or less successful in conveying his state of mind and everything pertaining to his person; some parts in fact may be outstanding because they are expressed profoundly and clearly, with assurance and grace. General topics, such as God and fatherland, the boundlessness of nature and her countless manifestations, impress us in some poems of young writers, the moral value and praiseworthy technique of which we readily acknowledge.

Yet this is precisely where the danger lies, for many young people with the same aspirations will embark together on a joyful journey, without first asking themselves if their destination is not too far beyond the horizon.

Unfortunately, a sympathetic observer will soon notice that the youthful enthusiasm suddenly begins to diminish. The clear, fresh spring is muddied by sadness over lost joy, by pining for what is lost, yearning for the unknown and unobtainable, by discontentment, railing against any and all obstacles, and the struggle against ill-will, envy and hostility.[3] The happy group disbands and scatters as misanthropic hermits.

How difficult it is therefore to explain to someone with any degree of talent in any field that the muses are glad to accompany life but are totally unable to guide it. Eventually we enter an active and vigorous phase of life which may be unpleasant at times, where we all inevitably feel that we are but parts of a greater whole. If we then want to cling to all our past dreams, wishes, hopes and the comforting security of youthful fantasies, the muses will abandon us. They seek out the one who gladly practices a certain resignation and whose soul is easily restored, who sees good in every season and knows that there is a time for skating on the frozen pond, for strolling in the rose garden, who alleviates his own suffering and casts about for opportunities to soothe suffering and be host to happiness.

Then his years will no longer separate him from the muses, who while delighting in timid innocence, yet stand by the side of farsighted wisdom, who while fostering the development of promising talent, yet delight in the ultimate in excellence. And so I may conclude these outpourings with this little verse:

When heart and mind are blithe and free
O youth, of this take timely heed:
The Muse affords you company,
But does not ever take the lead.[4]

Further Advice For Young Poets[1] (1832)

We think of him as our master under whose constant guidance we practice our art and who, as we progress, imparts to us step by step the principles which will most surely enable us to attain our goal.

In this sense, I have never been a master to anyone. But if I am asked to define what I have been to Germans in general, and particularly to young poets, then I could call myself their liberator. For they have through me become aware that, just as man must live from within, the artist must express his own self by revealing—no matter how he does it—only his own specific individuality.

If he proceeds in a natural and positive manner, he will manifest what is of high value in life, his nobility or grace, or perhaps even the graceful nobility granted him by nature.

I can recognize quite well, incidentally, whom I have influenced. This influence has produced natural poetry,[2] so to speak, and only in this manner is originality possible.

Fortunately, our poetry is on such a high level technically, and the importance of worthwhile content so obvious to everyone, that we are witnessing the emergence of wonderfully successful works. The situation may improve even more, and there may well be no limit. But every writer must get to know himself, learn to judge himself, because for this no outside standard can be applied.

The most important point can be briefly stated: The young poet should give voice only to what lives and can and will live on, whatever its shape or form. He should refrain from all contrariness, all antagonism and condemnation, anything which merely negates, because that is unproductive.

I cannot recommend to my young friends emphatically enough that they see to it that as their poems acquire a certain facility in rhythmic expression they also gain significantly in content.

Poetic content, however, is the content of one's own life. That content cannot be given us by anyone; others may mar it perhaps, but not spoil it. Vanity, that is, every form of complacency without merit, will be treated as the worst offense.

To declare oneself free is a great presumption. In doing so one declares the intention to rule oneself, and who is able to do that? On this point, I wish to tell my friends the young poets the following: At present, there is no standard for you—you must create it for yourselves. Ask yourselves with every poem if it contains something you have experienced and if that experience has made you grow.

You will not grow if you keep on mourning a beloved whom you have lost through separation, unfaithfulness or death. It is a useless poetic pursuit, no matter how much skill and talent you may lavish on it.[3]

Let us take the flow of life as a guide, and on occasion examine ourselves. Then we can see instantly whether we are truly alive, and, reflecting later in life, whether we have been truly alive.

PART THREE

Observations on Art and Literature

On Dilettantism[1] (1799)

The dilettante always shies away from serious study, avoids acquiring essential knowledge in order to get to actual practice, and confuses art with subject matter. For example, one will never find a dilettante who draws well. If he did draw well, he would be on the path to art. On the other hand, there are those who draw badly and paint decently. Dilettantes frequently favor mosaic and encaustic wax painting because they mistake permanence for art. They often take up etching because the technique of reproduction fascinates them. They seek out cunning devices, mannerisms, various techniques and arcane means because they usually cannot free themselves from the notion of technical skill and think that if they just knew the trick, they would have no more difficulties. Precisely because most dilettantes lack a true concept of art, they prefer quantity and mediocrity, the unusual and costly to what is select and good. Many dilettantes have large collections. We might even say that all large collections owe their existence to dilettantism. For the dilettante's desire to collect, particularly when supported by great wealth, usually deteriorates into an obsession to amass as much as he can. He wants only to possess, not to select judiciously and be satisfied with less, but of good quality. Two unfortunate traits often encountered among dilettantes can also be ascribed to lack of a true concept of art. First, they want to dictate standards; that is, their judgment is to be definitive, they determine who deserves the name of artist. Second, in contrast to the artist and the true connoisseur, who have a total, wholehearted committment to the seriousness of art and the work of art, the dilettante's interest is always halfhearted, and he pursues his artistic activities as a game, a pastime. Usually, he has an ulterior motive, wants to satisfy a private inclination or is acceding to a whim. He tries to escape his responsibility to the world and the requirements of taste when, in acquiring a work of art, he means to perform a worthy service. Supporting a promising artist, helping a poor family—those are usually his reasons for having purchased this or that piece. So he either seeks to display his taste or excuse it. In addition, dilettantes frequently have patriotic intentions; a German dilettante is often interested exclusively in German art, hence our collections of engravings and paintings of only German masters.

In all arts there is an objective and a subjective element, and depending on whether one or the other predominates, dilettantism has some value or is worthless.

Where the subjective element is in itself important, the dilettante invariably resembles the artist, for example in dance, music, oratory, lyric poetry.

Where the reverse is true, there is a more marked distinction between artist and dilettante, and dilettantism can be harmful, as in architecture, drawing, the dramatic arts, and epic or dramatic poetry.

Art creates its own laws and sets the standards of the time; dilettantism follows the trend of the time.

When leading artists themselves stray from the path of true taste, the dilettante will all the sooner believe that he has reached the level of art.

Because the dilettante's urge to create derives solely from the effect which works of art have on him, he confuses this effect with objective causes and motives. And so he now believes it possible to use the emotional state into which he has been transported as a means of being productive—which is tantamount to trying to produce a flower by means of its fragrance. For the dilettance, the essential element of art and the basis of his own work is what speaks to the feelings; this, to be sure, is the ultimate effect of all artistic creation but it also presupposes the mustering of all art's resources.

In general, the dilettante in his mistaken assessment of himself wants to replace the active with the passive, and since he is highly susceptible to the effects of art, he believes he can himself produce effects with the effects that affected him.

Wherever art itself does not yet have a useful system of rules, as in poetry, horticulture or the dramatic arts, dilettantism does more harm and becomes more presumptuous. The worst case is in the dramatic arts.

In principle, dilettantism is legitimate if the dilettante is willing to submit to strict rules at the beginning and complete all levels in sequence and with the greatest of care, which he is quite capable of doing, since first of all, no goal is demanded of him, and secondly, if he wishes to abandon his efforts at some point, he has prepared himself in the best way possible to become a connoisseur. Contrary to prevailing assumptions, the dilettante must submit to even stricter criticism than the artist, who because he is firmly based in his art can deviate from the rules with less danger and can thereby expand the dimensions of art itself.

The true artist stands firmly and securely on his own. All his endeavors are directed towards the ultimate in art. He will always find himself far from his goal and is therefore by necessity ever modest in regard to art or the higher idea of art; he will confess that he has as yet achieved very little, no matter how excellent his work or how great the feeling of his own worth in relationship to the world. Dilettantes or out-and-out incompetents, by contrast, do not seem to strive for a goal or look ahead, but see only what is happening in their immediate surroundings. That is why they constantly compare, are lavish with their praise, inept in their criticism and have immense respect for each other. They give themselves an air of kindness and fairness, while all they are doing is enhancing their own image.

Once he has done what his abilities will allow, the dilettante by way of excuse will usually say that his work is not quite complete. But it never will be complete, for it was never really begun. The master presents his work with a few strokes; finished or not, it is complete. The most clever dilettante gropes in uncertainty, and as his work goes forward the inadaquacy of his original conception becomes more and more evident. Only at the end is the mistake recognized, which cannot now be remedied, and so the work can never be finished.

What the dilettante truly lacks is the talent for form in the highest sense, that productive power which creates, develops and organizes. He has an inkling of it, but he surrenders himself totally to his material instead of being master of it.

One finds that ultimately the dilettante is mainly concerned with order and neatness, with the finishing of something that already exists, whereby he can delude himself that the something is worthy of existence.

Toying with the serious and important corrupts man. [The dilettante] skips some levels, lingers on others which he regards as goals, and he thinks he is justified in judging the whole from this vatange point, thus impeding his advancement. . . . Yet dilettantism counteracts complete lack of cultivation. It is an inevitable product of already established art, and it can also become the germinal phase of art. Under certain conditions it can help stimulate and develop true artistic talent. While it degrades art itself, it elevates handicraft to a certain semblance of art.

Architecture. Because it is quite difficult to lend character to architecture and to give it variety and beauty, the dilettante, who cannot do this, will either slip into the prosaic and bombastic or the ponderous and vacuous, depending on the circumstances of his time. However, a work of architecture, owing as it does its whole existence to beauty, is artistically meaningless if it fails to produce beauty.

Architectural dilettantism, unable to fulfill architecture's aesthetic goal, usually does harm to its physical goal: usefulness and comfort.

Visibility and durability of works of architecture make their [dilettantism] more general and lasting, and perpetuate false taste because here, as in all the arts, that which is available and widespread serves in turn as a model. [Yet] where lack of cultivation prevails, it awakens a certain artistic sense and spreads it to areas that the artist himself normally would not reach.

Poetry. In this art form there is a greater danger than in others of confusing mere dilettantish skill with true art. If this happens, the individual is worse off than in any other dilettantish endeavor because he lacks all authenticity: a poet devoid of seriousness and artistic qualities is nothing.

Because there are no objective rules yet for either the inner or outer structure of a poem, the dilettante, more so than the master, must adhere to accepted models and imitate the good that exists rather than strive for originality.

Dilettantism can be of two kinds. It either neglects indispensable technical skills and believes it is sufficient to show imagination and feeling. Or it seeks poetry only in technical skill, and is without imagination and substance. Both are harmful. But the former does more harm to art, the latter to the individual himself.

All dilettantes are essentially plagiarists. They undermine and destroy all natural beauty in language and thought by mimicking and aping it in order to cover up their own vacuity. Thus language gradually becomes filled with an assortment of plundered platitudes and meaningless clichés: One can read whole books written in a beautiful style without content.

On Acting[1] (1824)

Enunciation

Just as in music the correct, exact and pure production of every individual sound is the basis of all artistic presentation, so in dramatic art the pure and distinct enunciation of every individual word is the basis of all forms of recitation and declamation.

Enunciation is complete when no syllable of a word is suppressed, but each is given its proper value.

Enunciation is pure when all words are pronounced in such a way that the audience grasps the sense easily and precisely. Purity and completeness combined make enunciation perfect.

The actor should try to acquire perfect enunciation, bearing in mind that a swallowed syllable or an indistinctly pronounced word often makes the whole sentence ambiguous, destroying the illusion and often provoking the audience to laughter even in the most serious scenes.

Faulty or incorrect memorization is the cause of faulty and incorrect enunciation for many actors. Before committing something to memory, the actor should read the text slowly and deliberately. In doing so, he should avoid all emotion, declamation and play of imagination. He should merely try to read correctly and memorize accurately. Later, many errors will be avoided regarding both accent and enunciation.

Recitation and Declamation

By recitation we mean a method of delivery that lies halfway between passionless, detached speech and speech that is highly emotional; it does not soar with feeling, yet it is not completely devoid of expression. The audience must always be aware that the actor is simply reciting a text.

To be sure, passages calling for recitation must be presented with the appropriate expression of the sensations and feelings which the poem inspires in the reader through its content. But this must be done with moderation and without that complete surrender to the role that is called for in declamation. When the actor recites, his voice is of course guided by the poet's ideas and by the impressions made on him by various subjects, gentle or horrible, pleasant or unpleasant. He adopts a horrified tone for what is horrible, a tender tone for what is tender, and a solemn tone for what is solemn, but only to demonstrate the consequences and effects of the impression made on him by the subject. He does not change his own character in the process, nor disown his nature or his individuality, and he may be compared to a piano which is played in the tone natural to that instrument. One is forced by the way a passage is composed to observe the *forte* or the *piano, dolce* or *furioso;* but one does this not by making use of the pedals, but only by the transmission of the soul into the fingers which, through their responsiveness—that is, through stronger or gentler pressure on the keys—transmit the spirit of the composition into the particular passage, arousing the sensation which can be produced by its content.

However, declamation, or hightened recitation, is quite a different matter. Here you must relinquish your innate character, disown your nature and enter completely into the situation and mood of the person whose part you are speaking. The words you say must be delivered with energy and the liveliest expression, so that it seems that you are actually experiencing every emotion.

Here the player uses the pedals and all modulations of sound that the instrument affords. If he uses them with taste, and appropriately, and if beforehand he has studied their possible uses and effects with understanding and dilligence, then he can be sure of the most beautiful and accomplished result.

One could call declamation a kind of music in prose, for it has in fact much in common with music. But we must make the distinction that music by its very nature has more freedom. The art of declamation is far more limited in the range of its sounds, and it serves ends other than its own. The actor who declaims must always bear this basic fact in mind. If he changes pitch too rapidly, if he speaks either too low or too high, or uses too many halftones, he approaches singing. On the other hand, falling into a monotone is also wrong even in simple recitation. Here we have two extremes, one as dangerous as the other, and between them a third lies concealed, namely preaching. In trying to avoid the first two, one easily becomes a victim of the last.

It is of great advantage to the beginning actor to speak as deeply as possible whenever he declaims. In this way he will develop great range and will consequently be able to produce other gradations of pitch with ease. But if he begins too high and grows accustomed to the upper register, he will lose his masculine tones, and with them the proper expression of the sublime and the spiritual. And what success can he hope for with a shrill, piping voice? But if he has mastered declamation in a deep voice, he can be confident of being able to do complete justice to every possible modulation.

Speaking Verse

All rules and suggestions concerning declamation apply here as a basis as well. It is, however, particularly characteristic of speaking verse that the text requires an even more passionate intensity of delivery. Every single word must be enunciated with a certain degree of emphasis.

But the actor must beware of stressing the meter or the end rhymes too much. Rather, he should preserve the sense of continuity, as in prose.

If he has to declaim iambic poetry he should indicate the beginning of each line by a short, scarcely perceptible pause, though it should not interfere with the flow of the declamation.

Position and Movement of the Body on Stage

Above all, the actor must remember that he should not only imitate nature but also present it in an idealized way. That is to say, in his presentation he must unite reality and beauty.

For this reason he should have control over every part of his body so that he can use every limb freely, harmoniously and gracefully, depending on the effect he wants to achieve.

His posture should be erect, his chest thrust out, his upper arms to the elbow held rather close to the torso, his head turned slightly toward the person he is addressing, but with three quarters of his face always turned toward the audience.

For the actor must always remember that he is there for the sake of the spectators.

Therefore actors should not, from a sense of misunderstood realism, play to one another as if no third party were present. They should never act in complete profile nor with their backs to the audience. If this is done for the sake of characterization or out of necessity, let it be done with discretion and grace.

The actor ought also to take particular care never to speak upstage, but always toward the audience. For he must divide himself between two parties: the person to whom he is speaking and the spectators. Instead of turning his head completely, he should use his eyes expressively.

When two actors are engaged in dialogue, it is very important that the one speaking lean back slightly while delivering his lines, and when finished, lean forward. If the actor uses this technique prudently and practices it until it becomes natural, he will achieve the best results both in regard to the visual effect of his delivery and to its intelligibility. Actors who have become masters in this will produce gratifying results and enjoy a great advantage over those who have not.

When two persons are speaking, the one on the left should be very careful not to crowd the one on the right. This side is reserved for respected persons—women, older people, or those of higher social standing. Even in ordinary life we keep our distance from those we respect, and not doing so reveals a lack of breeding. The actor should appear well-bred and should therefore adhere strictly to this rule. The person on the right should insist on his priviledge and not let himself be pushed towards the wings, but stand firm and, if need be, signal the offender with this left hand to move back.

One beautiful contemplative pose suitable for a young man is the following: the entire body erect and the chest out, feet in the fourth position,[2] head tilted slightly to one side, eyes fixed on the ground, both arms hanging loosely.

Position and Movements of Arms and Hands

In order to ensure free movement of hands and arms, the actor should never carry a cane.

The recent habit of putting one's hand into the flap of one's trousers should be abandoned completely.

It is highly incorrect to place one hand on top of the other, or to rest them on the stomach, or stick one or both into the vest.

The hand itself must neither be clenched in a fist nor held flat against the thigh, like a soldier standing at attention. Rather, some fingers must be half bent, the others kept straight, but they must never appear cramped.

The two middle fingers should always be kept together, and the thumb, index and little finger should be slightly bent. In this way, the hand is in its proper position, one suitable for all movements.

The upper part of the arm should always be pressed lightly to the torso and move much less than the lower part, which should possess the greatest suppleness. For if you raise your arm only slightly when talking about everyday things, how much greater the effect will be when you raise it all the way. If you do not moderate your movements when delivering lines of less importance, you will not have any gestures strong enough for those that are more emotional, with the result that all gradations in the effect will be totally lost.

Furthermore, the hands should never return to a position of rest before completion of a speech, and even then only gradually, similar to the way a speech comes to an end gradually.

The movements of the arms should always be sequential. First the hand should be raised or moved, then the elbow, and then the entire arm. The arm should never be raised all at once, otherwise the movement will be stiff and unsightly.

It is advisable for the beginner to force himself to keep his elbows as close to his torso as possible. In this way he will gain control over this part of his body and be able to make gestures in accordance with the above rule. He should also practice outside the theater and always keep his arms back—when he is by himself, even tied back. While strolling or during moments of leisure, he should let his arms hang loose, never press his hands together, but always keep his fingers in motion.

The descriptive hand gesture ought to be rarely used, though not omitted entirely.

In allusions to the body, the actor should never indicate with his hand the part of the body referred to. For example, when Don Manuel in *The Bride of Messina*[3] says to the Chorus:

> Select a mantle also, woven of
> Shimmering silk and gleaming with pale purple;
> And at the shoulder clasp it with a golden
> Cicada. . . .

it would be highly inappropriate for the actor to touch his shoulder at the mention of the word.

Descriptive gestures are necessary, but they must seem unintentional. In certain cases there are exceptions here too, but the above can and should be adopted as a basic rule.

The descriptive gesture of pointing the hand to the breast to indicate oneself should be used as rarely as possible and only when the meaning absolutely requires it, as for example in the following passage from *The Bride of Messina:*

> I—have brought no more hatred with me now,
> I hardly know what made us quarrel so.

Here the first 'I' can be fittingly indicated by the descriptive gesture of raising the hand to the breast.

To make this a beautiful gesture, care should be taken that the elbow is held away from the torso as the arm is raised, but that the hand not be extended too far in being brought to the chest. The hand should not be placed flat on the chest, only the thumb and ring finger should touch it. The others must be held arched above the surface of the chest, pointing to it, as it were.

In gesturing the actor should try to avoid covering his face or other parts of his body with his hand.

If a handshake is required and the right hand is not explicitly called for, the left can be used. For on stage there is no right or left. What is important is to avoid spoiling the visual effect by assuming an unattractive position. But if it is absolutely necessary for the actor to use his right hand and he is so positioned that he would have to reach across his body, he would do better to step back a little before shaking hands so that he remains facing the audience.

The actor should always remember on which side of the stage he is standing and adjust his gestures accordingly.

If he stands on the right side, he should gesture with his left hand, and vice versa, so that his chest is covered by his arm as little as possible.

In emotional scenes, when he is gesturing with both hands, he must still try to follow this rule.

For the same purpose of keeping the chest turned to the audience, it is advisable to put one's left foot forward when standing on the right side, and vice versa.

Gesture and Expression

To develop proper mimetic technique and be able to judge it properly, the following rules should be noted.

Stand before a mirror and speak the passage to be declaimed softly, or better, just think the words. The advantage of this method is that one is not carried away by declamation, but rather can easily notice any wrong movement which does not reflect what is thought, or softly spoken. The actor can then also select attractive and appropriate gestures and lend impact to the entire mimetic action through movement that is artistically analogous to the meaning of the words.

But it must be presumed that the actor has first carefully studied the character and the situation of the person to be represented, and that he has gone over the material thoroughly in his mind. For without this preparation he will not be capable of either declaiming or moving correctly.

In order to gain practice in mimetic action and to make his arms mobile and flexible, it is advisable for the beginner, without any recitation, to try to make his role intelligible merely by pantomine; then he is forced to select the most suitable gestures.

Rules for Rehearsals

In order to learn to move the feet lightly and gracefully, one should never rehearse in boots.

The actor, especially the younger one who plays the lover and other roles requiring agility, should keep a pair of slippers in the theater for rehearsals. He will soon notice results.

Even during rehearsals nothing should be allowed that is not acceptable in performance.

Actresses should not carry their handbags.

No actor should rehearse in a cloak, but should have his hands and arms free, as he will during performance. For the cloak not only hampers him in making proper gestures, but also forces him to adopt inappropriate ones, which he will then unwittingly repeat in performance.

The actor, even in rehearsal, should make no movement that is out of character.

Whoever sticks his hand in his bosom during the rehearsal of a tragic role runs the risk of groping for an opening in his armor during performance.

Bad Habits to be Avoided

Among the most flagrant blunders to be avoided is that of the seated actor who in order to move his chair forward reaches between his thighs, grasps the chair, raises himself a little, and in that position pulls it forward. This is an offence not only against esthetic sensibilities, but even more against decorum.

The actor should never display his handkerchief on stage, still less blow his nose, still less spit. It is terrible to be reminded of these natural functions in the context of art. He should keep one of those currently fashionable small handkerchiefs handy for an emergency.

Conduct Offstage

The actor should remember that even in everyday life he is on public display.

For this reason he should guard against acquiring mannerisms of gesture, pose, position of the arms, and carriage. For if he must focus on avoiding such mannerisms during a play, he will tend to neglect what is most important.

It is therefore absolutely necessary that an actor be free of any mannerisms, so that during a performance he can identify completely with his role and his mind can focus on his adopted personality.

On the other hand, it is an important rule for the actor that he make an effort to carry his training over into everyday life—in the use of his body, in his behavior and all his daily activities—as if he were engaged in a constant rehearsal. All aspects of his art will thereby benefit greatly.

The actor specializing in dramatic roles will improve immensely by seeking to retain a certain accuracy in regard to both emphasis and enunciation whenever he speaks and a certain lofty style in all his gestures. Of course he must not exaggerate, or he will make himself an object of amusement to others, but in general they will recognize behind such practices the artist developing his art. His conduct will by no means reflect poorly on him. On the contrary, people will gladly tolerate his peculiar behavior offstage, if they have the opportunity to admire him on stage as a great artist.

Because everything on stage must be presented not only realistically but also esthetically, and because the eye of the spectator demands pleasant groupings and poses, the actor should strive for these even offstage. He should always imagine himself in front of an audience.

While he is committing a part to memory, he should always pretend to be facing an audience. Even when by himself or in company at the dinner table, he should always try to create a tableau, pick up and put down objects with a certain grace as if he were on stage. And so he should be mimetic in everything he does.

Positions and Groupings on Stage

Stage and auditorium, actors and audience—only together do they form a whole.

The stage should be seen as a bare tableau in which the actor supplies the living figure.

Therefore he should never play too close to the wings.

Nor should he step out onto the proscenium. This would be the gravest error, for it would mean that the actor leaves the space within which, together with the painted scenery and the other actors, he helps form a whole.

When the actor stands alone on stage, he should bear in mind that he too is only part of a whole, all the more since attention is concentrated on him alone.

Just as soothsayers divided the sky into various sections with their staffs, the actor can divide the stage in his mind into various areas which can be sketched on paper as rhomboids. The stage floor then becomes a kind of checkerboard, and the actor can determine which squares he will enter. He can jot down his moves in advance, and is then certain not to rush about aimlessly during this emotional speeches, but rather combine beauty and significance in his positionings.

Whoever enters the stage for a monologue from an upstage wing, does well to move in a diagonal line towards the opposite side of the proscenium. In general, diagonal movements are very attractive.

Whoever enters from the rear wing to join another actor already onstage should not move parallell to the wings but slightly toward the prompter.

All these rules pertaining to technique and language should be adopted where applicable as general guidelines and practiced until they become habit. There should be no trace of stiffness, and the rule must become the imperceptible basis of living action.

It is obvious that these rules must be especially observed in portraying noble, dignified characters. On the other hand, there are characters who are to be portrayed as the opposite of dignified, such as peasants, boors, etc. The actor will be able to play these roles even better if, artistically and consciously, he does the reverse of what decorum requires, always remembering, however, that his performance should be idealized and not merely a realistic imitation.

On World Literature[1]

1. National literature is no longer of importance; it is the time for world literature, and all must aid in bringing it about.

2. Everywhere we read and hear about the progress of the human race, of good prospects for the future regarding relations among nations

and human beings. Whatever the situation may be in this respect—which is beyond my province to judge or investigate—I wish nonetheless to point out to my friends that I am convinced that a world literature is beginning to develop, in which an honorable role is reserved for us Germans. All nations are paying attention to us; they praise and criticize, accept and reject, imitate and distort, understand or misunderstand us and open or close their hearts to our concerns. We must accept this with equanimity because it is of great value to us.

3. If we have dared proclaim the beginning of a European, indeed a world literature, this does not merely mean that the various nations will take note of one another and their creative efforts, for in that sense a world literature has been in existence for some time, and is to some extent continuing and developing. We mean, rather, that contemporary writers and all participants in the literary scene are becoming acquainted and feel the need to take action as a group because of inclination and public-spiritedness. However, visits more than correspondence will bring this about, since only personal contact can establish and solidify true relationships.

4. Every nation has idiosyncracies which differentiate it from others and make it feel isolated from, attracted to or repelled by them. The outward manifestations of these idiosyncracies usually seem strikingly repugnant, or at best ridiculous, to another nation. They also are the reason why we tend to respect a nation less than it deserves. The true character of a nation, on the other hand, is seldom recognized or understood, not by outsiders or even the nation itself. Nations, like human beings, are unaware of the workings of their inner nature, and ultimately we are surprised, even astounded at what emerges.

I do not pretend to know these secrets, nor would I have the courage to define them if I did. I wish only to say that in my opinion the characteristic traits are now most evident in the French nation, and for that reason it will again exert a great influence on the civilized world.

5. [In reply to a letter from a recently founded literary society in Berlin]

That a group of Germans gathered to take note specifically of German literature was completely proper and highly desirable because all of them, as educated men well-informed about other kinds of writings and public affairs in Germany, were indeed qualified to identify and select literature for their intellectual pleasure.

One can say therefore that the literature of another nation cannot be understood and felt without being aware at the same time of its general social conditions.

We can achieve such awareness in part by reading newspapers, which tell us in great detail about public affairs. But that is not enough. We must also discover what attitudes and opinions, what views and judgment critical journals and reviews express regarding their own nation as well as others, especially the German nation. For example, if we wanted to become acquainted with current French literature, we would have to read lectures delivered and published during the last two years, such as Guizot's "Cours de l'histoire moderne," Villemain's "Cours de la littérature française," and Cousin's "Cours de l'histoire de la philosophie."[2] Their views about themselves and about us emerge most clearly there. Even more helpful, perhaps, are the newspapers and journals that appear more frequently, such as *Le Globe, La Revue Française* and the recent daily, *Le Temps*. They are all indispensible if we wish to have a clear picture of the ebb and flow of the ever-shifting tides of opinion in France, and their subsequent impact.

German literature, as can be seen from our own dailies and the two latest literary magazines, offers only exclamations, sighs and interjections produced by well-meaning individuals. Views are expressed according to temperament and education. There is hardly any concern for more universal or loftier matters. Almost no mention is made of social conditions, not much of the national state of mind and none of the concerns of church and state. We do not wish to criticize these practices, but draw attention to them for what they are. I mention them to point out that French literature, like all forms of French writing, does not for one instant isolate itself from the life and passions of the whole nation: in recent times this appears as an encounter of opposing forces, mustering all talent to assert themselves and defeat the other side. It stands to reason that the established power need not be very imaginative in its response.

But if we follow the course of these lively exchanges of views, we gain an insight into French affairs. And from the way they speak about us, whether favorably or unfavorably, we learn to judge ourselves; it can certainly do no harm if for once someone makes use think about ourselves.

Frankly, I believe more is gained by this than by entering into correspondence with foreign poets. The best of them still remain individuals limited by their particular circle, and if we like their work, they can do little more than say a gracious thank-you. If we should criticize their writings, our relationship is immediately severed.

But if we follow the course proposed above, we will soon be well informed of everything that has been or will be published. Considering the efficiency of today's book trade, any work is readily obtainable. It happens frequently that I have read a book long before I receive a courtesy copy from the author.

Anyone will agree that gaining a real understanding of modern French literature is obviously no small task. The literature of England and Italy would in turn require special approaches, for the conditions there are quite different.

6. But if such a world literature develops in the near future—as appears inevitable with the ever-increasing ease of communication—we must expect no more and no less than what it can and in fact will accomplish.

The world at large, no matter how vast it may be, is only an expanded homeland and will actually yield in interest no more than our native land. What appeals to the multitude will spread endlessly and, as we can already see now, will be well received in all parts of the world, while what is serious and truly substantial will be less successful. However, those who have devoted themselves to higher and more fruitful endeavors will become more easily and more intimately acquainted. Everywhere in the world there are men who are concerned with what has already been achieved and, using that as a basis, with working toward the true progress of mankind. But the course they take and the pace they maintain is not to everyone's liking. The more forceful members of society want to move faster and therefore reject and prevent the furtherance of the very things which could aid their own advancement. The seriousminded must therefore form a silent, almost secret congregation, since it would be futile to oppose the powerful currents of the day. But they must maintain their position tenaciously until the storm has subsided.

Such men will find their main consolation, even their ultimate encouragement in the fact that what is true is at the same time useful. Once they themselves have discovered this connection and can demonstrate it convincingly, they will not fail to have a strong impact, and what is more, for years to come.

7. Although it may be appropriate not to present our thoughts to the reader directly, but rather indirectly to awaken and stimulate his own thinking, it may be advisable to re-examine the above remarks, written some time ago.

The question whether this or that occupation is truly useful is often asked. It is especially relevant at the present when people are no longer permitted to live as they like, quietly, contented, with moderation and free from pressure. The world is in such a turbulent state that every individual is in danger of being sucked into its vortex. In order to satisfy his own need, he finds himself compelled to attend directly and promptly to the needs of others. The question remains whether he has adequate skills to fulfill these pressing obligations.

At this point, all we can do is tell ourselves that only egotism pure and simple can save us. But this egotism requires a confident, considered and calmly formulated decision.

Everyone should ask himself for what he is best suited and develop this talent with the utmost diligence. He should consider himself first an apprentice, later a journeyman, a foreman, and only in the very end and most tentatively, a master.

If with prudent modesty he increases his demands on the world in strict conjunction with the growth of this abilities and thus ingratiates himself by being useful, he will step by step attain his purpose, and once he succeeds in reaching the top will be able to lead a comfortable, productive life.

If he is attentive, life will teach him about the opportunities and obstacles offered and created by the empirical world. But this much the practical individual should always bear in mind: to drive oneself frantically in order to gain the approval of the day brings no advantage for the morrow or the day after.

8. The extravagances to which the theaters of the great and vast city of Paris feel themselves driven prove harmful to us too, although we have by no means reached that point yet. But there we have also the results of an advancing world literature, and our only consolation is that although the general effect is harmful, certain individuals will derive great benefit from it. I have seen convincing evidence of that already.

9. The phenomenon which I call world literature will come about mainly when the disputes within one nation are settled by the opinions and judgments of others.

10. For some time there has been talk of world literature, and properly so. For it is evident that all nations, thrown together at random by terrible wars, then reverting to their status as individual nations, could not help realizing that they had been subject to foreign influences, had absorbed them and occasionally become aware of intellectual needs previously unknown. The result was a sense of goodwill. Instead of isolating themselves as before, their state of mind has gradually developed a desire to be included in the free exchange of ideas.

11. Poetry is cosmopolitan, and the more interesting the more it shows its nationality.

POSTSCRIPT

The essays on art and on literature that Goethe wrote over the years reflect the process that underlay his creative work. There are quite distinct lines of development in his critical thought which match his poetic practice. Yet the essays have a life of their own. They do not anticipate the practice, nor do they serve as its justification, but are themselves the product of forces that produced the poetic works.

The earliest and most celebrated of the essays, "On German Architecture," for example, not only effectively marked the break with tradition that made possible the major writings of the early period, *Urfaust, Götz von Berlichingen, The Sorrows of Young Werther,* but was written in a style and form commensurate with them. The piece is pure *Sturm und Drang* in its unbound expressiveness and spirit of revolt. Yet in the very act of creation, which it demonstrates in its own style as it glorifies the act in the work of art before it, the essay uncovers a truth, all but formulates a theory, that seems to transcend its original and conscious intent. "Art is creative long before it is beautiful," it states, almost abruptly, in the midst of its paean to the cathedral at Strasbourg, the reputedly monstrous Gothic form of architecture which the estheticism of the times rejects but the essay has come to honor. The statement represents not a compromise but an important process of thought. It is as if the essay in the intensity and profundity of its own creative urge has parted the waters and seen to a depth where the forms that have surfaced as beauty in art are found in their awkward originality, and forms of a beauty not yet realized are oddly prefigured. These are not, of course, the pure forms of Platonic philosophy or of eighteenth-century esthetics but the primal forms of evolutionist thought. Upon that thought, here barely emerging in his work, Goethe erected his developmental theory of art (e.g. "Simple Imitation, Manner, Style," "Justus Möser: Superstition and Poetry"), defended his concept of classicism ("Ancient versus Modern"), and affirmed his historicism against the absolutist principles of an earlier tradition ("Winckelmann and His Age").

The deeper process in his thought persisted. Goethe had a way, indeed, of producing his greatest thoughts in *not* thinking, at least not on the surface. We take a further example from the opposite end of the spectrum of his critical thinking. Here the thought seems less the product of inspired insight than the result of influences and experiences long in tow joining new concerns from new experience and producing the unexpected observation. In a conversation of a much later period, with the art historian S. Boisserée, Goethe remarked: "Art is on its highest level when it is wholly absolute, when its subject matter is no longer of importance and has become simply a vehicle." The remark is striking in its modernity and is often quoted for that reason alone. But it is also striking in its apparent conflict with the early view we have just described. Subject matter had been the stepping stone for Goethe in his break with the past. He had been willing to sacrifice beauty and order to the deeper necessity of an authentic statement, and this in his own practice of literature and not merely in his critical pronouncements. His *Faust* from beginning to end, both in the sense of its composition over sixty years and in the final product as we have it, is not ordered and was too creative in content to have been so. And for all that beauty and order meant to him at the height of his classical period, it was never as principles or qualities apart. It was not the art in the sculpture and architecture of the ancient Greeks, but the awe expressed through the art, in their statues for the human body, in their temples for the gods, that he most revered.

The diminishing importance of subject matter was hardly in itself, therefore, a sign of progress in art. Goethe had taken a deeper purchase on the question. He had long abandoned, with the Romantic era as a whole, the concept of art as simple imitation and looked to it for a form of truth as valid as that reflected in science or expressed through reason, but stated differently, sensuously. Yet his instinctive manner of thought caused him to grasp this question also in its evolutionary aspect. The question for him was not whether art, ideally, should separate itself as far as possible from the things of the objective world but whether in any given artist, age, or culture it had sufficiently freed itself from its origins in imitation to be able independently to express its distinctive values, its own truth. He treats this question in "Simple Imitation, Manner, Style." It is raised here, however, to suggest a mode of thinking. For abstract art, as much as Goethe might have rejected its appearance, was yet presupposed in the implications that emerge from his casual remark to Boisserée. His critical separation of subject matter from artistic values, like his vision of creativity as prelude to beauty, throws twentieth-century art in general into new, evolutionist perspective. His conclusions, in short, tend to comprise new beginnings. It was this quality above all that distinguished his critical thought, and it is a quality that relates to life and to growth rather than to theory.

We pay a price for this natural birth of Goethe's critical ideas. No abstract, articulated framework of thought accompanies or explains his insights into literature and art. Nor do they gain by association with the esthetic theories of the age, which they sometimes resemble in their influence but not in their origins. They are the product of experience, an experience as sound and coherent for all its variety as any systematic construct, but stubborn in its demand to be understood in context. The context for the essays on art or on literature, however, was formed as often as not simply by occasion. Goethe wrote certain pieces clearly with the intent of presenting a critical position or theory. Some have been mentioned. He also created the journal *Propylaea* for the acknowledged purpose of forcing himself to give shape to thoughts on art which he had long carried about with him. But he did not write abstractly on subjects such as Beauty, as had Diderot, or on the Sublime, like Burke or Schiller. He was not, in that sense, at all an eighteenth-century thinker. Most often it was a recently published book, a newly arrived set of prints, that set him to writing. The book, the prints, in turn brought the critical obligations of explanation, identification, background or summary which sometimes reduced the generic idea or insight that had initially prompted the writing to a single paragraph or a passing observation. Time and place had their influence in a broader sense also. Goethe in tiny Weimar, despite his worldwide renown, seems generally to have conceived of his audience as a small, interested public rather than a cosmopolitan group well enough versed in particulars to desire and expect generalities and theory. His essays, especially those on art, have a distinctly utilitarian flavor. They 'rendered a service'—to use an expression he favored in his late years. And when there was no avoiding, so to speak, a discussion of the philosophical or theoretical in the interest of true progress in literary or artistic taste, he could draw upon a practice from a long tradition and seek to amuse while he instructed. Thus "The Collector and His Circle," a novella in letter form which gently mocks taste in art by matching preference to station in life, to age, to personality or profession, and so reproduces the esthetic climate of the day.

Occasion, which may often have determined the choice of subject for his essays, did not determine their importance. Occasion itself had taken on special meaning for Goethe. As a poet he believed that all poetry should be occasional, created by and for an occasion, whether it be the more common occurrence of birth or death, or the uncommonly moving personal experience, the uncommonly important event. Art was thus joined with life in the manner in which it surely had its origin; it was thus the more authentic. The confessional, autobiographical element in his own writing, which one usually associates with a romantic disposition, can as well be understood in this quite different, profoundly practicable, way as the urge to give expression to immediate experience as the only certain thing that time and place afford the poet in an ever changing world. What Goethe found disturbing in the romanticists was not the subjectivity of their approach in itself but in its application that was often neither personal nor real. As a young poet, in reviewing a book that resembled Sterne's *A Sentimental Journey,* he wrote: "Sterne feels; this writer sits himself down to feel." The remark anticipates his later, celebrated equation of romanticism with sickness and classicism with health. In the figure of Euphorion in *Faust,* who represents Byron, he depicts a daemonic poetic spirit (the offspring of Faust and Helen of Troy) who in an attempt to fly, leaps and falls dead at the feet of his parents. It is not that he has attempted the impossible, which in *Faust* is a virtue, but that he has attempted it outside his element; that makes his act unreal.

We are concerned with Goethe the critic, not the creative writer. But his views on the uses of poetry are reflected in his criticism. He never abandoned his faith in experience as the basis of knowledge. "In the beginning was the deed," he has Faust translate from the Bible. Experience remained the beginning and end of his philosophy of life and of art. It provided him with knowledge of self in relationship to self through the autobiographical content of his early works; of self in relation to society in the more objective dramas and novels of the middle years; and, with history and the observation of nature, which are the extensions backward and outwardly from the individual, of self in relation to the most broadly comprehended whole. The completed *Faust* represents this attempt at summation. It was as if he had not only sought coherence in his thought and art but had systematically planned for it. And yet the reverse was equally true. The order and integrity of his development derived from principles that only manifested themselves in action. Truth came after the fact, or with it.

Goethe's criticism does not reveal quite the same pattern of growth as the body of his creative work, in that it is the product mainly of his later years. It nevertheless illustrates, as criticism rarely does, this crucial last point. There is a movement in his essays on art and on literature, though more clearly in the former than the latter, from a subjective to an objective approach, from the particular to the general, but also beyond to what may be called the essentially true, the true independent of theory.

The trip that Goethe made to Italy in September 1786, where he stayed until June 1788, had the most profound influence on his understanding and appreciation of art. It had a lasting effect on his life, his work and his thought. In the *Italian Journey* he speaks time and again of the spiritual clarity and intellectual revelation which his experience in this new land has brought him.

But the experience was not merely that of an impressionable young genius. Goethe was thirty-seven years old when he began his journey and already famous enough to prefer to travel incognito, as a painter. The register for his lodgings read: *Filippo Miller, tedesco, pittore*. The experience marked a stage in an extraordinary development that seemed never to decline nor come to rest, so that there always lay in tension beneath the surface of its achievement the forces that would produce the next achievement, create the next stage. Beneath the experience of the splendor of art in Italy lay the ingredients for a critical impasse. Goethe had brought with him not merely a preference but a passion for realism in art, the art of the North. He speaks in his autobiography of his obsession with the Dutch masters and, for a period, of "living with Rembrandt alone." In the art of Italy, both in its ancient classical and its modern form, he was confronted with a realism that was idealized, with forms of art so highly perfected as to seem eternal. He appears to have been tempted in Rome to acknowledge the existence of an order of beauty that transcended time and place, in the philosophical and not merely the popular sense. And this is an apparent negation of his earlier insight into the evolutionist nature of art and an implied acceptance of the neoclassical precepts he had roundly condemned as a younger man. But he was forced in his botanical research in Italy to abandon his hope of finding a single plant from which all others derived, his *Urpflanze*. He similarly stopped short in his esthetic philosophy in believing in a form of beauty from which all others should or could derive.

He resolved the potential conflict within a broader framework of meaning. There was in fact no inherent contradiction between his former esthetic theory, to the extent that it had become theory, and the recognition of eternal or transcendent forms of art. For these forms, in his view, were the result of a process of achievement within time which time then could not alter, and not the expression or realization of a discerned and discernible idea of beauty outside of time. Goethe does not make this arguement directly, but it is evident from the first critical essay he wrote after his return from Italy that he had weighed the implications of his earlier views against those of his new experience.

The argument in "Simple Imitation, Manner, Style" not only serves to clarify his former intuitive sense of the developmental character of art but sets that development within the individual artist as the tangible or palpable basis for its broader reflection in the history of art in general. The artist is possessed of the urge to imitate but also of a desire to express an individualistic sense of reality. There inevitably arises from these separate tendencies toward the slavishly imitative and the artificially free a tension which can only be resolved in a higher achievement. Goethe calls this achievement simply Style. Style raises simple imitation to the level of true art, yet not beyond to mannerism. Not that imitation in this higher guise was now to be considered the final purpose and end of art. Even in the most primitive artistic forms Goethe recognized a religious, spiritual, or ideal motive which preempted or at least preceded the simple urge to imitate. In architecture, an art which is not imitative of nature but is an art in and of itself, as he noted in an unpublished fragment on architecture of the year 1795, he found the same developments, tensions and resolutions as in sculpture and painting, as though in all forms of art the idea of beauty was sought and realized not in and through nature but parallel with it. Indeed, it was a concept of the new age and new esthetic that the artist was in essence a creator and not an imitator. The basic principle on which Goethe took issue with Diderot, whose *Essais sur la peinture* he translated and commented on, was imitation and the tendency in earlier ages to confuse, "to amalgamate," as he put it, nature and art, which in fact are separate entities. He makes this point on the separation of powers, so to speak, simply and cogently in the dialogue "On Realism in Art." Here the advocate of the new esthetic soon disabuses his naive opponent of the belief that the pleasure he has always derived from art was as a substitute for reality.

The resolution of tensions in a higher achievement was a phenomenon or law or model which Goethe saw in the inner workings of nature as well as in the development of art. He described the phenomenon as polarity and heightening. As a phenomenon of nature it thus expressed itself in action rather than in thought. And the principle which he ultimately formulated as the capstone of his esthetic philosophy, in the sense that it served to reconcile the opposing tendencies in his own thought, similarly took the form of an exhortation to action. For the evolutionist principle, though it provided for the freedom to develop which he and his literary generation had championed from the beginning, led of itself to no resolve. In fact, it tended in its relativism to encourage irresolution and lack of rigor. How opposed he was to such expressions of dilettantism may be judged from the exacting demands he made upon the artist and the connoisseur of art alike in his introduction to the *Propylaea;* the fragmentary "On Dilettantism," which he composed together with Schiller, makes comparable points. Yet for all that he himself may have succeeded in managing the new freedom in his own "poetic production," as he liked to call it, and in his own mind, he had not raised the question as such and stated his position.

Now he does in "Ancient versus Modern." The relationship of manner to style, of trompe l'oeil to realism (the former "something more surprising than pleasing," as it is so nicely put in "The Collector and His Circle"), of beauty to truth, which Goethe had earlier identified in individual artists, he now enlarges as a concept to include the art of whole ages and cultures. Thus the division here between "ancient" and "modern." Like the single artist in his own development, or like one artist as opposed to another, a culture in its movement from primitive imitation to higher forms might reach truth in its art and imperceptibly pass beyond. The Greeks themselves, he claims, could be called mannered in their late development. Or an age might remain rooted in less than perfection, not for want of talent but because of circumstances or attitudes of mind. Raphael, as opposed to his contemporaries Leonardo and Michelangelo, throughout his life maintained a mental harmony and vigor that translated itself into the harmony and perfect clarity of his works. His great contemporaries neglected the full exploitation of their extraordinary talent, the former in the pursuit of technical perfection, the latter in that blind eccentricity which led him to squander endless hours in stone quarries, seeking out the ideal block of marble for his sculpture. Goethe here indulges a preference, some would say a prejudice, since Raphael had died in the prime of his life. But the point was not to demonstrate, either that an age of itself determined the course and achievement of its art, or that surpassing talent and balanced character alone accounted for the highest accomplishments. The point was to settle the Quarrel, as the conflict between neoclassical and modern opinions on learning and art had come to be known.

For Goethe the matter was clear. The ancients were to be recognized as the creators of the greatest art yet known to man, and imitated, but in spirit, not to the letter. The moderns with their less stable sense of reality were to be recognized for their achievements in their own right, and admired and emulated for having reached supreme heights in eras favorable to art, understood and accepted in their inevitable limitations in less propitious times. Hence the pronouncement that consolidates the modern position, yet in the light of the great tradition: "Let everyone be a Greek in his own way!" But hence also the exhortation that lends to the pursuit of the new a formidable respect for the accomplishments of the past: "But let him be a Greek!"

Theory once aside, Goethe could concentrate on appreciation. Not that he in fact reserved his thoughts on individual artists until he had put forth his theoretical views, rather the contrary. And he was of the opinion in any event, as he says in a preliminary note to his essay on *Laocoon,* that to speak of any work of art is to speak of all art. The essay itself provides an example of theory after the fact, or with it. Goethe speaks here of the attributes that he believes all great works to have in common, but he is concerned to show that these qualities, which we assume to be the product of artistic intention and surpassing capability, derive from an urge to truth rather than to beauty. This, of course, was the question at issue in the *Laocoon* group, a beautiful artifact that depicted an ugly scene. The contorted but artistically harmonious figures in the group, in his view, owe their very movement, or illusion of movement, to the central fact of the serpent at that very moment biting the hip of the main figure and sending a tremor through his body which animated the whole. Not the desire and ability of the sculptor to render the muscular beauty of the straining human body, Goethe believed, but the choice of the "true," the "characteristic" moment best explains the genius of the work. From the truth derived the beauty. The concern in his description of Leonardo's *The Last Supper* was again with the position, posture, gesture and head movement of the figures, much as a novelist might conceive the setting, with less attention to the beauty of the rendering than to the reality to be depicted. There was little concern in the essay with color. Yet this neglect was also typical of an age which in its reaction to the gaudy extremes of the Baroque had come to prefer the sculptured to the painterly in art, the line to color. The call for "noble simplicity and quiet grandeur" with which Winckelmann roused the late eighteenth century is most understandable in this light. It was the light in which Goethe would have seen his own change from an early insistence upon naturalism and realism to his later conversion to the idealism of the classical style.

Occasion, we said, mainly determined the choice of subject matter for his essays. A landscape with which he was particularly familiar in the real world, when reproduced in painting might occasion a discussion of that genre, as in "Two Landscapes by Philipp Hackert." When in his view speculation about fragmentary or lost monuments of art remained wholly inadequate or had become too misguided, he might undertake to solve a problem or redirect an inquiry, through not always successfully. Thus "A Grave Near Cumae" and "Myron's Cow." Artists whose work he had admired over a lifetime would under one or another circumstance elicit an essay on an aspect of their genius long apparent to him perhaps, but never explicitly stated. Thus "Ruisdael as Poet" and "Rembrandt the Thinker." It was a set of excellent sketches from *The Last Supper,* which Goethe had seen in Italy in unrestored form, that brought on the detailed description and appraisal of that work. Discussion of a proposed victory monument on which he had been consulted led to his comment on a question seldom raised in criticism, i.e. the relationship between art and public consciousness. Thus the unusual "A Challenge for a Modern Sculptor." Also concerned, not with what was, but what might be, was the essay "Christ and Twelve Figures," which conceives of a cycle of sculpted figures in an imposing setting. The magnitude of the conception and the detail in which it is described again suggests the fascination that art held for him and, coming at the end of his life, attests to the regret he must have felt in not being able himself to accomplish what he so enjoyed and admired in others. For he had hoped, planned and studied as a young man to be a painter. He could say in his autobiography that "art above all things has given me the greatest pleasure of my life."

The essays in this volume are meant to represent this life *in* art and not merely at its critical periphery.

"Art is creative long before it is beautiful."—"Art is on its highest level when it is wholly absolute." These were the poles, the beginning and the ultimate end, that Goethe envisioned for the course of art. It was a broad vision. It allowed for the initial ungainliness of creativity, for the individual achievement of perfection and its reattainment in new forms, and for the ideal of a beauty unattached. Yet beauty, like light, as we are told in *Faust,* "clings to objects." The ideal of absolute art was less a goal to be set by individual artists than a hope that there might arise in the development of a given culture circumstances in which the freest and highest expression of genius would meet with the needs and desires of the broadest public. Goethe in his "classicism" never forgot time and place.

A word must be said separately on Goethe as a critic of literature. The views he held on art in general he applied to literary forms, of course, and rarely bothered to mark distinctions. "Ancient versus Modern," which was occasioned by a literary event, namely a criticism of his own poetic development, illustrates and resolves its question with examples from painting and sculpture. His earliest essay, the piece on German architecture, was read at the time, and is still read, as a celebration of enthused and inspired *poetic* genius. The same general insights that appear in the essays on art might as well have appeared in those on drama or poetry. Yet they do not. The essays on literature are different in approach, tone and manner, for they inevitably reflect a different relationship to their subject matter.

It is not simply that Goethe was a student of the one, even in the best humanistic sense of the word, and a master of the other. The difference between the essays on literature and on art is not one of quality but of impact. Goethe functioned as a critic of literature as much through his poetic work as through his pronouncements on literature. There were implied standards set by his literary accomplishments. But these were not set gradually. It was his first novel, *Werther,* that became the model of expression for the new sensibility of the age, his first drama, *Götz von Berlichingen,* that was to mark the beginnings of a national theater. His later development, or rather, later new beginnings, for his development was a series of such, was likewise original and exemplary at once. *Iphigenia* was not merely a product of Weimar Classicism, it became its symbol. *Wilhelm Meister* initiated and defined the tradition of the "Bildungsroman." And as Goethe's achievements began to impress no less by their variety than their apparent spontaneity, they appeared to others inhibiting, almost preemptive. "Goethe is simply in my way," the young Schiller said. Yet in breaking the impasse, both for himself and an important new generation of writers, Schiller only enhanced the image of his older contemporary. In his essay *On Naive and Sentimental Poetry,* he spoke of Goethe as a "poet in whom nature functions more faithfully and purely than any other, and who, among modern poets, is perhaps least removed from the sensuous truth of things.'' Goethe was in effect relegated to the high order of poets of the classical world, while Schiller reserved for himself, as more typically a product of the modern era, the task of regaining the effect of spontaneity through unending conscious effort. The standard was thus clarified, the way made clear, but the ideal remained formidable.

Goethe himself had little to do with the shaping of this image of his genius, the effects of which on later German literature and literary theory were immeasurable. Yet the factors that went outwardly to create the image, went inwardly to establish the basis for his formal judgment and criticism of literature. He felt himself to be on equal footing with the very great, and when he addressed himself to their work and their particular essence it was in the way that geniuses tend to regard one another, which is as human entities and not as phenomena of nature. His remarks on Dante, on Calderon, on Sterne derive their importance from his conception of these figures of world literature as best understood and appreciated primarily in terms of their times or their particularity of being, so that what defined and accounted for their individual greatness at the same time circumscribed its limits. Only Shakespeare appeared to him unbound. ''Nature! Nature! Nothing so like Nature than Shakespeare's figures!'' This was the youthful expression of an admiration that went, in more reasoned form, into the later essay ''Shakespeare Once Again.'' The admiration was general as well as personal, however. Goethe found in Shakespeare not only a poet whom he revered throughout his life but also the most representative literary genius of the modern era, as the essay in its interpretation of the tragic in Shakespeare and in its view of the essential nature of his poetry makes clear. Only Byron seems to have affected him uncertainly. There is praise and careful appraisal in the essay on *Cain,* but ambivalence in the remarks on *Manfred.*

What had provided Goethe with the confidence, one might say, to see the truth, lent him special credibility in expressing it. He was never the lyric poet criticizing the novelist with little understanding of the latter's form, never the novelist demanding of the dramatist what the drama cannot afford, or the reverse. For these crafts and forms were his crafts and forms as well. When he wrote ''On Epic and Dramatic Poetry,'' it was only after, and perhaps directly upon, completing *Hermann and Dorothea,* an epic in classical form with contemporary content. ''On Didactic Poetery'' had similar origin. Not that this knowing from experience in itself rendered his judgments valid. But it did add to the weight usually afforded the poet as critic a dimension that was perhaps unique. There was the appearance and presumption of total freedom from vested interest in his literary essays. When, further, he seemed to turn his back on poetry in concentrating his energies on science, the picture of Olympian detachment was complete.

Yet his view of the purpose of literature was clear, and anything but Olympian or elitist. He had no desire to create a literary hierarchy. His first literary essay proper, "Response to a Literary Rabble-Rouser," defends German writers against the charge that they had not produced prose works that could be called "classical." Goethe asked, What is a classic? and in his reply listed a set of required circumstances, social, political and cultural, which together suggested that such a work *happened* to a writer as much as he produced it. This developmental concept was less original with Goethe than with Herder who, as the "father of modern historiography," championed the idea of cultural relativism against the normative or absolutist tendencies of his day. What was new with Goethe was the extention of the concept, which had served him and Herder earlier as justification for a national literature and national concerns, to include a further step in the developmental process. This step was toward a "world literature."

"National literature is no longer of importance. It is the time for world literature," Goethe remarked to Eckermann in 1827. He did not mean by that term what is generally assumed today, rather the opposite. World literature was to include not only the works of surpassing greatness to which the tradition had given almost sole attention but also products of less importance which nevertheless brought alive the conditions, the context, the life of a nation that had produced and was producing the greater works. World literature was to be inclusive: it would seek the universal through comprehension, that is, through taking in all. The reading of newspapers, journals, literary reviews, of history and biography, was recommended and the public acquisition of this material encouraged. The essay on Carlyle's *German Romance* is a declaration in praise of translation and translators, those purveyors of mutual understanding. Goethe quotes the Koran, "God has given every nation a prophet in its own language," and adds, "Thus every translator is a prophet among his people." "Plato as Party to a Christian Revelation" suggests through the very anachronism in its title the distortions of meaning that arise precisely from a lack of understanding of historical or foreign contexts. Even the apparently specialized discussion of form in "Greek Tetralogies" has broad implications. The emphasis and ready acceptance which it gives to the disparate elements in Greek theater throws into peculiar relief the assumption of purity of purpose in ancient drama upon which European playwrights had built, Goethe himself in his classical period not excepted. This openness to variety and change was as much a condition for his idea of world literature as it was its result. He had long concerned himself with the poetry of other nations and with the indigenous, yet isolated literature of his own. Thus "A

German Gil Blas'' and ''Justus Möser,'' which latter essay he put to wider purpose with a discussion of the relationship between poetry and superstition.

World literature was to be social, or political, in its ultimate purpose. Nations were to better understand one another, not through their common humanity so much as through their obvious and their subtle differences, differences which Goethe believed were best reflected in their literatures. That concept was of the age, ready to be born. An earlier time had sought understanding through emphasis on the universality of purpose which supposedly underlay the actions, thought and art of all nations and men, and had failed. Witness the wars and the violent social and political upheaval that Goethe himself had experienced in his lifetime. Not the universal, but the particular in its own right and yet as part of a greater whole to be, would mark the future. The Germans themselves, Goethe noted, had only lately moved toward a national literature, and the eyes of the world were now upon them. In this new setting he appeared even to forget his own differences with the Romantic poets of his day; most of the writings he welcomed in the four volumes of Carlyle's *German Romance* as national contributions to a literary world view were of the substance, and by the authors, he had condemned on other occasions.

The concept and vision of a world literature, coming at the end of a long career that had found its purpose and direction in development and change, provided an apt conclusion. The concept seems in retrospect to have evolved naturally and inevitably from the idea of a national and indigenous literature and art with which Goethe had first identified, just as his classicism evolved from the subjectivism and romanticism of his early life and works. His visions, his idealism, his life itself in the immense variety of activities and interests which it simultaneously entailed reveal the same natural growth. His very conception of the ideal had the attributes of life rather than thought. For him the ideal was not a preconceived notion to which one as poet, or critic, or human being sought to make the things of art or of life conform, but a projected image, always only imperfectly conceived, which the experience of life or of art constantly modifies to make apparently attainable. The ideal is what induces to action.

John Gearey

NOTES

The translations are based on the texts in vols. 13 and 14 of the *Gedenkausgabe der Werke, Briefe und Gespräche,* ed. Ernst Beutler (Zürich, 1948ff.), "Schriften zur Kunst" and "Schriften zur Literatur," respectively.

In preparing the notes I have consulted a number of editions of Goethe's works. The Hamburg edition, vol. 12, "Kunst und Literatur," eds. Herbert von Einem and Hans-Joachim Schrimpf, which contains a detailed bibliography, including many English titles, and the Berlin edition, vols. 17–18, "Schriften zur Literatur," and vols. 19–20, "Schriften zur bildenden Kunst," ed. Siegfried Seidel, proved most helpful.

PART ONE: ESSAYS ON ART

On German Architecture

1 "Von deutscher Baukunst" appeared as a pamphlet in 1772, anonymously. It was dedicated to Erwin von Steinbach, whom Goethe believed to be the sole architect of the Cathedral at Strasbourg, to which the essay is devoted. The title, "On *German* Architecture," reflects the erroneous assumption that Goethe made at the time, that the style of architecture before him was intrinsically German. "Gothic" would have been the more appropriate adjective, but the term *stilo gotico,* which was current in the age, was derogatory and meant little more than the "barbaric," i.e. Goths' style.

2 *Anno Domini. . .*"In the year of our Lord 1318, on January 17 [the 16th calendar day before February], Master Erwin died, who was planner of the Cathedral at Strasbourg."

3 *Acts* 10 (v. 11–12). Peter "saw heaven opened, and a certian vessel descending unto him, as it had been a great sheet knit at the four corners, and let down to earth: Wherein were all manner of four-footed beasts of the earth, and wild beasts, and creeping things, and fowls of the air."

4 *à la Grècque. . .*With decorative motif from antiquity, i.e. with precisely the same artificiality contained in his theories of architecture.

5 The *new French school* represented in Goethe's mind by the Jesuit scholar Marc-Antoine Laugier, the "dear Abbé" mentioned below, whose *Essai sur l'architecture* (1753/55) was known to Goethe in the German translation of 1768; also his *Observations sur l'architecture* which appeared in 1765. The latter featured an engraving depicting the muse of architecture sitting atop the ruin of an ancient temple and

pointing toward a simple hut consisting of four upright tree trunks and a pointed roof of branches as the essential form of architecture. Goethe takes exception to this supposition. However, he had not read far enough in Laugier to find the detailed appreciation of the Strasbourg cathedral that is contained in Chap. IV of the *Essai.*

6 Johann Georg Sulzer in his dictionary of art terms (1771) writes of 'Gothic' in the manner that Goethe here dismisses. Sulzer is also the "German scholar" and the "modern esthetiziser" below. In reviewing Sulzer's writings in the *Frankfurter gelehrte Anzeigen,* Goethe began: [His works] could easily be translated into French and just as easily have been translated from the French."

7 The allusion is to the theory that Homer simply compiled the creations of an oral tradition.

8 It is not clear whether Goethe has a specific church in mind. The S. Marie Madeleine in Paris was hardly begun when this essay was written. Goethe may have seen plans for this church that were published in 1765.

9 An allusion to the portrait painters of the Rococco period.

10 Again a biblical allusion, *Psalm* 139 (v. 9).

11 *Psalm* 17 (v. 12).

12 The artist in Goethe's time had become "a second maker, a just Prometheus, under Jove," in the words of Shaftesbury, whose esthetic theories were most influential in the *Sturm und Drang* movement at the end of the eighteenth century. See "Soliloquy" in Shaftesbury's *Characteristicks of Men, Manners, Opinions, Times* (1711).

ON GOTHIC ARCHITECTURE

1 "Von deutscher Baukunst" in *Über Kunst und Altertum am Rhein und Main,* Vol. IV, 1823. Goethe edited this journal with the so-called Weimar Friends of the Arts from 1816 on. We translate the word *deutsch* in the title as *Gothic* since the essay deals with the Cologne Cathedral. Cf. the earlier essay "On German Architecture" and the first note.

2 When Goethe speaks of both concealed and revealed relationships in architecture, he has something specific in mind. He expressed to his friend Wilhelm Humboldt his belief that one can walk through an architectural structure blindfolded and yet sense its inner design, as evidenced in a letter of Humboldt to Schiller of Nov. 9, 1795.

3 François Blondel, whose *Cours* appeared 1675/83, was the French architect of renown in the seventeenth century and an opponent of the Gothic style.

4 That is, in the early essay on German architecture that is mentioned again at the end of the present piece, with a hint at its republication.

5 In the interim, Goethe's enthusiasm was reserved for Andrea Palladio (1508–1580), the "classical" Italian architect, on whose work and theories he had begun an essay in 1795. It is there that Goethe spoke

of architecture as a "fiction," that is, as an art form that imitates, not nature but itself.

6 Johann Sulpiz (1789–1854) and Melchior Boisserée (1786–1851), art historians and collectors.

7 Georg Moller, an architect who published newly discovered original plans for the Cologne Cathedral in 1818. Begun in 1248, construction of the cathedral was halted in the middle of the sixteenth century. Goethe's essay may have had its influence, since construction was begun again in earnest in 1842.

8 Heinrich Friedrich Karl von und zum Stein (1757–1831), Prussian statesman of great influence at the beginning of the nineteenth century.

9 Gottlieb Büsching, *Versuch einer Einleitung in die Geschichte der altdeutschen Baukunst* (1821).

ON THE LAOCOON GROUP

1 "Über Laokoon" in *Propyläen,* Vol. I, 1798. Laocoon warned the Trojans against accepting the gigantic horse in which Greek soldiers were hiding. The gods who see their plan of destroying Troy thwarted send two snakes from the sea which catch the priest and his two sons in their coils and suffocate them.

2 The group had been taken by Napoleon to Paris as part of the peace settlement with Italy and Pope Pius VI in 1797. Goethe does not mention the *Laokoon* in his *Italian Journey* but it is assumed he saw the sculpture in the Vatican while in Rome.

3 Goethe uses, respectively, the following words for the qualities he describes: *lebendige, hochorganisierte Naturen; Charaktere; in Ruhe oder Bewegung; Ideal; Anmut; Schönheit.*

4 The group is attributed by Pliny in his *Natural History* to the artists Hagesander, Polydoros and Athenodoros of Rhodes, 1st century B.C.

5 The references are to a Roman copy of the group by Praxiteles [?], *Niobe and Her Daughters* in the Uffizi in Florence; to the *Spinario,* a Roman bronze in the Municipal Collections in Rome; to a marble group of *Wrestlers* in the Uffizi; to the wrestling satyr and hermaphrodite of the twin statues in Dresden.

6 The sculpture, a Roman copy of a late Greek statue, depicts Dirce, Queen of Thebes, tied to a bull and being brutally dragged to death. The promised discussion did not materialize.

7 Milo, the Greek athelete. Goethe may have had in mind the statue by Falconet, in whose work he had taken interest in early years. See "Nach Falconet und über Falconet" in *Aus Goethes Brieftasche* (1776).

MYRON'S COW

1 "Myrons Kuh" in *Über Kunst und Altertum,* Vol. II, 1818.

2 In *Anthologia Graeca,* a tenth-century collection of ancient poems, which Herder translated into German (1785/86).

3 Phidias, 5th century B.C. sculptor who designed the ornamental art for the Parthenon; Polyclitus, noted 5th century sculptor.

4 Goethe's theory found little credence even in his own day. The coins of Dyrrhachium could hardly have had a connection with Myron's statue. The drawing is by K. A. Schwerdgeburth, who had earlier done a series of drawings after sketches by Goethe.

5 These goddesses have in fact been depicted in the manner which Goethe here thinks demeaning. (See the *Hamburger Ausgabe,* vol. 12, p. 625.)

6 Amalthea was the name of the she-goat who nurtured Zeus; Chiron the teacher of the great heroes of antiquity, e.g. Hercules, Achilles, Jason.

7 Zeuxis, famous painter of the 5th century B.C.; Skopas, sculptor of the 4th century B.C.

8 The emblem of Rome, a brass metal statue of Greek or Etruscan origin in the 6th century B.C. The human offspring, Romulus and Remus, were added in the Renaissance.

9 The remark was directed not so much against the motif as religious subject matter as against contemporary Romantic treatments of it. In print Goethe omitted a passage from the manuscript which makes that clear.

10 Gilles Ménage (1616–1692), French writer and philologist.

11 Inachus' daughter, i.e. Io. According to Greek mythology, Zeus fell in love with Io and transformed her into a beautiful white cow. Hera had her pursued by a horsefly.

12 Admetos was the mythic king of Pherae. His herds were multiplied by Apollo, who had once served as his shepherd.

A GRAVE NEAR CUMAE

1 "Sendschreiben des Herrn Geheimen Rats Goethe . . . über ein neu entdecktes griechisches Grabmal bei Cumae" in *Curiositäten . . . für gebildete Leser,* Weimar, 1812. The archeologist Friedrich Karl Ludwig Sickler discovered an ancient grave at Cumae, near Naples, with a three-part relief, possibly from the 1st century A.D. He announced his findings to Goethe in a letter and published them in the periodical *Curiositäten.* This essay is Goethe's open response to Sickler.

2 Sickler's article encouraged this interpretation by referring in the title to the bas-reliefs as depicting 'bacchanal celebrations.'

3 *Zeuxis,* see "Myron's Cow," note 7. Hecuba, wife of Priam, bore him nineteen children.

4 This does not seem to have been a common practice.

5 Orion, the hunter of mythology, was placed in the heavens after his death, to continue his chase.

6 Cerberus is the three-headed dog that guards the entrance to Hades.

7 "Better, I say, to break sod as a farm hand for some poor country man . . . than lord it over all the exhausted dead" (*Odyssey* XI, trans. Fitzgerald).

8 The original sequence of the reliefs was in fact different from what Goethe assumed.
9 The ancient city of Herculaneum was destroyed in 79 A.D. by an eruption of Mt. Vesuvius. Archeological excavation begun in 1719 provided important knowledge of the ancient world.
10 Philostratos Flavios and his grandson produced the *Eikones,* poetic descriptions of paintings that purportedly existed in Naples in the third century and dealt with the feats of gods and titans.

GIUSEPPE BOSSI: ON LEONARDO DA VINCI'S LAST SUPPER AT MILAN

1 In *Über Kunst und Altertum,* Vol. I, 1817. Giuseppe Bossi (1777–1815), painter at the academy in Milan, was commissioned to make a copy of the *Last Supper* in the size of the original fresco that Leonardo had painted for the refectory of the Dominican monastery between 1495 and 1497. He published a book on his research, 'The Last Supper of Leonardo da Vinci,' in 1810. The Duke of Weimar possessed three of Bossi's tracings from other copies of the *Last Supper.* The original Bossi copy was destroyed in World War II. Goethe had seen the fresco in the Dominican monastery during this stay in Italy. The illustration on page 41 is of the Morghen print referred to in note 4.
2 The Byzantine style, *maniera bizantia,* was the predominant style in the Italian middle ages.
3 Leonardo was commissioned to paint a mural depiciting the victory of the Florentines over the Lombards at Anghiari in 1440, and Michelangelo a mural that would face it of a victory at Cascina in 1364. A cartoon for the former exists only in fragments; the cartoon for the latter is lost. The *Madonna and Child with St. Anne* is in the Louvre.
4 Raphael Morghen completed a print of the *Last Supper* in 1800.
5 *Matthew* 26 (v. 21); *John* 13 (v. 21).
6 Michelangelo Bellotti (died 1744), Milanese painter.
7 Antonio De Georgi (1720–1793), Milanese painter.
8 Giuseppe Mazza (died 1796).
9 Herostratus set fire to the Temple of Artemis at Ephesus in order to gain fame.
10 Eugène Beauharnais, the son of Josephine Beauharnais, who married Napoleon in 1796.
11 The "almost thirty" copies has now been reckoned at forty-two, including Bossi's. See L. Steinberg, "Leonardo's *Last Supper,*" *Art Quarterly,* XXXVI, 1973; for Leonardo's preparatory drawings for the fresco, see L. H. Heydenreich, *Leonardo: The Last Supper* (1974).
12 Marco d'Ogionno (or d'Ogiono), Lombard painter. The larger copy to which Goethe refers is today generally attributed to another pupil

of Leonardo's, Giampietrino, as is the copy that Goethe attributes to Pietro Lovino (Luini).
13 That is, the viceroy, Eugène Beauharnais.
14 The mosaic was eventually created by Giacomo Raffaelli (1753–1836) and brought to Austria in 1818. It is in the Minoritenkirche in Vienna.
15 Alessandro Verri (1741–1816), a writer on art.
16 Goethe had earlier read Leonardo's treatise on painting, *Trattato della pittura*. His reference to a new edition of the treatise at the end of the essay does not indicate first acquaintance.
17 Goethe identifies the apostles according to Bossi.
18 In his portraits of the ancient philosophers and scientists in this painting, Raphael seems to have suggested figures from his own age: Donato Bramante, architect of St. Peter's, in the face of Euclid; Michelangelo in the philosopher Heraclitus.
19 Not as closely as Goethe assumed. His interpretation was misled in some particulars by details ommitted from the original.
20 Friedrich Müller, called *Maler Müller,* i.e. Müller the Painter (1750–1825), is best known as a poet of the *Sturm und Drang*.
21 Leonardo's treatise on painting, edited by Guiglielmo Manzi (Mansi), from the manuscript in the Vatican library.

GIOTTO'S LAST SUPPER

1 "La Cena, pittura in muro di Giotto" in *Über Kunst und Altertum,* Vol. V, 1824.

2 An informal group that figures often in the essays. See "Introduction to the *Propylaea,*" note 1, as well as "The Collector and His Circle," note 1, for Goethe's activities in promoting the arts. It has been suggested that the essay is indeed not by Goethe but by another member of the group, Heinrich Meyer (1759–1832), artist and art historian in Weimar and close friend of Goethe's. See *Berliner Ausgabe,* vol. 20, p. 705.

3 Both Johann Anton Ramboux (1790–1866), pupil of David in Paris, and Ferdinand Ruscheweyh (1785–1845) were associated with the Romantic movement and with a group of German painters known as the "Nazarenes" for their theory that only through a devout and moral way of life could art be renewed in the modern era.

RUISDAEL AS POET

1 "Ruisdael als Dichter" in *Morgenblatt für gebildete Stände,* No. 107, Tübingen, 1816. With Allart van Everdingen and Meindert Hobbema, Jacob van Ruisdael (1628?–1682) represents the second great period of Dutch landscape painting. Goethe has a wrong birth date for Ruisdael.

2 The *Dresdener Galerie,* where Goethe saw these paintings.

3 *The Jewish Cemetery* (near Ouderkerk).

REMBRANDT THE THINKER

1 "Rembrandt der Denker" in the posthumous collection of Goethe's works, 1832, vol. 44. *The Good Samaritan,* a drawing, 1633. Goethe had a lifelong interest in Rembrandt. Rembrandt, Raphael and, somewhat unexpectedly, Rubens seemed to him "veritable saints," he said in 1776 in "Nach Falconet und über Falconet."

2 Giuseppe Longhi (1766–1831), engraver and art historian. The quotation is from his volume on copper engraving which is the first part of *Concerente la teorice dell'arte* (1830).

TWO LANDSCAPES BY PHILIPP HACKERT

1 "Zwei Landschaften von Philipp Hackert" in the *Jenaische Allgemeine Literaturzeitung,* Nos. 19/20 (1804). Philipp Hackert (1737–1807), German landscape painter, lived in Naples in the latter part of his life. Goethe studied drawing with him after they had met in 1787. In his will Hackert gave autobiographical material to Goethe with the request that he publish it. See *Philipp Hackert.* Biographische Skizze, meist nach dessen eigenen Aufsätzen entworfen von Goethe (1811).

2 By the "Duke" is meant here as elsewhere Karl August of Sachsen-Weimar-Eisenach (1757–1828), Goethe's patron since 1775.

3 The terrain, villas, and other features of the landscape that Goethe describes were familiar to him from his extended stay in Rome. He knew the surroundings of Florence less well. His own knowledge of the subject matter of these paintings is relevant to the distinction he makes in this essay between landscape painting and the painting of scenes or views, "Abbildungen der Gegend." Contrast "Ruisdael as Poet."

SIMPLE IMITATION, MANNER, STYLE

1 "Einfache Nachahmung der Natur, Manier, Stil" in *Teutscher Merkur,* February 1789. The short treatise 'On the Artistic Imitation of Beauty,' *Über die bildende Nachahmung des Schönen* by Karl Philipp Moritz (1788), with whom Goethe had discussed such matter during their acquaintance in Rome, is reflected in the present essay. See the study of this interesting figure by Mark Boulby, *Karl Philipp Moritz: At the Fringe of Genius* (1979).

2 After Cézanne we can no longer think of still-life painting in this way.

3 See "Two Landscapes by Philipp Hackert" above.

4 These ideas are further developed in the "Introduction to the *Propylaea*" and "The Collector and His Circle."

5 Jan van Huysum (1682–1749) and Rachel Ruysch (1664–1750), Dutch landscape and still-life painters, examples of whose works Goethe saw in the Dresden collection.

ON REALISM IN ART

1 "Über Wahrheit und Wahrscheinlichkeit der Kunstwerke" in *Propyläen,* Vol. I. 1798. The title translates more literally as "On Truth and Verisimilitude in Art," but Goethe is clearly dealing with the misconception that exact imitation most truly represents reality, which is the crucial question in the matter of realism in art.

2 The great master is Zeuxis (5th century B.C.). The story is told by Pliny in his *Natural History*. There, however, the cherries are grapes.

INTRODUCTION TO THE PROPYLAEA

1 "Einleitung" to the *Propyläen. Eine periodische Schrift, herausgegeben von Goethe,* 1798. "Propylaea" after the Greek meaning an architectural threshold to a temple. Six issues of the journal were published between 1798 and 1800. The *we* of the Introduction is a plural, not an editorial *we*. Goethe worked together with a group who would later call themselves the Weimar Friends of Art: Heinrich Meyer, artist and art historian, professor at the Weimar art academy, and closest collaborator; Wilhelm von Humboldt, the philologist and statesman; Friedrich August Wolf, classical philologist at Halle; and Schiller, more as a consultant than as a contributor. Goethe reflects the agreed opinion of this consortium in his Introduction and thus the views on art of Weimar Classicism at its height. See Victor Lange, *The Classical Age of German Literature* (1982).

The journal had little success. The bland pedagogical tone of the Introduction may suggest a reason for the limited readership. There was an undeniable pedantic streak in Goethe which was not suppressed in his essays. Gerhart Hauptmann, the German dramatist, perhaps had that in mind when he remarked, "It is nice when the genius in Goethe outshines the guild master."

2 Goethe hoped that his own *Theory of Color* (which was completed only later, 1810) would have practical application for the artist. See the English edition by Herbert Aach, trans., and Ruprecht Matthei, ed. (1971).

3 This is the essay 'On the Choice of Subject in the Visual Arts,' "Über die Gegenstände bildender Kunst," by Heinrich Meyer.

4 The reference is to Goethe's own essay "On the *Laocoon* Group."

5 "Meyer [Heinrich] has remarked that all the forms of visual art were driven toward painting, in that through perspective and color it alone could make imitation seem wholly true. One also sees in the development of poetry that everything pressed toward drama, toward something truly present." (Goethe to Schiller, December 23, 1797.)

6 This did not occur until much later. In collaboration with Schiller, Goethe did write "On Epic and Dramatic Poetry," "On Dilettantism," and planned larger projects.

7 In 1796/97, by Napoleon when he invaded Italy.

ANCIENT VERSUS MODERN

1 "Antik und Modern" in *Über Kunst und Altertum,* Vol. II, 1818. In a previous essay in the same issue of the journal, Goethe speaks of the competition between poetry and the visual arts to illustrate and celebrate ancient mythology as leading to the highest accomplishments. The competition between ancient and modern art is thus conceived as similarly conducive to great accomplishment. Cf. "Philostrats Gemälde," which deals with the *Eikones* of Philostratus Flavius (Cf. "A Grave near Cumae," note 8).

2 Schubarth (1796–1861), philologist and writer on esthetics, published *Zur Beurteilung Goethes mit Beziehung auf verwandte Literatur und Kunst* in 1817. Schubarth joined Goethe in the publication of *Über Kunst und Altertum* in 1820.

3 Daniel Nikolas Chodowiecki (1726–1801), painter and engraver, director of the art academy in Berlin.

4 See note 9 to "A Grave Near Cumae."

5 Pietro Vannucci (1446–1523), called Il Perugino.

6 It is also true that Pope Julius lost interest and discontinued the project. *Moses,* at the tomb of Julius II in Rome.

7 Of the Carracci family, artists between 1560 and 1619 in Bologna. Annibale and Agostino and a cousin, Ludovico, were representative of the Italian Baroque.

8 Goethe referred to Rubens, along with Rembrandt and Raphael, as "veritable saints" in his early acquaintance with art. "What the artist hasn't loved, doesn't love, he must not, cannot paint. You find Rubens' women too fleshy! I tell you, they were his women, and had he peopled heaven and hell, the sky, earth and the sea with idealizations, he would have been a worse husband," Goethe wrote in "Über Falconet und nach Falconet" in 1776.

A CHALLENGE FOR A MODERN SCULPTOR

1 "Anforderung an einen modernen Bildhauer" in *Über Kunst und Altertum,* Vol. I, 1817. The city of Rostock decided in 1814 to erect a memorial to its hero from the Wars of Liberation, Fieldmarshal Gebhard von Blücher. Goethe was asked to suggest appropriate scenes from the war. The sculptor was Johann Gottfried Schadow (1764–1850), director of the art academy in Berlin. Public questions and controversy arose in the matter, to which this unusual piece is a response.

2 The allusion is to the Thessalian mountain people of Greek legend who did battle with the centaurs, a motif often repeated in Greek art and literature. The centaurs are often depicted as savage and lusting for women and wine.

3 As in the reliefs on the monument of Lysicrates (c. 334 B.C.) in Athens.

4 The reference is to the Column of Trajan in Rome that celebrates his victories over the Tracians in the 2nd century A.D.

5 Polidoro Caldara da Caravaggio (died 1543), not the later, renown Michelangelo Merisi da Caravaggio. No such painting has been identified.

6 In motifs from Virgil's *Aeneid* for frescoes in the Palazzo Fava, 1580–1585.

7 *Matthew* 2 (v. 16).

8 Goethe indulges a general European prejudice of his day. Contact with the Ottoman Empire had been limited to the battlefield. There were three wars with Austria and Russia between 1736 and 1792. The Turks were still the "infidels."

9 The Revolutionary Wars (1775–1783).

10 Tippoo Sahib, the Sultan of Mysore, was killed by the English in 1799 and his kingdom became an English colony.

11 Eteocles and Polynices, sons of Oedipus who killed each other in combat for the rulership of Thebes. The Furies are imagined as encouraging this fratricide.

CHRIST AND TWELVE FIGURES

1 "Christus nebst zwölf alt- und neutestamentlichen Figuren, den Bildhauern vorgeschlagen" in the posthumous collection of Goethe's works, vol. 44 (1832). Between 1821 and 1827, the Danish sculptor Bertel Thorvaldsen (1768–1844) created a cycle, *Christ and the Twelve Apostles* (Copenhagen, Thorvaldsen Museum), of which Goethe saw certain reproductions. Remarking on the unimaginative way in which these figures were usually treated in sculpture, he said: "The one apostle is always more or less like the other, and yet the least of them have enough life and deeds behind them to lend them character and meaning. For my own amusement I have been trying recently to imagine a cycle of twelve biblical figures in which each would be important, each different and therefore each a thankful subject for the artist" (*Eckermann*, March 16, 1830).

2 Goethe's general opposition to religious subject matter in art has to do with the manner in which such motifs were treated in his time by members of the Romantic movement, especially the so-called Nazarenes. See note 3 to "Giotto's *Last Supper*." Perhaps Goethe felt that sculpture, not because of the nature of the genre but simply because it had not identified itself with religious subject matter in his time, could reclaim a role that had been usurped.

3 The original cycle by Raphael has not been preserved. Goethe knew the paintings from engravings.

4 *Matthew* 8 (v. 5–13).

5 In the manuscript, a final sentence is included: "Even if a beginning has to be made by confectioners on Christmas Eve—if a joke may be allowed."

WINCKELMANN AND HIS AGE

1 The essay was part of a larger project which was undertaken with two of the other Weimar "Friends of Art," Heinrich Meyer and Friedrich August Wolf (see note 1 to "Introduction to the *Propylaea*") and included letters of Winckelmann and further essays. Its title: *Winckelmann und sein Jahrhundert. In Briefen und Aufsätzen herausgeben von Goethe* (Tübingen, 1805).

2 Johann Joachim Winckelmann (1717–1786) was born in the country town of Stendal, near Magdeburg. Little is known of his early years. His murder, in Trieste, is not mentioned by Goethe although it was known as a fact soon after it occurred. An excellent biography in English is by Wolfgang Leppmann, *Winckelmann* (1970).

3 Cloris, daughter of Niobe, called the "blossom child," and Thyia, "the stormy," a Delphic nymph.

4 The reference is to Winckelmann's student in Magdeburg. Winckelmann was 25 years old when he met Wilhelm Peter Lamprecht.

5 A statue by Phidias, of gold and ivory, from the 5th century B.C., now lost.

6 Winckelmann served Heinrich von Bünau as secretary as well as taking care of his considerable library.

7 Winckelmann was 37 years old when he converted.

8 In this work (1755) appeared the renown formulation of the essential nature of Greek art, its "edle Einfalt und stille Größe"—"Noble simplicity and quiet greatness." I take the English title from Leppmann (*op. cit.*).

9 The artists mentioned here were influential academic artists, all of them in Dresden. Winckelmann was close by at the residence of Count von Bünau, and studied with Adam Friedrich Oeser (1717–1799), who later was also Goethe's teacher. The classical principles that Oeser taught persisted importantly in Goethe's development despite the apparent casual dismissal of the man and his views in the present context.

10 The influence of the Italian experience on Goethe himself was profound, as he well knew and reiterated in his *Italian Journey*. But a lasting, 'objective' result was also the sense of understanding other peoples and their literatures, not for one's own sake but for theirs as well. This is one of the first anticipations of the concept of world literature that Goethe developed toward the end of his life. See "Observations on World Literature" and "On Carlyle's *German Romance*."

11 The year, 1755.

12 Goethe himself arrived in Rome incognito, posing as an artist.

13 Wilhelm von Humboldt, who was Prussian representative in Rome from 1802 to 1808. The quotation is from a letter to Goethe, August 23, 1804.

14 The ancient name for modern Tivoli, near Rome.

15 Anton Raphael Mengs (1728–1779), painter at the Court of Dresden, practitioner and promoter of classicism, and opponent of the Baroque. He became director of the painters' academy in Rome (1754), where Winckelmann met him. The *History of Ancient Art* is dedicated to Mengs.
16 This plan and the plan for a study of Phidias were not carried out.
17 Goethe quotes from Paterculus' *Roman History* (29 A.D.), Part 1.
18 Marcus Fabius Quintilianus (lst century), author of *Education of an Orator,* from which Goethe quotes (Bk. 12). The painters and sculptors cited by Quintilian span a period from the 5th through the 4th century B.C. Their works are known only from contemporary descriptions.
19 The cardinals and ecclesiastics mentioned in this and the following section were connected with the libraries, antiqarian collections or art treasures at the Vatican.
20 Via Sacra because the street was lined with temples in ancient times. The Palatine is one of the Seven Hills of Rome.
21 Roman Emperor from 117 to 138.
22 The reference is to the plundering of the Villa Albani by the French in 1796. Not all the treasures, as Goethe seemed to believe, found their way back.
23. These ancient cities were destroyed in 79 A.D. Excavations of the ruins were begun in the early eighteenth century. After visiting the sites Winckelmann wrote an 'Open Letter on the Most Recent Discoveries made at Herculaneum' (1762).
24 Baron Philipp von Stosch, residing in Florence, gained international fame for his collection of gems. Winckelmann published a *Catalogue of the Engraved Gems of the Late Baron Stosch* (1760).
25 The East German edition of Goethe's works (*Berliner Ausgabe*) lists in a note to the text the following: 'Letters from Rome,' 'Commentary on the Oldest Greek Coins,' 'On the Restoration of Statues and Other Works of Antiquity,' 'On the Present State of the Liberal Arts and Sciences and on Scholarship in Italy.' 'Treaties on Corrupted Taste in the Arts and Sciences,' and 'How to Travel With Profit in Italy.'
26 English translations of Winckelmann's writings are limited. In citing titles I have followed Leppmann's (*op. cit.*) renderings from the German. The *History of Ancient Art* appeared in 1856 in a translation by G. Henry Lodge.
27 At Halle, he had heard Christian Wolff (1679–1754), the popular philosopher of the German Enlightment, and Alexander Baumgarten (1714–1762), the founder of Esthetics as a separate field of study.
28 Johann Friedrich Christ (1700–1756), professor of classical archeology, the first to teach the subject at a German university.
29 *Monumenti inediti* ('Unpublished Ancient Monuments, explained

and illustrated by Winckelmann') first appeared in Italian in 1767.
30 At the end of the Seven Years' War, 1763.
31 Frederick the Great had earlier sought to appoint Winckelmann as his librarian in Berlin. When a yearly stipend of 2000 Thaler was requested by Winckelmann, the king who had invited Voltaire to his court but had ignored Lessing, is said to have replied: "For a German, 1000 is enough."
32 Gerlach Adolf von Münchhausen founded the Göttingen Academy of Sciences and Göttingen University.
33 These included Johann Heinrich Füssli (1772–1825), poet and artist, the creator of paintings based on Milton's works, and Salomon Gessner (1730–1788), poet and engraver, best known for the 'Moral Stories and Idylls by Diderot and S. Gessner' which appeared in German and in French in 1773.
34 A gate on the passageway to the underworld. Cf. *Odyssey*, Bk. XI.

THE COLLECTOR AND HIS CIRCLE
1 "Der Sammler und die Seinigen" in *Propyläen*, Vol. II, 1799. For purposes of reading continuity the letters have been identified as to writer and addressee. Goethe had no need for such clarification. As editor of the *Propylaea*, in which these ficticious letters appeared, he would be assumed to be involved in the fiction. Schiller collaborated closely in the writing of the piece. He is unmistakably identified with the "philosopher" in Letter 5, though not throughout. The relationship to the world of reality in this novella cum essay is commensurate with the point it has to make, namely that the understanding of art is a human activity as much related to time, place, social status, character and personality as to pure critical perception.
2 Johann Heinrich Füssli, the Swiss painter and poet, who had done a set of engravings for Shakespeare's *A Midsummer Night's Dream*, one of which is alluded to below as "my Titania."
3 Goethe could not know at the time that his journal would last only through two more issues. See note 1 to the "Introduction to the *Propylaea*."
4 The "stranger" is to be identified with Aloys Hirt (1759–1839), art historian, who had visited Weimar in 1797 and published two articles in Schiller's journal *Horen* ('Horae'). Passages from these articles are repeated in his 'conversations' that follow.
5 In his essay "Laocoon"; for Winckelmann's formulation see note 8 to "Winckelmann and His Age."
6 Niobe, whose many children are killed; Dirce, who is dragged to death by a bull; and the *Laocoon* group, in the illustration, p. 19.
7 Angelo Fabroni, *Dissertazione sulle Statue . . . di Niobe* had just appeared, 1797.

8 A reference to Lessing's argument in his essay "How the Ancients Pictured Death" that not death but sleep, i.e. peace, is represented by the figures that stand by ancient tombs.
9 This is "Schiller" speaking. The fullest representation of his views on art are to be found in his *On the Aesthetic Education of Man*.
10 The "new breed" are Kant and his followers. The Kantian philosophy was often referred to simply as the "neue Philosophie" as well as the "kritische Philosophie."
11 The idea of a 'productive sense' is also suggested by Goethe's response to Eckermann's assumption that a great deal of experience of the world must have gone into the creation of *Faust*: "That may be. But had I not through anticipation already carried the world within me, with seeing eyes I would have remained blind, and all exploration and experience would have been nothing but a totally dead and vain endeavor" (*Eckermann,* February 26, 1824).
12 Depicting Christ with a crown of thorns standing before Pilate. Pilate is said to have exclaimed, "ecce homo"—'Behold the man.'
13 William Hogarth had claimed in his *Analysis of Beauty* (1753) that something resembling an S-shaped line informed all true beauty.
14 Goethe's reference to his *Faust,* Part II as "these very serious jokes" and Schiller's concept of a "Spieltrieb" in human nature which is central in the esthetic education of man come to mind. The lighthearted names and characterizations in the "Collector" also represent 'serious play.' Goethe to Schiller, June 22, 1797: "If one were now to make Michelangelo a *Phantomist,* Correggio an *Undulator,* Raphael a *Characterizer,* these categories would gain unbelievably in depth, in that one would see these outstanding men in their limitations and yet as kings or high representatives of whole forms and genres." See, for example, the short piece on Dante.

PART TWO: ESSAYS ON LITERATURE

SHAKESPEARE: A TRIBUTE

1 "Zum Shakespeares-Tag"—Goethe spelled *Schäkespear* and *Schäckespear*—appeared in print for the first time in 1854. It had been composed in 1771 as a speech to be delivered among a group of friends in 'festive' celebration of Shakespeare's name day, October 14 (Wilhelm). Herder was also to write a speech for the occasion, though the speech seems not to have materialized. More important, Herder had brought Shakespeare to the attention of the younger writer, with the result that a play in the Shakespearean vein, *Götz von Berlichingen,* and the original version of *Faust,* the *Urfaust,* came into being at the

same time and in the same spirit in which the tribute to Shakespeare was written.

2 That is, an effeminate marquis imitating the warrior Alcibiades is like Corneille imitating Sophocles.

3 Goethe uses "Raritätenkasten," 'raree show.'

4 Christian Martin Wieland (1733–1813), the most established German writer of the day, whom Goethe gently mocked in a later piece, "Gods, Heroes and Wieland," a satire of 1773.

5 The mocking complainer of the *Iliad*.

6 In the Luther Bible, *Tobias* 6 (v. 3); the King James Bible has a different reading.

SHAKESPEARE ONCE AGAIN

1 "Shakespeare und kein Ende" in *Morgenblatt für gebildete Stände*, May 12, 1815; Part III in *Über Kunst und Altertum*, Vol. V, 1826. Goethe had first-hand knowledge of Shakespeare as a playwright through forty years of association with the Weimar Theater, the greater part (1791–1817) of which he spent as its director. For the Shakespeare plays he produced see Marvin Carlson, *Goethe and the Weimar Theatre* (1978).

2 Ludwig Tieck (1773–1853), who with August Wilhelm Schlegel (1767–1845) wrote the standard German translations of Shakespeare's plays between 1797 and 1810, earned a reputation as a master reader of Shakespeare.

3 Romantic in the sense that Schiller intended the word in *On Naive and Sentimental Poetry* (1795) where "sentimental-romantic" meant self-reflective and self-divided.

4 In *Wilhelm Meister's Apprenticeship*, Bk. 4, chap. 13.

5 Hecate, the goddess associated with witchcraft.

6 Heinrich Blümner. His study appeared in 1814, the review in the *Literaturzeitung* No. 12, 1815.

7 Schiller's hope for the theater is related to the role he envisioned for theater in humanistic education. See *On the Aesthetic Education of Man* (1795) and "What Can a Good Permanent Theater Really Effect?" (1784).

8 In *Henry IV*, Part 2, (IV, iv).

9 The coarseness and, with it, the humor are removed from these two figures in Goethe's adaptation of the play for the Weimar Theater. See Carlson, *op. cit.*

10 Goethe relied on Tieck's *Alt-Enqlisches Theater* (1811). More recent scholarship has shown that the old version of *Lear* included there was not the basis for Shakespeare's play. Note the concluding paragraph to this essay.

11 Friedrich Ludwig Schröder (1744–1816), actor and theater director in Hamburg, to whom Goethe would turn for advice in theater matters.

LAURENCE STERNE

1 "Lorenz Sterne" in *Über Kunst und Altertum,* Vol. VI, 1827.

2 Speaking of Oliver Goldsmith as well as Sterne in a letter of December 25, 1829, Goethe said: "[They] influenced me in the main line of my development. Their goodwilled irony, their justness along with all their broadness of view, their gentleness in all adversity, their constancy in all change, and whatever other related virtues, taught me much; and in the end it is such attitudes that finally lead us back from the false starts in our lives."

BYRON'S MANFRED

1 "*Manfred.* A dramatic Poem by Lord Byron. London 1817" in *Über Kunst und Altertum,* Vol. II, 1820. Byron to his publisher, June 1820: "Enclosed is something which will interest you; to wit, the opinion of the greatest man in Germany—perhaps in Europe—in short, a critique of Goethe's upon *Manfred.*"

2 Byron knew only *Faust,* Part I, which was completed in 1808. Part II was not completed until the last year of Goethe's life, 1832.

3 Goethe rendered in German the lines which we give here, somewhat abridged, in the original. What he recommended for practice in declamation, provided him with an exercise in translation, one of the few he did of verse, though his translations of works of prose are numerous and substantial in length. *Manfred* in German does at times sound like *Faust.* The passage is from Act II, sc. ii.

BYRON'S CAIN

1 "Cain. A mystery by Lord Byron" in *Über Kunst und Altertum,* Vol. V., 1824.

2 The *Moniteur Universel,* a political newspaper, was established in 1789. D'Olivet's belief that he had "refuted" Cain was announced in the title of his book: "*Cain* . . . traduit en vers français et refuté dans une suite de remarques philosophiques. . . ."

3 The last three words, and their context, are as follows:

CAIN: And *he* who lieth there was childless. I
Have dried the fountain of a gentle race . . .
O Abel!
ADAH: Peace be with him!
CAIN: But with *me*!—

The "imaginative friend" in the last paragraph of the essay is probably Ottilie Goethe, his daughter-in-law, who welcomed Byron's friends in Weimar. See E.M. Butler, *Byron and Goethe* (1956).

DANTE

1 The title "Dante" comes from Eckermann and should not be construed as an encapsulation of Goethe's view of the Italian poet. The

essay was written as a note to be forwarded to Karl Streckfuß, whose translation of the *Divine Comedy* appeared 1824/26.

2 Giotto (1266?–1337), contemporary of Dante (1265–1321), began a new age in European art with his frescos in Florence.

3 *terza rima* . . . the compact verse form in which Dante composed his *Divine Comedy*.

4 Cebes, Greek philosopher of the 4th century B.C., compared human life to a cone-shaped mountain with labyrinthine paths which human beings must climb in order to reach happiness. Following Vasari's *Lives* Goethe believed that the frescos (at the Campo Santo in Pisa) were by Andrea Orcagna; they have now been attributed to Francesco Triani, also a contemporary of Dante.

5 Goethe, of course, gives the German from the Streckfuß translation. We quote from a standard verse translation, by Geoffrey L. Bickersteth, published in 1932.

6 Trento, city on the Adige river in northern Italy.

7 Dis, Roman god of the underworld.

8 Minotaur, the monster, half man, half bull, of the mythical labryinth on Crete.

9 Chiron, a centaur, renown as the teacher of the great heroes.

CALDERON'S DAUGHTER OF THE AIR

1 "Die Tochter der Luft" in *Über Kunst und Altertum,* Vol. III, 1822.

2 Jakob Balde (1604–1668), Jesuit and neo-Latin poet whose poems Herder had translated under the title *Terpsichore* (the muse of dance and poetry) in 1795.

3 Calderon's life (1600–1681) spans almost the whole of the Golden Age of Spanish culture and power. Goethe's supreme praise of Calderon: ". . . if poetry were to disappear completely from the world, it could be reconstructed from *The Constant Prince*." (To Schiller, Jan. 28, 1804.)

4 See "Shakespeare Once Again," pp. 167–68.

5 J.D. Gries (1775–1842), translator of Spanish and Italian literature. This seemingly gratuitous praise, suddenly introduced in an essay not concerned with translation is the less obtrusive when seen as an anticipation of Goethe's concept and program of world literature which he was soon to formulate and in which translations and translators play the foremost role. See, for example, "On Carlyle's *German Romance*."

A GERMAN GIL BLAS

1 "Der deutsche Gil Blas" in *Über Kunst und Altertum,* Vol. III, 1821. The "German" Gil Blas is the autobiography of the servant and journeyman Johann Christoph Sachse (1761–1822) to which Goethe gave the title. The French *Gil Blas* ("Histoire de Gil Blas de Santillane"), a picaresque novel by Alain-René Lesage, appeared in 1715.

2 Of which Goethe was also witness, at first hand. See his *Campaign in France*. The "unfortunate Champagne" mentioned below is both the region that suffered and the campaign that failed when conservative allied Europe moved against revolutionary France in 1792.

FAUST

1 "Faust. Tragédie de Monsieur de Goethe, traduite en français par Monsieur Stapfer, ornée de XVII dessins par Monsieur Delacroix" in *Über Kunst und Altertum*, Vol. VI, 1828.

2 A deluxe edition of the French translation of *Faust* by Frédéric Albert Stapfer with illustrations by Eugène Delacroix, the French Romantic painter, appeared in 1828. The translation was of Part I, as Part II was not completed until 1832. The whole *Faust* took some sixty years to complete. Even the first part to which Goethe here refers would stir memories from many years. An unpublished version was written around 1773; a *Fragment*, so called, published in 1790; and *The Tragedy*, Part I completed in 1808. These thirty plus years anticipated some twenty-five more years to come.

RESPONSE TO A LITERARY RABBLE ROUSER

1 "Literarischer Sansculottismus" in *Die Horen*, Schiller's journal, Vol. I, 1795. Goethe participated anonymously.

2 The ironic approval of printing the "immature effort" plays on the title of the publication in which it appeared, 'Berlin Archive of the Times and Its Taste.'

3 From a letter of Wilhelm von Humboldt to Schiller, August 15, 1795, it is clear that names were named, including Goethe's, but were scratched at publication.

4 Goethe uses the word *Schriftsteller* as opposed to *Dichter*, just as he uses *Poet* and *Prosaisten* in the following paragraph. The distinction is between creative writers (artists) and lesser writers of note.

5 Christoph Martin Wieland, see note 4 to "Shakespeare: A Tribute."

6 The plural for *Smelfungus*, the always complaining traveler of Sterne's *Sentimental Journey*.

7 Much later Goethe sketched out a plan for a study of German literature between 1750 and 1820, "Epochen deutscher Literatur."

8 The philosophy of Kant.

ON EPIC AND DRAMATIC POETRY

1 "Über epische und dramatische Dichtung" appeared first in *Über Kunst und Altertum*, Vol. VI, 1827, although it was written much earlier, in 1797, and represents, along with "The Collector and His Circle" and "On Dilettantism," the cooperative work of Schiller and Goethe in that period.

2 For Goethe's comparison between the drama and the novel, see *Wilhelm Meister's Apprenticeship*, Bk. 5, chap. 7.

DIDACTIC POETRY

1 "Über das Lehrgedicht" in *Über Kunst und Altertum,* Vol. VI, 1827.

2 The reference is to the mock epic *King Coals' Levee or Geological Etiquette* (1819) by John Scafe. Goethe made a didactic poem famous with his "Metamorphose der Pflanzen" (1798). For an English version of the poem, see "Metamorphosis of Plants," trans. Michael Hamburger, in *Goethe. Selected Poems,* ed. Christopher Middleton (1983).

ON GREEK TETRALOGIES

1 "Die tragischen Tetralogien der Griechen" in *Über Kunst und Altertum,* Vol. IV, 1823.

2 The reference is to the *Oresteia* by Aeschylus.

3 Carlo Goldoni (1707–1793), comic dramatist. Five plays of his were produced at the Weimar Theater in Goethe's time, albeit not in the manner that he describes here.

ON INTERPRETING ARISTOTLE'S POETICS

1 "Nachlese zu Aristotles' Poetik" in *Über Kunst und Altertum,* Vol. VI, 1827.

2 For the words "pity," "fear," and "neutralization of emotions," i.e. catharsis, Goethe uses the German *Mitleid, Furcht* and *Ausgleichung solcher Leidenschaften.* Often the controversy around this famous passage from Aristotle centered on the Latin or French or English equivalents for these words. For example, Lessing's dispute with Corneille's interpretation concerned the difference between fear and terror, between purifying and purging. See *Hamburg Dramaturgy,* No. 74.

3 The difference in the case of Alcestis is that he is brought back to life, not merely saved from death, by a god as are Isaac and Iphigenia.

4 See "On Greek Tetralogies."

5 Goethe's polemics against Newton were notorious, however. Yet it is true that on the subjects of art and literature he sought to be constructive in his criticism. "There is destructive and productive criticism. The former is very easy. One simply formulates in his mind some kind of measure, imagines any model, no matter how limited, and then announces with assurance, 'This work does not satisfy the requirements and is therefore worthless. . . .' Productive criticism is a good deal more difficult. It asks, 'What is the intent of the work? Is that intent intelligible as well as intelligent? How far has it succeeded in its purpose?' " (from Goethe's review of Manzoni's romantic tragedy *Il Conte di Carmagnola* in *Über Kunst und Altertum,* Vol. III, 1821.)

6 An oratorium, 1736.

PLATO AS PARTY TO A CHRISTIAN REVELATION

1 "Plato als Mitgenosse einer christlichen Offenbarung" in *Über Kunst und Altertum,* Vol. V, 1826. The essay was written earlier but not published, in 1797.

2 Friedrich Stolberg (1750–1819), jurist and poet, an early acquaintance of Goethe's who later converted to Catholicism, published a selection of Platonic dialogues in 1795 which was accompanied by a sanctimonious preface. Goethe's essay is a late response.

3 Christoph Martin Wieland, the representative writer of the German Enlightenment and as a literary figure kindred to Horace, published *Satyren des Horaz* in 1786.

STAGES OF MAN'S MIND

1 "Geistesepochen, nach Hermanns neusten Mitteilungen" in *Über Kunst und Altertum,* Vol. I, 1817. *Geistesepochen,* more literally, "Epochs of the human spirit." These anticipations of Oswald Spengler's *The Decline of the West* (1918) are an elaboration on ideas put forward by the classical philologist Johann Gottfried Hermann (1772–1848) in a dissertation on ancient mythology. Hence Goethe's subtitle.

JUSTUS MÖSER: SUPERSTITION AND POETRY

1 "Justus Möser" in *Über Kunst und Altertum,* Vol. IV, 1823. We add a subtitle in order to identify the subject matter of the essay. Justus Möser (1720–1794), statesman and historian, whose 'History of Osnabrück' appeared in 1768, made a strong impression on the young Goethe, who in a letter (June 21, 1781) claims that in forming opinions he often asked himself "What would Möser have thought of that?"

2 Origines (185–254), church father.

3 "Superstition is the poetry of life; that is why it does not hurt the poet to be superstitious" (from *Maxims and Reflections*).

4 Astraea, goddess of justice, fled to her original home in the skies when men began forging weapons of war.

5 Goethe includes a passage from Byron's *Manfred* (I,i), which he translates beginning with "Wenn der Mond ist auf der Welle" and offers it as an illustration of his last point.

ON CARLYLE'S GERMAN ROMANCE

1 "German Romance. Volumes IV. Edinburgh 1827" in *Über Kunst und Altertum,* Vol. VI, 1828. Goethe corresponded with Carlyle, who by this time had translated *Wilhelm Meister* (1824) and written his *Life of Friedrich Schiller* (1825).

2 Karl August Musäus (1735–1787), author of 'Folktales' (1782), is the only writer in the collection whose works have not survived as German classics.

3 The reference is to remarks he had repeated often in these years on the subject of world literature, which was taking ever clearer shape in his mind. See "Observations on World Literature."

ADVICE FOR YOUNG POETS

1 "Wohlgemeinte Erwiderung" in *Über Kunst und Altertum,* Vol. VI, 1832.

2 Cf. "Response to a Literary Rabble-Rouser." On the development of the German language as an instrument for literary expression, see the important study by Eric Blackall, *The Emergence of German as a Literary Language* (1959).

3 Of the young poets of the day, Goethe remarked to Eckermann, Sept. 24, 1827: "[They] all write as if they were sick and the whole world an infirmary. . . . That is a real misuse of poetry, which is given to us after all to reconcile the differences in life and to make human beings accept the world and their condition."

4 "Jüngling, merke dir in Zeiten,/ Wo sich Geist und Sinn erhöht:/ Daß die Muse zu begleiten,/ Doch zu leiten nicht versteht."

FURTHER ADVICE FOR YOUNG POETS

1 In the posthumous edition of Goethe's works, vol. 45 (1833), the essay appears under the title "Noch ein Wort für junge Dichter," since there it follows the preceeding essay which is titled "Für junge Dichter."

2 Goethe uses the word *Naturdichtung*. The concept of an *Erlebnisdichter,* a poet who creates from the stuff of immediate experience, became the standard term in German literary history to describe Goethe himself and those he influenced.

3 Cf. "On Byron's *Manfred*."

PART THREE: OBSERVATIONS ON ART AND LITERATURE

ON DILETTANTISM

1 These "observations" are selected from the notes, schemata, and preliminary drafts by both Schiller and Goethe for a planned treatise on dilettantism in all the arts. The introductory scheme lists poetry, music, dance, drawing, painting, sculpture, architecture, theater and horticulture. The advantages and disadvantages of dilettantism in each particular art were to be examined; further, the advantages and disadvantages for the individual as well as society, i.e. from a subjective as well as an objective point of view. The notes for the general scheme were first published in Schiller's posthumous works, vol. 4 (1841), those for particular subjects in Goethe's posthumous works, vol. 44 (1832). The selection here is from "Über den Dilettantismus" in the *Gedenkausgabe,* vol. 14, except for the first observation in our third grouping which is from *Maxims and Reflections*.

ON ACTING

1 Goethe was the director of the Weimar Theater from 1791 to 1817. It was under his direction that the original amateur undertaking, the *Liebhabertheater,* became a professional theater. See Carlson, *op. cit.*. Goethe's notes on acting were first published in his posthumous works,

vol. 44 (1832). The selection here is virtually complete; mainly where linguistic matters were involved and the point could not properly be made in translation have some rules been omitted, e.g. on enunciation or declamation. An impression of Goethe's theater as he experienced it, and thus of the German theater of the day, emerges from his rules for actors perhaps more clearly than might be the case with an expository account.

2 The fourth position in ballet.

3 This and the following quotation are from Schiller's *The Bride of Messina* (I,vii), trans. Charles E. Passage (1962).

On World Literature

1. The concept of *world* literature originates with Goethe. His many comments on the subject occurred in letters, conversations, critical pieces, and *Maxims and Reflections*. The selection here is from "Allgemeine Betrachtungen zur Weltliteratur" in the *Gedenkausgabe,* vol. 14 and from "Goethes wichtigste Äusserungen über Weltliteratur" in the *Hamburger Ausgabe,* vol. 12. Our Nos. 2–7 are from the former, Nos. 1, 8, 9, 10, from the latter. No. 11 in a letter to Count Stolberg, June 11, 1827.

2 François Guizot, Abel Villemain and Victor Cousin, professors of history, rhetoric and philosophy, respectively, at the Sorbonne, published these works between 1828–30.

ILLUSTRATION ACKNOWLEDGEMENTS

Strasbourg Cathedral: New York Public Library

Cologne Cathedral: New York Public Library

Engraving of the Laocoon statue: Reproduced by courtesy of the Warburg Institute

Myron's Cow and the Greek Grave near Cumae: Artemis Verlag AG, Zürich

Leonardo da Vinci's *Last Supper:* Photograph by Giacomo Brogi, Florence

Giotto's *Last Supper:* Padova, Cappella degli Scrovegni

The Jewish Cemetery: The Detroit Institute of Arts

The Good Samaritan: Rotterdam, Boymans Museum

Goethe's *Faust:* New York Public Library

INDEX

GPSR Authorized Representative: Easy Access System Europe - Mustamäe tee 50, 10621 Tallinn, Estonia, gpsr.requests@easproject.com

www.ingramcontent.com/pod-product-compliance
Lightning Source LLC
LaVergne TN
LVHW102158101026
849957LV00026B/224
9780691292182